WordPress for Journalists

WordPress for Journalists presents an in-depth and accessible introduction to using the content management system WordPress to produce journalism today. LJ Filotrani, an experienced multimedia journalist and website editor and creator, gives readers guidance on using the wide-ranging functionality of WordPress to create news and other forms of journalistic content.

Readers will find everything they need to set up both a .com and a .org site, from naming the site and buying a domain to choosing a hosting package and keeping hackers at bay. Chapters also cover house style, how to create posts and pages, hyperlinking, embedding content, setting up widgets and sidebars and working with themes, plugins and SEO. There are sections on troubleshooting, HTML/CSS, RSS and curation, alongside advice on audience engagement and commercialisation.

Chapters feature:

- step-by-step instructions on setting up and managing a professional website, with illustrative images throughout;
- comprehensive lists of the most useful apps, themes, sites and plugins;
- a guide to producing multimedia content online, including images, info-graphics, videos, podcasts and live streaming;
- expert interviews with professional journalists working successfully online;
- a glossary of terms.

By bringing together real-world advice, detailed walkthroughs and practical tips and tools for best practice, *WordPress for Journalists* will inspire young journalists and content producers who are looking to widen their skill set and build their presence online.

LJ Filotrani is Senior Lecturer at London South Bank University, UK. She is Course Director for the BA (Hons) Journalism course, specialising in building sites in WordPress and producing video, audio and text for digital journalism platforms. She is a former site editor for the *Guardian* and was responsible for creating and launching the multimedia microsite Careers Guardian.

WordPress for Journalists
From Plugins to Commercialisation

LJ Filotrani

Routledge
Taylor & Francis Group

LONDON AND NEW YORK

First published 2018
by Routledge
2 Park Square, Milton Park, Abingdon, Oxon OX14 4RN

and by Routledge
711 Third Avenue, New York, NY 10017

Routledge is an imprint of the Taylor & Francis Group, an informa business

British Library Cataloguing-in-Publication Data
A catalogue record for this book is available from the British Library

Library of Congress Cataloging-in-Publication Data
Names: Filotrani, Laura-Jane, author.
Title: WordPress for journalists : from plugins to commercialisation / Laura-Jane Filotrani.
Description: London ; New York : Routledge, 2018. | Includes bibliographical references and index.
Identifiers: LCCN 2017060627| ISBN 9781138652019 (hardback : alk. paper) | ISBN 9781138652026 (pbk. : alk. paper) | ISBN 9781315624471 (ebook)
Subjects: LCSH: WordPress (Electronic resource) | Web sites–Authoring programs. | Blogs–Computer programs. | Web site development. | News Web sites.
Classification: LCC TK5105.8885.W66 F55 2018 | DDC 006.7/8–dc23
LC record available at https://lccn.loc.gov/2017060627

ISBN: 978-1-138-65201-9 (hbk)
ISBN: 978-1-138-65202-6 (pbk)
ISBN: 978-1-315-62447-1 (ebk)

Typeset in Scala and Scala Sans
by Swales & Willis Ltd, Exeter, Devon, UK

Printed in the United Kingdom
by Henry Ling Limited

Contents

Walkthroughs

How to use this book

Apart from the first section on the initial set-up of a site, this is not a book which you need to work through page by page chronologically. It is a book designed to be used when needed. You won't need to know everything in here right at the start – so you don't need to read from beginning to end in one go. There will be functions that will make no sense to you until you have a need for them. You do need to be sat in front of your computer, however, as this is not a conceptual text. It is a practical step-by-step account, so you will need to be ready to work through the examples as explained. The other thing that is advisable is to get up the accompanying website (wpforjournalists.com), as this will give you easy access to all the resources mentioned. You will find everything you need hyperlinked.

The book is pitched at someone with little knowledge of content management systems and no real experience of producing content online. It is not aimed at would-be developers or designers; it is aimed at journalists, those who are involved in news content production and factual storytelling. The book draws on my own experience of working as a multimedia newspaper journalist and it is centred around what I found useful. Because of this you may

> You should pick and choose what you use – it is not meant to be gospel – and you will find your own ways of working which suit you. So please don't be scared to do it your way.

find it a bit idiosyncratic. Much of what you will find here is my preference.

It is expected that you as a journalist, in whichever sector you are working in, are able to work in any media and on any platform, and as such this book is directed towards the process of creating stories online. Whether you are in television, or on radio, or writing for a newspaper, or working for a PR company, the process of getting content online is the same.

While the book will be useful for anyone producing content online, the examples used to illustrate points and to provide inspiration are mostly centred around news organisations. You will find suggestions for themes, for example, that are designed with news content in mind, feeds which are news and interviews from newspaper journalists.

Just a quick note on timeliness. Because of the nature of the topic – that of a continually developing technology – you may find some of the plugins and themes covered in the book are not working or not being updated, or not in the marketplace at all, by the time you are reading this. This is to be expected and where this is the case you will find an alternative on the website. In any case, what I have tried to do is give you an overview of what is possible in terms of WordPress, to provide you with some inspiration; you can use the examples given to investigate alternatives yourself.

While the textbook covers both the setting up of free blogs and self-hosted sites, and how to maintain them and how to grow them, it is mainly targeted at self-hosted sites as it is these sites which allow for extended functionality with added plugins.

The book starts with a brief web history and gives some context for the developments in online journalism. You will then find everything you need to set up both a .com site and a .org site. These chapters include everything from naming your site and buying a domain to choosing a hosting package and keeping a site safe from hackers. There is also advice on how to improve the speed of a site and all of the essential plugins that make a website run efficiently and safely.

Chapters also cover house style, how to create posts and pages, how to hyperlink, how to use the media library, how to embed content, how to use categories and tags, how to set up widgets and sidebars, how to import and export, working with themes and search engine optimisation (SEO), and there is a troubleshooting chapter where the most common errors are explained – what a 404 error would mean, for example, and what to check for in the wp-config file. The majority of this section is applicable to both the free blogs on .com and the self-hosted sites using .org.

Also included is a chapter on plugins, covering the standard plugins that are activated by default with the .com blogs and then the essential plugins that I turn to when I start a new site. You will also find quite detailed advice on improving the performance of your website, making sure your site works on mobile devices and how to connect to your social media accounts.

A note on why mobiles fall within the site set-up section rather than under managing content. These days you cannot have a website that does not work on mobiles: "The mobile/tablet now outstrips the computer. We have

reached the mobile tipping point with a publisher like the BBC reporting that around 70% of traffic now comes from mobile devices" (Digital News Report (2016), Reuters Institute for the Study of Journalism). You need to make sure this is one of your first considerations when building a site – so this is why it is covered in the site set-up. However, all the way through the text there are references and advice reinforcing this mobile-first attitude that you should adopt.

There is also a section explaining how WordPress works and the most important files to be aware of, and while it is not my intention to teach journalists to be website developers I think it is important for anyone using WordPress professionally to at least be familiar with the terminology and have a basic understanding of how the content management system works. This is mostly in order to troubleshoot when issues arise. This basic knowledge is imperative when dealing with developers and hosts so that you can explain what problems you are having and apply suggested fixes.

You will find out how to deal with content – how to create and upload content on your newly created website. This whole chapter offers examples of good multimedia journalism content online and explanations of how pieces have been put together. There are sections on layout, HTML/CSS, RSS, syndication, curation, images, video, streaming, audio, live blogging, infographics and maps.

Your users are also covered. Understanding the visitors to your website should be key in determining your content strategy or, rather, defining who you are trying to reach. This chapter highlights some tools to help you. It looks at metric apps such as Google Analytics and how you should use them to guide editorial decisions based on traffic. It will also cover engagement through using comments and plugins to promote content in order to combat bounce.

Lastly, commercialisation is explained. It is not easy to make money from a website (and it may not even be a consideration for you – but if it is, and if you are predominantly running a news site, making it sustainable financially is no mean feat). There are, however, plugins that you will find useful so these are covered in this chapter, and I have also included a few different methods of generating revenue streams, all tried and tested by me (some more successful than others).

The book concludes with a glossary of terms. So, if you come across something you are not sure of, have a look in the glossary (and if it isn't explained for you, log on to the website and let me know and I'll add it to the site).

All the way through the book you will find tips and advice and if you see an italicised word, this normally means there is a definition for you in the glossary.

Please let me know via the website wpforjournalist.com if you find a reference to a site/plugin/theme in this book that doesn't work, and I'll make sure there is an up-to-date link on the website.

CHAPTER 1

Why WordPress?

THE BIRTH OF THE CMS

WordPress was created and launched in 2003 by developers Matt Mullenweg (just 19 at the time!) and Mike Little. It was a response to another blogging platform (b2/cafelog)[1] closing and it was a chance comment on a message board by Matt, which Mike responded to, that became the start of what is now the biggest blogging platform of the internet.

But what actually is it? It is a *content management system* – a *CMS* – which is needed to power a website. Essentially a CMS allows someone with little knowledge of any code to create and publish content online – it is the user-friendly dashboard where you can create posts and upload images, and the system that will then translate what you have uploaded into code and files stored in a database. It is like a translator for people who do not understand code and do not have the knowledge to build the architecture needed for a website to function properly.

The platform offers two different ways of working with it. The first is a simple blogging platform – WordPress.com, and the second a more complex platform – WordPress.org.

WordPress.com is the place where you can set up a free blog – everything you do on it is *hosted* on WordPress. All your files, all your content, everything – it's all hosted and run by WordPress. WordPress.org, on the other hand, is the place which gives you the WordPress code to upload onto your own self-hosted website.

Using this method, you are in charge of everything – from uploading your *themes* to troubleshooting any issues. The reasons for choosing one over the other are covered in Chapter 3.

For the moment though, here are a few differences to consider (Figure 1.1).

There is also the copyright consideration when choosing between .com and .org. If you host your site using the free platform WordPress.com you are beholden to the terms of service as set out by parent company Automattic (which essentially owns your site):

> By submitting content to Automattic for inclusion on your website, you grant Automattic a world-wide, royalty-free, and non-exclusive license to reproduce, modify, adapt and publish the content solely for the purpose of displaying, distributing and promoting your blog. If you delete content, Automattic will use reasonable efforts to remove it from the website, but you acknowledge that caching or references to the content may not be made immediately unavailable.[2]

And there is also a question about termination – more from the terms of service: "Automattic may terminate your access to all or any part of the website at any time, with or without cause, with or without notice, effective immediately."

There are, however, many positive reasons for using .com – it's free, for a start, and you

WordPress

.com   .org

X

ACCESS TO FILES

This is the biggest issue with the free blogs - you do not have access to all your files. Essentially you don't own your site - which in the worst case scenario would mean it could be shut down at any time without your permission ....

With a self-hosted site you own your site - you are in control - you have access to all your files and can download a site in entirety. You can back-up, clone, transfer - take down ... anything you like. It's yours.

X

THEMES

You cannot upload any new themes - you can only use the themes that are uploaded for you - some are commercial themes which you can pay for but you cannot buy a theme from another site and upload it. Nor can you do any modifications to existing themes.

You can upload any theme you like and most importantly you can edit any theme that you activate - even all the free ones offered to you from WordPress

X

PLUGINS

Same as the themes - you cannot upload any new plugins - you can only use the plugins offered by WordPress.

You can upload any plugin you like and like themes you can edit any plugin that you activate - even all the free ones offered to you from WordPress

COMMERICIALISATION

You cannot create an e-commerce site, nor can you add any affiliate marketing links. You are not allowed to sell any ads on your site.

Freedom to do what you like!

X

MEMBERSHIP

You cannot create a membership site

Freedom to do what you like!

Figure 1.1 Differences between the free blogs and the self-hosted WordPress sites on .org.

are less likely to get hacked. More on the positives in the next chapter.

There is actually a third way of working with WordPress – that's WordPress.com VIP, but this is a premium service which is aimed at large, well-established companies (with big budgets). For the purposes of this book we'll just cover setting up and using WordPress.com and WordPress.org.

When you are thinking about creating a website, WordPress is not your only option, of course. There are quite a few content management systems to choose from, including Drupal and Joomla, but by far the biggest and most powerful is WordPress. Figures from WordPress itself published in 2016 suggest that on its free platform (WordPress.com) users published more than 595 million posts and more than 457 million comments in 2016.[3]

It powers more than 29% of the web in comparison to just 3.2% by Drupal and 1.8% by Joomla[4] – according to builtwith.com there were 74 million sites powered by WordPress, roughly 50% on WordPress.com and 50% on WordPress.org.

A lot of companies have their own bespoke content management systems but there are more and more big players (particularly within publishing) who are moving part or all of their website platform to WordPress. The *Sun* (News UK) is one of the latest to make the move, citing the requirement to make frequent changes to its *homepage* as one of the main motivators for moving to the platform. It follows competitors such as *Metro* (metro.co.uk), which made the move in 2013.

Martin Ashplant, digital director for metro.co.uk, said:

We moved to WordPress because it offered us a much nimbler, reactive CMS than we were using at the time and we wanted to benefit from the wider developer community

> **WordPress revolutionized the way our journalists were working – suddenly they were able to work remotely – being able to upload content via their mobile phones directly – it fundamentally changed the culture of the newsroom. WordPress essentially gave the keys of publishing to all levels of staff.[6]**

who constantly feed into the platform. We also needed something that was delivering mobile content much faster than we were able to – WordPress offers this. Soon after we switched over to the CMS we saw a spike in traffic and we became the fastest growing national newspaper website in 2013.[5]

Since 2005 WordPress has been owned by Automattic (also founded by Matt Mullenweg). Automattic is the creator of many of the *plugins* that you can upload (if you are on WordPress.org) to extend the functionality of the core files. For more on plugins see page 62.

HOW WORDPRESS WORKS AND WHO USES IT

Using WordPress you can create posts and pages, upload images, embed video content and audio content, create interactive maps, communicate with your visitors via comments, send out regular newsletters, create polls, live blog an event ... The list of what you can create is really only limited by your imagination. All of this functionality was once only available to developers and website designers. The launch of WordPress opened up this publishing capability to the layperson.

For inspiration on creating websites using WordPress.org, check out some of the biggest media companies currently using the CMS:

- **BBC America** This is actually a multisite (see page 24 for help with setting up a multisite). Each programme has its own area which is powered by the main site. David Anderson, the senior product development manager at BBC Worldwide at the time of the move to the platform in 2013, explained:

Our previous platforms locked us into very rigid options. Changes were expensive and took a long time to implement. Now, we have a solid platform that is flexible and constantly being improved.

The ability to create custom content through the WordPress interface (and not have to create custom HTML code) streamlined 80% of the work which in the past had occupied a huge amount of time for a team of four editors. The result is that editors now have more time to focus on content creation instead of figuring out how to edit (or troubleshoot) code.[7]

- **Quartz** Business news, mobile-first platform, launched in 2012.
- **MTV News** Celebrity news, gossip, exclusive interviews and pictures from the world of music and entertainment.
- **Time.com** Breaking world news and analysis.
- **CNN** Breaking US news.
- **Reuters blog** Blogs from a variety of Reuters journalists on a range of topics.
- **MSNBC** This is the website for the American cable and satellite television network covering news and political commentary from NBC News on current events.
- **Spotify** A digital music service that gives you access to millions of songs.
- **The Fair Go** This is the official website for the Liberal Party in Australia. If you like what you see, you can buy the theme! It uses the theme Newspaper. (For help with installing a new theme, see page 30.)

REFERENCES

1   Matt Mullenweg. (2017). The Blogging Software Dilemma. [online] Available at: https://ma.tt/2003/01/the-blogging-software-dilemma [Accessed 12 Nov. 2017].

2   WordPress.com. (2017). Terms of Service. [online] Available at: https://en.wordpress.com/tos [Accessed 12 Nov. 2017].

3   The WordPress.com Blog. (2017). WordPress.com in 2016: A Year in Review. [online] Available at: https://en.blog.wordpress.com/2016/12/16/wordpress-com-in-2016-a-year-in-review [Accessed 12 Nov. 2017].

4   Trends.builtwith.com. (2017). WordPress Usage Statistics. [online] Available at: https://trends.builtwith.com/cms/WordPress [Accessed 12 Nov. 2017].

5   Pressgazette.co.uk. (2017). *Metro* Fastest Growing UK Newspaper Website, *Mirror* Daily Total Exceeds 2m, *Mail* Online Stays Top – *Press Gazette*. [online] Available at: www.pressgazette.co.uk/metro-fastest-growing-uk-newspaper-website-mirror-daily-total-exceeds-2m-mail-online-stays-top [Accessed 12 Nov. 2017].

6   Ashplant, M. (2017). Digital director of metro.co.uk, interview by LJ Filotrani.

7   WordPress.com VIP. (2017). Case Study: BBC America Runs on WordPress. [online] Available at: https://vip.wordpress.com/2013/05/01/bbc-america-runs-on-wordpress [Accessed 12 Nov. 2017].

CHAPTER 2

Journalism online

THE CURRENT CLIMATE AND FUTURE TRENDS

It goes without saying that the way a journalist works now is completely different to the way a journalist worked pre the web, but I think it is worth just giving some context in order to understand just how much impact the online environment has had on the profession. So before we launch ourselves into a site set-up, let's consider how the working practice of a journalist has changed and therefore why it is so necessary to learn how to use a CMS such as WordPress. I want to also take a brief look at future developments – where storytelling is going online – so that we can think about what trends could become common practice.

A bit of web history first. The World Wide Web was created in 1989 by an English scientist working at CERN (the European Organization for Nuclear Research), Tim Berners-Lee (now Sir Tim Berners-Lee). Not to be confused with the internet – the birth of which can be traced to much earlier (the first recorded 'conversations' between computers are commonly attributed to a scientist at MIT in 1962, J.C.R. Licklider) – the creation of the World Wide Web was the game-changer. With the development of *Hypertext Markup Language* (HTML), uniform resource identifiers (URI; now commonly called *Uniform Resource Locators* or URLs – essentially web addresses), and

Hypertext Transfer Protocol (HTTP – the way linked content is retrieved from across the web), the online community was born.

On 30 April 1993 CERN put the World Wide Web software in the public domain. CERN made the next release available with an open licence, as a surer way to maximise its dissemination. Through these actions, making the software required to run a web server freely available, along with a basic browser and a library of code, the web was allowed to flourish.[1]

Since then the look and feel of the web has changed dramatically. In the beginning, everything was simply text with a few symbols and a few basic links. (Amazon was one of the early adopters – it started selling books online in 1994!) In 1995, with the development of *browsers*, images started to play an important part in the design of web pages. At the same time a new programming language called Javascript was created by American technologist Brendan Eich. This new language allowed developers and designers to make web pages dynamic, for example by adding functionality such as pop-ups (Eich later went on to co-found the Mozilla Project). Following on from this, Macromedia launched Flash in 1996 (it was bought by Adobe in 2005 and is to be defunct very soon). Flash was a new technology which really marked the beginning of user interaction, animations and control over layout (this has now been superseded by HTML5).

By 1998, as websites were beginning to grow in size, designers were finding controlling the look and feel of a site simply using HTML a nightmare – there were too many pages to change individually. In response, the World Wide Web Consortium (W3C) created *cascading style sheets* (CSS). This allowed designers to define styles across a whole site from one style sheet – to make a site-wide change of font, for example, you could now just change the style sheet (.css file) instead of having to modify the HTML on every page.

Up to this point in time, it was really just developers who were able to create websites – you needed a pretty good understanding of code in order to build a functioning site and an excellent knowledge of HTML and CSS for it to look good. However, it wasn't long before content management systems such as WordPress changed all of this. It seemed as if almost overnight anyone could create a dynamic website. Suddenly anyone could publish anything at any time. No specialist coding knowledge was needed. No-one needed to be consulted (or paid).

Obviously, there were lots more technological developments over this rich period of growth – but what I want to get across is just how quickly the web changed from its simple text-format beginnings in the 1990s to its fully fledged format full of images and the possibilities for dynamic content just a few years later, and most importantly that it very speedily developed into a platform which was open in terms of publishing capability – to everyone.

IMPACT ON JOURNALISM

As the web grew, newspaper publishers started to take note and very soon online news websites began to proliferate. In the UK one of the earliest newspaper sites was that of the *Telegraph* – it launched in 1994; the BBC followed a couple of years later in 1996 and the *Guardian* in 1999. In the US the *New York Times* was one of the first nationals to go online – it launched in 1996. Like many of the early examples of

newspapers online, the *New York Times* used the website to house archives of past features and to republish what was in the printed paper.[2]

If we look to CNN though, and its coverage of the O.J. Simpson trial in 1996 (http://edition.cnn.com/US/OJ/), you can see the beginnings of how content would start to be handled on the web – and how it became apparent that publishing online was not simply a case of uploading printed articles, as demonstrated by the *New York Times*, but instead offering the reader a much richer experience by pulling in different sources and giving background material to support a story – a 'multiplicity of perspectives', to borrow a phrase from academic and journalist Dr Aleks Krotoski.[3]

By the time WordPress had started to gain traction, social media was beginning to change the way news was being accessed and the way content was being produced. Social networking sites such as Friends Reunited in the UK and Classmates in the US – both from the decade before – gave some indication of the huge impact the capability of social shares was to have on news online. But it was the next wave of technologies that really swept us into the arena of *user-generated content* (UGC), social shares, *content curation, aggregation* tools and live, 24-7 media consumption.

Looking back, it was a whirlwind – all the technologies we now take as fundamentals for producing content online were launched within the space of a decade: Skype in 2003, Facebook 2004, Flickr 2004, YouTube 2005, Twitter 2006, Justin.tv (now called Twitch) 2007, SoundCloud 2007, Pinterest 2010, Instagram 2010, Snapchat 2011. I cover all of these later in the book when we look at managing content, and there are more of course, but what I want to stress is just how quickly the landscape changed. With the launch of all of these new applications and platforms we as consumers expected our news to be 24-7, for our coverage to be live and for us to have access to whatever we liked (and for free). And we wanted to be involved: we wanted to contribute our stories, our lives, to the news.

And now we as an audience don't want to wait. We want real-time.

The development of the World Wide Web opened up horizons, allowing people to connect globally. It enabled direct access to data hitherto locked away and it allowed people to build networks, to build communities, albeit virtual. And, with the development of content management systems such as WordPress enabling real-time publishing, the web fundamentally transformed the working practices of a journalist and in turn the types of content being produced.

So, what has been the impact on journalists? The content producers? The reporters? No longer is a reporter following a lead from a news wire, writing a story and handing it over to be subbed to be published the next day. The reporter is now sourcing their own leads, filling in Freedom of Information (FOI) requests, mining data, researching, writing, filming, recording, editing, sourcing images, cutting, cropping, writing posts, *hyperlinking* and publishing – while at the same time managing social media accounts, promoting content, encouraging dialogue, responding to comments, following links and networking, ready to react at any time, on any day. This is what it means to be a journalist now. The stories we produce are multimedia, multiplatform and multifaceted. A story is explored through many angles with supporting video, snippets of audio, infographics, polls, surveys and UGC.

Consequently, not knowing how a CMS works is not an option if you want to work as a journalist. And to this end, learning WordPress is an excellent way of understanding how to publish content, how to engage an audience and how to connect with an audience. With so much content being produced, so much of everything on the web, you need to know what you are doing in order to find your audience. Without an audience, you may as well stick your stories up on your bedroom wall.

LOOKING FORWARD

So where are we headed? What's the next wave ready to toss us around? Here's Richard Silvester, managing director of infographic company Infogr8, nicely summing up all the major trends of the moment:

In 2017, interactive and data-driven content is changing fast. Content that is triggered by scrolling, not clicks, is on the up as an increasing number of users access the web on small screens. Thanks also to the growth of mobile, 'destination' interactive data visualisation websites are less popular now than a few years ago, though they remain a powerful way of engaging audiences with complex datasets.

Personalisation is a key trend and an increasing amount of content is personalised using data from social media, or data submitted by users. Emerging formats such as interactive video create new opportunities. Over the next few years, the rise of chatbot-based messaging apps and other conversational user interfaces (CUIs), facial recognition and virtual reality (VR) experiences will create new and exciting forms of interactive content.

Big players like the *New York Times* and the *Economist* have created virtual reality experiences. The *Economist's* first VR story allowed viewers to stroll around an Iraqi museum, looking at treasures since destroyed by ISIS. The Fight for Falluja – [an app] produced by Pulitzer Prize-winning Ben C. Solomon for the *New York Times*, has been downloaded around two million times, with users spending an average of over six minutes in the app.[4]

(For more on Ben C. Solomon and the making of The Fight for Falluja, see the Pulitzer Centre website: http://pulitzercenter.org/education/meet-journalist-ben-c-solomon)

For journalism, immersive storytelling using VR is exploding. The *Guardian*, for example, has its own head of VR, Francesca Panetta. Panetta was part of the team who in 2013 produced 'Firestorm: The Story of the Bushfire at Dunalley',[5] a ground-breaking interactive multimedia story. Panetta was the driving force behind the *Guardian's* first hugely successful VR project in 2016 on solitary confinement, '6×9: A Virtual Experience of Solitary Confinement'.[6] The *Guardian* describes the purpose of '6×9' as "to demonstrate, using immersive journalism, how being in long-term solitary can affect the mind of prisoners held in segregation around the world, an estimated 80,000 to 100,000 of them in the United States alone".

The *New York Times* has also produced a number of brilliant interactives, as mentioned by Richard Silvester – check out its 'Antarctica' series.[7] For more interactives download the NYT VR app at www.nytimes.com/marketing/nytvr

So, VR is one trend making its way into mainstream content production – another is *augmented reality* (AR). In 2016 production studio Empathetic Media launched an AR storytelling app (available on both iOS and Android) alongside its partners, the *Washington Post* and Associated Press. The partnership aims to publish interactive news stories with videos, animations and infographics all overlaid with annotations, maps and audio clips. Check out the *Washington Post*'s first piece on Freddy Gray.[8] (For more inspiration on VR journalism projects, check out https://medium.com/journalism360)

One of the other biggest areas of growth is live coverage. Streaming content via social media platforms such as Facebook, Twitter and YouTube is finding its way into the mainstream. Live streams via Twitter's Periscope are regularly used on television news bulletins in the UK, for example, and gaming platforms such as Twitch.tv boast 100 million users every month.[9] It's easy to see why content producers and publishing companies are starting to experiment with how to use this technology. (See page 140 for advice on setting up streaming.)

And in terms of WordPress specifically, the roll-out of the Gutenberg block editor promises to fundamentally change the way we use the CMS. The plan so far is for it to be an optional plugin (there is some resistance to it becoming core), but who knows what impact it will have on content production and the direction of WordPress in the future (see page 110 for help with the plugin).

In website design generally in 2017, we have seen a move towards more minimalist sites, particularly with 'card' layouts in the style of Pinterest. More and more homepages, it seems, are becoming simple entry points – decluttered and reliant on visuals rather than text. There is also a move to eternally scrolling homepages, with some sites getting rid of *menus* altogether. With the rise in popularity of apps such as Snapchat there has been an explosion of animated GIFs, and a move away from stock images being used in favour of original photography, and there seems to be a general trend towards bigger text, bolder fonts, fewer buttons and more icons.

REFERENCES

1   CERN. The Birth of the Web. [online] Available at: https://home.cern/topics/birth-web [Accessed 19 Aug. 2017].

2   Lewis, P. (1996). The *New York Times* Introduces a Web Site. [Online] Available at: www.nytimes.com/1996/01/22/business/the-new-york-times-introduces-a-web-site.html [Accessed 8 Dec. 2017].

3   Krotoski, Aleks. (2011). What Effect Has the Internet Had on Journalism? [Online] Available at: www.theguardian.com/technology/2011/feb/20/what-effect-internet-on-journalism [Accessed 8 Dec. 2017].

4   Silvester, Richard. (2017). Managing director of infographic company Infogr8 – interviewed by LJ Filotrani.

5   *The Guardian*. (2013). Firestorm. [Online] Available at: www.theguardian.com/world/interactive/2013/may/26/firestorm-bushfire-dunalley-holmes-family [Accessed 8 Dec. 2017].

6   *The Guardian*. (2016). 6x9: A Virtual Experience of Solitary Confinement. [Online] Available at: www.theguardian.com/world/ng-interactive/2016/apr/27/6x9-a-virtual-experience-of-solitary-confinement [Accessed 8 Dec. 2017].

7   *New York Times*. (2017). The Antartica Series. [Online] Available at: www.nytimes.com/interactive/2017/climate/antarctica-virtual-reality.html?mcubz=0 [Accessed 8 Dec. 2017].

8   *Washington Post*. Events Leading to Freddie Gray's Death, Explained in Augmented Reality. [Online] Available at: www.washingtonpost.com/graphics/local/freddie-gray-augmented-reality [Accessed 8 Dec. 2017].

9   Twitchadvertising. Audience. [Online] Available at: http://twitchadvertising.tv/audience [Accessed 8 Dec. 2017].

CHAPTER 3

The basics

As outlined in Chapter 1, WordPress has two publishing arms – one which is free and one which requires you to have your own hosting account. In this section, we'll start with setting up a free site on WordPress.com and then move to setting up a self-hosted site on WordPress.org.

Although there are limitations to the free WordPress.com platform which are outlined on page 2, it is worth noting that there are some reasons why you would choose this way to host your website over WordPress.org. First and foremost, it's a great way to learn about the CMS, and second it will give you a sound understanding of how to handle basic multimedia content online. I advise anyone just starting out to set up a free site first to learn the basics.

One of the other reasons for choosing .com over .org is that it is free. Unlike.org, there are no start-up costs – you don't have to buy a *domain* name, you don't have to pay hosting fees each month, you don't have to buy themes and there is nothing to install, which means you can pretty much get started within a few minutes of signing up – there is no process, no system to get to grips with.

Another major reason for choosing .com over .org is that because WordPress.com is in charge of everything you don't have to

worry about making sure you are running the most up-to-date version of the CMS, nor do you have to worry about any security patches developed to address security breaches – one of the key steps against hackers. Because of this you are much more likely to be a victim of a hack on WordPress.org than WordPress.com, although it should be made clear that according to the terms of service on WordPress.com you as the owner of the site are still "responsible for maintaining the security of your account and blog".

Not everyone chooses to upgrade to .org – there are many really successful blogs running on .com and many established journalists who choose to use the free blogging platform. In a way, it is a much easier path to choose and requires much less maintenance on your part.

Many journalists use WordPress.com for personal blogs away from their employers. David Higgerson, publishing director at Trinity Mirror, is a prime example. His blog is davidhiggerson.WordPress.com and he uses the free theme Scrawl.

Richard Kendall, product manager for news brands for Johnston Press, uses the free theme Satellite for his site richardkendall.WordPress.

> You can check to see if your site has been hacked by running a basic scan with isithacked.com

com. Freelance journalist Meg Heckman uses the free theme Argent on her site megheckman. WordPress.com. Writer and broadcaster Kenan Malik uses premium theme Gridspace on his site kenanmalik.WordPress. com. Journalist Josh Stearns uses the free theme Sela on his site stearns.WordPress. com.

All of these sites are run on the free platform .com and with the exception of Kenan Malik, they use free themes too.

There are some premium add-ons that you can choose to pay for with WordPress.com, one of which is buying your own domain name. You still run your site on WordPress. com but you can opt for a different domain than the one given for free which has 'WordPress.com' at the end. (You can find out how much a domain would cost here: https://WordPress. com/domains. I explain more about this on page 16.) An example of a free . com site with a custom domain is that of US columnist at the *Globe and Mail* Sarah Kendzior. Her domain name is sarahkendzior.com – she uses the free theme Twentyten, as does Alison Gow, digital innovation editor at Trinity Mirror Regionals. Alison's domain is alisongow.com.

Both Kendzior and Gow's sites are run on WordPress.com but have custom domains. At the time of writing you can sign up for a personal account on WordPress.com, which will include a free custom domain, for $3 a month or you can simply buy a domain through WordPress which, depending on

> If you want to check out which theme a site is using, view the source code. To do this: If you are on Chrome click on View/Developer/ Source on the tool bar. Search for the word 'theme' and this should bring you to the name of the theme being used. You can tell pretty quickly if the site is a WordPress site – you will see 'wp-' every-where and the code is nicely spaced out. If the code is all jammed together with no line spacing it most probably is not a WordPress site.

what you want, can cost upwards of £15 a year. Before you do this though, read the next section on buying a domain.

Tip: to find out who hosts a particular site, use whoishostingthis.com

SITE SET-UP: FREE (.COM)

What you need: a computer, an internet connection and an email account.

A quick note on email accounts: you are going to need an email account for all your new online accounts, plugins, themes, everything really from here on in, so it is advisable at this stage to create a Gmail account. I recommend using Gmail because it makes everything easy as Google sign-ins are linked to so many different tools and platforms. Choose an email account name that is professional – your name is preferable. Keep it simple.

If you do start to grow your site and want an email address that shows your domain – for example, the journalism.london website for London South Bank University journalism students uses the email account editor@journalism. london – you can set this up with Google apps.

This is something you can set up at a later stage when you are ready. (You can of course get a custom email with your website host but I always advise not to do this because if you change hosts moving your email accounts over can become really complicated. Whereas if you set up a custom email account with Google it doesn't matter how many times you change host, your email accounts will stay the same.)

For now, just set up a free Gmail account that you can use with all the different accounts you are going to be signing up for.

Make sure all your social media accounts (and any account that you sign up for to use with your site) use the same email address that you have created for your website. One of the things that gets people in a mess is having lots of different accounts all registered to different email addresses. Keep it simple: one email for all accounts.

Once you have an email account you are ready.

To set up a free site with WordPress takes only a few minutes and you don't need anything other than to be online. Please see the Walkthrough on p. 12.

SITE SET-UP: SELF-HOSTED (.ORG)

What you need: a computer, an internet connection, an email account and a minimum of £25.

Please read the note on email accounts on page 10 before you go any further.

We should start by explaining what 'self-hosted' actually means. As outlined in Chapter 1, WordPress is a CMS – a user-friendly system which offers anyone the chance to create and manage a website. Both the free account (WordPress.com) and the self-hosted account (WordPress.org) use exactly the same system from WordPress, but the free version has restrictions that the self-hosted does not, namely access to files and the ability to add themes and plugins.

'Self-hosted' simply means that your site is hosted by yourself – i.e. not by WordPress. It does not mean, though, that you yourself actually host your sites (you can, but it is not advisable as you need to buy a server and have excellent and fast 24-7 internet). When we refer to self-hosted WordPress sites we mean hosted on an external host – a hosting company.

This means that all the files which are needed for the site to work plus the database are housed on this external host instead of with WordPress, giving you access to everything.

Some examples of self-hosted .org sites are:

- **thepoke.co.uk** Founded in Aug 2002 *The Poke* started life as a magazine to provide an outlet for upcoming comedy writers – 50,000 copies were printed and distributed at the Edinburgh Festival. Now its online version boasts 5 million unique users globally viewing up to 10 million videos, stories and pictures per month. The website uses a custom theme created by London-based Datadial.

- **thedailymash.co.uk** The Daily Mash is a satirical website which publishes spoof articles and uses a custom theme, Mashtastic, by OH Digital.

- **deadlinenews.co.uk** Deadline News is an independent news and picture agency based in Edinburgh. The site uses the theme Newspaper.

- **howtostory.be** How to Story is a fantastic site on visual journalism and storytelling. It uses the theme Newsdesk lite.

- **theundefeated.com** This is a WordPress VIP site.

- **simonrogers.net** Simon Rogers is a data journalist based at Google. His site uses the theme The Morning After, which is no longer available to buy. You can check on Woocommerce for alternatives.

- **jacklail.com** Jack Lail is the consumer experience director for the *Knoxville News Sentinel*. His site is hosted by Amazon and he uses the free theme Twentyseventeen. Jack moved over to WordPress in 2017. He said:

  I was using an old version of Movable Type (Movable Type Pro version 5.2.13) and it just wasn't up-to-date enough. I manage some WordPress sites at work (knoxblogs.com) so it was an easy switch. Some of the reasons for moving to WordPress are: it's a very flexible, stable platform with a robust library of plugins that

WALKTHROUGH ▶

Setting up a free site with WordPress.com

1 Go to http://WordPress.com
2 Click Create Website.
3 Pick a category for your website.

Categorising content: take some time to really consider where you want to be found. These are top-level categories, which are broad, and you will find that your content is more than likely going to spread across more than one category, so try to pick the area where the majority of your content could sit. These categories are not set in stone, and you can change your mind later on in the process, so don't spend too much time deliberating.

4 Pick your sub-category.
5 Choose what you want your homepage to look like. Although you are being asked to decide on what your homepage should look like now, you can change the layout at any time, so it doesn't really matter which one you choose at the beginning.
6 Choose a theme. We'll talk more about how to choose themes later in this chapter. For now, just pick the first one you like. You can change it any time you like.
7 Choose a domain. We'll talk more about choosing domain names in the next section but something you will be asked to decide at this stage is whether you want to stick with the free account or go Premium. Do not go Premium at this stage – I cannot stress this enough. Going Premium will give you a domain name without the addition of WordPress. com but, and it's a big but, it will not give you access to your files. This won't mean anything to you at this stage but trust me, having access to your files is key to the development of your site and the main reason that, if you are serious about running a website, you need to have a self-hosted account via WordPress.org not via WordPress.com. So choose your domain – if I wanted 'ljfilotrani' then using the free account my domain would be ljfilotrani.WordPress.com. You will also be offered the chance to add a domain that you already own to this account. *Do not do this either.* Don't be tempted. Stick with the free account while you are still learning about how WordPress works. Once you feel more confident you can move to a self-hosted account, which will give you all the benefits of WordPress with none of the restrictions.
8 Pick a plan. Stick with the free. Remember this is just a learning account, so don't spend any money yet.
9 Create your account. Make sure you pick a username you are happy for people to see, as you can't change it. (You can of course create a new user account so it's not a disaster if do you change your mind.)

Make sure you note your password and username somewhere as you will forget it.

You are ready to go. Please go to page 30 for the next step: choosing and activating a theme.

make it easy to customize for non-programmers or 'casual admins'. It's also actively updated.[1]

■ **blog.digidave.org** David Cohn is senior director at Advance Digital's Alpha Group – he uses free theme Twentythirteen on his site and it is hosted by LA-based InMotion.

■ **tellingthestoryblog.com** Another great site exploring storytelling by multimedia journalist Matt Pearl. He uses the theme Ubergrid.

Why does having access to your files matter?

As you become more and more proficient with your website, access to the files will become more and more important to you, particularly when things go wrong (which they will, often!). You will need access to the files in order to troubleshoot problems and you will want to be able to add your own theme and plugins to suit, which you cannot do with the free account.

There are three things that you need and that you are going to have to pay for:

1. **A host.** Your host is the place which will keep all your files safe. It is incredibly important to have a reliable host. Prices vary from as little as £1 a month anywhere up to £100 and above. A good ballpark figure for a small start-up website should be around £60 for the year. This is an ongoing cost which you can pay upfront – for 12 months or 24 months or sometimes even 48 months. Obviously the more you pay upfront the bigger the discount. I would advise just paying for 12 months to start off with – or go for the monthly option.

2. **A domain name.** The cost of your domain name is dependent on how popular the words in it are and what *top-level domain* (TLD) you want. The TLD is the '.com', '.co. uk', etc. – there are now lots more to choose from, so you could get something quite cheap. Mostly, though, if you are using your own name the likelihood is that only you will want it, so it will be cheap – around £10 or £15. This is per annum. It is an ongoing cost: you don't own the name, you lease it. So be prepared to pay for it each year.

3. **A commercial theme.** Obviously you don't need a commercial theme to get going. There are free ones you can use, but if you are serious about growing a fully functioning website you will need to invest in one. This is a one-off cost and the most popular ones are retailing at around £50.

So, all in all you will need:

■ £60 hosting fees for the year (or £5 a month),
■ £15 for a domain name, and
■ £50 for a theme (you could start off with a free theme first) *Prices correct as of Dec 2017.*

THE BASIC WORDPRESS INSTALL (.ORG)

After you have installed WordPress on to your website (page 14), let's have a look at what these files are, how they are organised and some of the functionality (Figure 3.4).

If you click into File Manager for your domain on the cloud-hosting dashboard on Tsohost you will see a file called public_html (this is called your root folder). This is the folder where all the WordPress files necessary to run your website have been created and stored.

All the content and functionality files are organised into three folders: wp-admin, wp-includes and wp-content.

Before we look at each of these folders I just want to turn your attention to a couple of files which you'll see floating next to these folders. The first one – and arguably the most important – is the wp-config file. This is one of the first files you will check if you get a database error. If your site isn't showing up anymore, check the details in your config file. The database username, the database password and the database host are listed in this file.

WALKTHROUGH ▶

Setting up a self-hosted site with WordPress.org

The first thing you need to do is pick a host.

1 Pick a hosting company

There are so many hosting companies to choose from with wildly differing benefits and costs. I have used lots of them – for my own sites and for other companies. My preferred host, and the one I am going to use as my example here, is Tsohost.

There are a number of reasons why I prefer this particular company – one of the primary reasons being that it is UK-based. This, I have found through experience, makes a huge difference in terms of how supported you feel as a customer. In the past, I have used companies based in the States with support offered via an online ticket system and, at a push, a long-distance call (though many companies now have call centres all over the world). While this can work, in reality you are always waiting for a response to a query raised instead of having direct access to a tech team.

Having your hosting company based in the same country as you means you can pick up the phone at any point during the day and receive instant help – this is particularly vital for new users with basic website knowledge. Tsohost also runs the standard ticket system online but having access to the tech team 365 days a week, 24 hours a day, at the end of a phone, is incredibly reassuring. There have been many 3am calls where I have had to troubleshoot a hack or some other bug which inevitably waits until sundown before raising its head!

But it's not just accessibility that separates Tsohost from the pack for me; it's the quality of the support offered as well. I don't know whether it is the fact that the company is employee-owned, which means that all employees have shares in the company, but it is by far the most efficient and helpful tech team I have ever used. It seems to me that many of the biggest hosting companies use call centres as a first response to technical problems, which is not helpful when you are stressed about a site going down. What you need is instant access to someone who knows what they are talking about. This is what you get in, my experience, with Tsohost.

The last consideration – which is not to be overlooked – is that its interface (what you use to manage your site on its platform) is very user-friendly. So many other companies, it seems, do not understand how important it is to have a well-designed, easy-to-use dashboard for its customers. So many of the other hosting companies I have used have messy, complicated, unhelpful dashboards which, unless you have some prior knowledge of how websites work, are impenetrable and therefore off-putting.

You can, of course, go with any hosting company you like (Figure 3.1) – but pick wisely because it will become very important to you and can make the whole experience of running a site incredibly frustrating.

Mosts hosts have offices and/or data centres in more than one location - however, if you can, choose a host which has its head office/main centre closest to you geographically. If you do not want to use TSO (particularly if you are not based in Europe) here is a selection of worldwide hosts. They are not tried and tested by me but they all offer specific support for WordPress sites and have generally good ratings. I have tried to loosely keep in mind different time zones.

Australia
Digital Pacific	https://www.digitalpacific.com.au/	based in Sydney
Aussie Hosts	https://www.aussiehosts.com.au/	based in Brisbane
Net Origin	https://www.netorigin.com.au/	based in Perth

Canada
Canspace	https://www.canspace.ca/	based in Toronto
Hostpapa	https://www.hostpapa.ca/	based in Burlington
Hostutopia	https://hostutopia.com/	based in Vancouver

US
Green Greeks	https://www.greengeeks.com	based in LA, California
Tadpole	https://tadpole.cc/	based in New York
a2hosting	https://www.a2hosting.com/	based in Ann Arbor, Michigan
actwd	https://www.actwd.com/	based in Houston
WpEngine	https://wpengine.com/	based in Austin

New Zealand
Umbrellar	https://www.umbrellar.nz/	based in Auckland

Asia
Vodien	https://www.vodien.com/	based in Singapore
Miles Web	https://www.milesweb.com/	based in Maharashtra, India
Net Space India	https://www.netspaceindia.com/	based in Mumbai, India
Xenyo	https://www.xenyohosting.com/	based in Kowloon, Hong Kong

Africa
Whogohost	https://www.whogohost.com/	based in Lagos, Nigeria
Hostking	https://www.hostking.co.za/	based in Cape Town, SA
Heberjahiz	https://www.heberjahiz.com	based in Casablanca, Morocco
Network Egypt	http://www.ne.com.eg/	based in Cairo, Egypt

Europe
home.pl	https://home.pl/	based in Szczecin, Poland
1&1	https://www.1und1.de/	based in Montabaur, Germany
Arsys	https://www.arsys.net/	based in Madrid, Spain
Kinsta	https://kinsta.com/	based in Amsterdam, Netherlands
tophost.it	https://www.tophost.it/	based in Rome, Italy
Ikoula	https://www.ikoula.com/fr	based in Boulogne, France
Blacknight	https://www.blacknight.com	based in Carlow, Ireland
DNhost	https://dnhost.gr	based in Athens, Greece

Figure 3.1 There are lots of hosts to choose from but my advice is to try and use a host from the same country that you live in.

A note on using another host. Although I am using Tsohost by way of illustration, the steps you will take will be replicated pretty much with whichever host you choose.

So if you can follow the process in my example, you will be able to replace Tsohost with your chosen host quite easily.

Before you go ahead and create an account with your new host, you should first choose a domain.

2 Choose a domain

It's better to buy your domain from your hosts if you can because it cuts down on the steps to getting yourself online. You can buy domains from a number of places – in the past I have often used 123-reg.co.uk, for example – but if you can, buy everything in one place.

Some things to consider when choosing a domain. What is your site for? If it is a portfolio site for you as a journalist – a place for you to house all of your content with a view of securing jobs – then stick with your name as the domain (for example, ljfilotrani.com) because this is about building you as a brand. If your site is about an area of news or a specific genre then think about the keywords associated with the content. Ask yourself what search words would you expect someone to put into Google in order to find your site. Consider using these words in your domain. Or perhaps you are creating a company, in which case this needs to be the domain name.

Try not to be too clever or cryptic. Keep it simple – be careful of potential spelling issues that may come up when people are searching for you, and don't use dashes or abbreviations if you can help it. Think about your users – you want your site to be found and your domain to be remembered.

Here's advice from Alex Price, founder of WordPress agency 93digital:

Choose the domain that is best suited to your business or organisation. Keep it short, easy to remember and use the TLD that is local to you. If you are based in the UK, then it usually makes the most sense to use the .co.uk. However, think about protecting your brand moving forwards. It makes sense to buy the major variations of your domain name if possible to stop others from buying them in the future. For example, you could buy the .com, .net and .org versions too.[2]

Let's go back to Tsohost – put in what you think you would like your domain to be and hit Search. The site will pull up a list of what is and what isn't available and will offer you all sorts of extensions, from '.com' to '.m.uk' to '.pro'. I advise you to get yourself either a '.com' or a '.co.uk' or both. If you are UK-based go for '.co.uk' because this establishes yourself with the UK – and if you want to further locate yourself with the capital you could try for a '.london' if it's available. If you are aligning yourself with a charity or non-governmental organisation then go for a '.org'.

Obviously the more popular the keyword the more expensive the domain (and most likely it won't be available). You have to think laterally. But I reiterate: keep it simple.

New TLDs are coming online all the time. You can check out the domains that are due to launch here: www.uniteddomains.com/domain/new-domains-launch-sequence

3 Pick a hosting package

Once you have decided on your domain, you need to buy a hosting package.

Hosting packages can vary in benefits from company to company and can also vary in costs. My advice is not to go for the cheapest. On Tsohost I always recommend my students go for the business cloud-hosting package as this offers a free domain and 10GB of webspace. The webspace is how many files you are allowed to store with it. As a multimedia journalist you are going to need space to store images (video and audio files will actually be stored on another host – YouTube and SoundCloud, for example – so these files won't take up space on Tsohost, but images can eat into space, so this is something to consider when choosing a package).

The other thing to consider is how much *bandwidth* you are allowed. Trying to work out how much bandwidth you will need is a bit tricky because the calculation is dependent on knowing how big your page size is, and this can vary greatly depending on what content you have on it. So, for example, if you had lots of images on a page, the size of the page is going to be much bigger than if it was just a page of text.

Let's say by way of illustration that your average page size is 50kb, and let's say each of your visitors to your site is going to look at 10 pages per month. Your average bandwidth per visitor per month is then 500kb. So, if you have a maximum bandwidth allowance of 5GB you'd have to have 10,000 visitors each month to hit this limit. This seems an enormous amount of *traffic* – way beyond what most people enjoy in terms of monthly visits. However, this calculation does not take into account all the other factors that add to the bandwidth usage, namely: larger file sizes; email usage; *File Transfer Protocol* (FTP) activity; search-engine crawlers; spam bots ... All of these will push your usage up and it is surprising just how quickly the 5GB limit can be reached, even with a relatively basic blog. My advice is to go for 10GB and above.

Tip: bandwidth usage, like most things online, can be scaled up or scaled down according to your use, so there is nothing to stop you starting off with the lowest bandwidth and therefore the cheapest hosting package while you are starting out.

On Tsohost go for cloud hosting rather than *cPanel* hosting because the interface is much easier to use and much more intuitive. CPanel is a web-based control panel which many hosting companies offer their customers in order to control their websites. Tsohost has built its own control panel for its cloud hosting and it is one of the nicest I have used.

4 Create your account

Once you have decided on your domain name and chosen a hosting package, you are ready to create your account. Add the hosting account to your shopping cart on Tsohost and you will then be asked to create an account. If you get stuck at any stage call the tech team and it will help you.

5 Make sure your domain is active

Before you can add your domain to your hosting account and begin the process of building your WordPress site, check that the domain that you have bought/claimed on Tsohost is showing as active. To do this, make sure you are logged on by clicking My.tsohost and then click on My Domains. Your domain should say 'Active' – if it doesn't, give Tsohost a call (Figure 3.2).

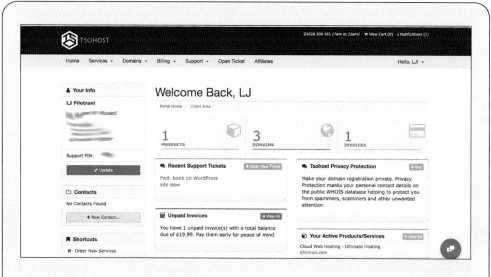

Figure 3.2 All hosts use pretty much the same system, so if you can follow these instructions for Tsohost you will be able to apply that knowledge to another host.

6 Add your domain to the hosting account

On My.tsohost click on Products. This will show the hosting package you have signed up for. Click on the hosting package name and then Manage to log in to the control panel. This opens up the cloud-hosting dashboard and it is in here where you will find all your files for your site. You can add a number of websites to your hosting package – if you have chosen the professional package you can add up to six sites for free.

To add a new site simply click on Add a New Website. Put in your active domain and hit Next.

Use the recommended operating system, Linux.

What is Linux? Linux is an operating system. It basically allows communication with your computer (hardware) and the program it runs (software).

Once you have added the site you will see a dashboard giving you many options for controlling your website. If you click on File Manager, you will see a folder called public_html. It is empty at the moment, but this is where all the WordPress files will be stored once you install the platform.

At this point in the process your website still doesn't exist – if you try to find your domain you will get a page saying 'This site can't be reached', or a parked page. This is because you haven't actually created a website yet – you have only chosen the address.

To create the site, you need to install the CMS WordPress.

On your dashboard, click on your domain. That will bring all your options back up. The first block you see is Basic Management Tools, the second is Advanced Management Tools, the third is Database Tools and the fourth (and the one that you are looking for) is Application Options. You need to select Install Applications.

When selecting a hosting company (if you decide not to use Tsohost) make sure it offers one-click installs to make the process of creating a WordPress website as easy as possible (all the hosts on page 15 offer one-click installs).

Make sure WordPress is selected and then hit Install. Leave Install in Path blank. Just hit Install Application (Figure 3.3).

Figure 3.3 The application is installed successfully.

Tip: some hosting companies offer you the option to install a basic version of WordPress or a deluxe version (it can be called other things). Always go for the basic – this will give you all that you need and no more. With deluxe installs you will get lots of themes and plugins that you will never use or need, but you will have to continually update them or delete them. So just go for the basic. You can add in anything you choose later.

Your site has now been created. Please take a note of the username and password in the green box. Write it down!

You can click on Login and it will reveal your log-in URL or you can access the dashboard to your website from anywhere by adding '/wp-admin' to your domain – for example, http://yourdomain.com/wp-admin. Once you click on this link you will be taken to the log-in page where you can put in the username and the password you were given by Tsohost.

If your site cannot be found at this stage, don't panic! Give Tsohost a call – you may have missed something.

All of this information needs to correspond to the information on your host (Tsohost, in your case) and if it doesn't then the site can't be loaded. We'll talk more about databases on page 24 but for now all you need to know is to be very careful with this file.

On Tsohost you can view the content of the file by clicking on Edit File. In the future you will be looking at these files via an FTP server rather than on Tsohost, but more on that later (see page 42). For now, click on Edit File and you will see the contents of the config file (Figure 3.5).

Another important file is the .htaccess file. The .htaccess file is primarily used for creating pretty *permalinks* (Figure 3.6).

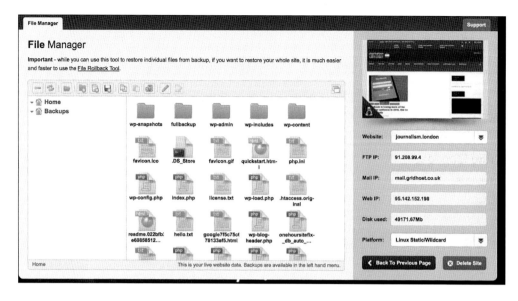

Figure 3.4 The core WordPress files.

What is a permalink? A permalink is simply a URL which is automatically created when you create a new post or a new page. For example, instead of a new post that you have just created being given the url http://yoursite.com/?p=45 – which is the default way WordPress handles content – you will have a link created that uses the title of the post and date, so it would look more like this: http://yoursite.com/2016/07/this-is-my-first-post. This has obvious benefits in terms of searches and in terms of archiving – using keywords is much better than random numbers. See page 76 on *search engine optimisation* (SEO) for more on this.

The other file that can be important is the robots.txt file, which you may or may not see. This file instructs search engine bots and can have an effect of stopping too much activity on your site from spiders, crawlers, robots and bots which can spike your traffic and eat into your bandwidth allowance. Restricting some crawlers

A good practice to get into right from the beginning is to always make a copy of the text in a file before you start making any changes. This way if you break your site you can revert back to the original file with the original code.

can be useful, especially if your site seems sluggish and slow to load. Instructions for restricting crawlers will be listed in this file.

Important folders include:
wp-admin In the wp-admin folder there are numerous HTML, CSS, PHP and JavaScript files which allow you to control the administration of your site.

wp-includes The wp-includes folder also holds a number of HTML, CSS, PHP and JavaScript files but these are the ones that actually control how your site works.

Both wp-admin and wp-includes should be left alone. They contain the files known as the 'core' files, and tampering with any of them isn't advisable unless you know what you are doing. I hardly ever go into these folders.

wp-content This is the folder that you'll become most familiar with. It houses the themes, the plugins and any images that you upload.

In a basic WordPress install you get a couple of default themes and a couple of plugins.

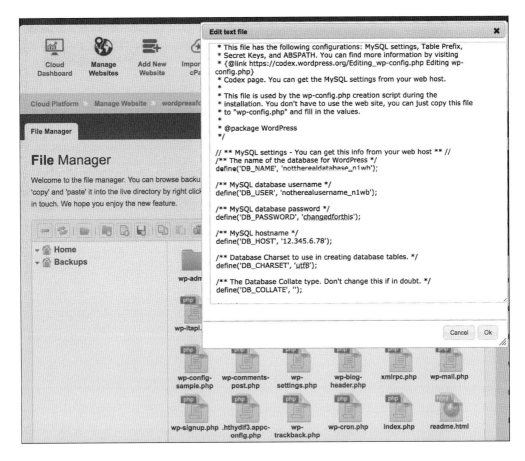

Figure 3.5 The config file is one of your most important files. If you are getting a database error, your first check should be the config file showing the database information as outlined above.

If you click into the wp-content folder and then the Themes folder you will see which themes you have installed – at the time of writing the default themes are Twentyfifteen, Twentyfourteen and Twentysixteen. No doubt by the time this book goes to print there will be Twentyseventeen and Twentyeighteen as well.

At this point you should go to your website dashboard – to do this go to your log-in page http://yoursite.com/wp-admin, put in your username and password, and then you should see the site dashboard (Figure 3.7).

On the left menu you will see Appearance. Hover over this and it will bring up a drop-down menu – click on Themes. (We will be looking at themes in more detail on page 30; this is just to illustrate the correlation between what you are looking at on Tsohost and your site.)

You will see that the themes on offer for you to use are the same as the ones in the folders on Tsohost. Whenever you upload a theme this is where it will appear.

Go back to Tsohost and the file manager and now click on Plugins (wp-content/plugins) (Figure 3.8).

Then go back to your website dashboard and find Plugins (underneath Appearance). If you click on Plugins you will see a list of plugins – some active, some not active – that have been uploaded to your site. This list should correspond to the folders in your plugins file on Tsohost.

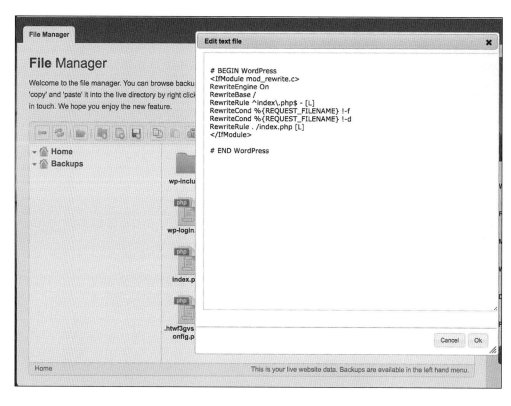

Figure 3.6 The .htaccess file is one of the most important files in a WordPress install.

Figure 3.7 The WordPress dashboard – this is where you control all your content.

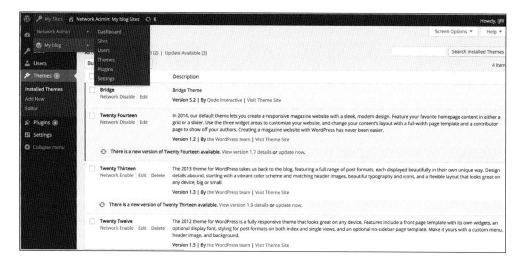

Figure 3.8 WordPress comes with a number of default plugins already installed.

Figure 3.9 Activating your multisite.

```php
                    wp-config.php — Edited

/**#@-*/

/**
 * WordPress Database Table prefix.
 *
 * You can have multiple installations in one database if you give each a unique
 * prefix. Only numbers, letters, and underscores please!
 */
$table_prefix  = 'r0zo_';

/**
 * For developers: WordPress debugging mode.
 *
 * Change this to true to enable the display of notices during development.
 * It is strongly recommended that plugin and theme developers use WP_DEBUG
 * in their development environments.
 */
define('WP_DEBUG', false);

define ('WP_ALLOW_MULTISITE', true );

/* That's all, stop editing! Happy blogging. */

/** Absolute path to the WordPress directory. */
if ( !defined('ABSPATH') )
        define('ABSPATH', dirname(__FILE__) . '/');

/** Sets up WordPress vars and included files. */
require_once(ABSPATH . 'wp-settings.php');
```

So how does your website actually work?

WordPress uses two things – PHP code (the core) and an SQL database to store the data. Each WordPress site has one database. All the information, such as user accounts, passwords, tags, categories, posts and comments, is stored in the database. The rest of the content, such as anything you upload, is stored in the core files (the PHP files). When a visitor comes to your site, their browser will request the page that they have clicked on. This page is brought up by the PHP and finds the appropriate data in the database – everything is then combined PHP and a mix of HTML to output the result for the visitor.

This is what is known as the loop – essentially it carries out this function again and again until there is nothing new to serve up. On a *static page* – for example, an About page where there is no dynamic content (no *widgets* or anything with updated stories or information) – it may just loop once and that's enough. But on a page where there is lots going on – content changing and updating constantly – the process will keep going, searching, retrieving and outputting.

WordPress source code – the code that actually makes the site function properly – consists of PHP, JavaScript and CSS code. When we talk about the code being 'open-source' it simply means that anyone can see the code, making it easy to understand, amend and approve (and hack . . . more on this in the chapter on security; see page 80). The thing to remember about the WordPress source code is that it is being constantly updated, improved upon and developed, so you absolutely must keep on top of any new release. The other great thing about WordPress being open-source is that it allows developers all over the world to contribute to it – this is what makes is such a rich source.

Don't worry if this doesn't make any sense at the moment. You will start to get the hang of things as you spend more time on your site. I don't think you need to know too much more at this stage. As we go through the book you will be introduced to the database and to some of the core files that you need to know in more detail.

You are ready now to choose, upload and activate a theme. So please skip to page 30.

MULTISITES

This is not a section for beginners, so if you have only just started out on WordPress, my advice is to get to grips with running a single site first before attempting a multisite launch. This is primarily because the multisite function is not enabled by default on the standard WordPress install and requires some changes to the core files.

I am assuming you know how to use an FTP server (see page 38 if not), that you know how to locate the wp-config file (see page 13 if not) and that you know how to activate/deactivate plugins (see page 73 if not).

First things first: a definition. A *multisite* is a system of allowing many separate websites to run off one domain – with one WordPress installation but with the ability for each site to run mostly independent of one another. So one main website can run a network of other sites off it using the same domain as the root with the addition of a site name. For example, http://yourdomain.com/newsite

Why would you want to do this? Having the ability to create new websites under the umbrella of a main site means that you are able to control all the sites from one dashboard. This will have enormous benefits when it comes to updating WordPress, plugins and themes, and it also means that as the super admin you are able to access and share content from all the sites and can control the users. All of this while allowing these individual sites or microsites, which is what they are, to develop and grow independently of each other. One of the biggest examples of a multisite network in action is WordPress.com – every new blog created is essentially running off the main site, the main domain: http://WordPress.com

At London South Bank University our journalism students all get given a microsite to use for the duration of their degree. The super admin can see and control all the sites, with each student having control over their own site and being able to activate whichever theme they want from an approved list. (As the super admin you are in control of what themes and plugins are available to use cross-network and by individual sites.)

This is one of the biggest advantages of running a multisite – the ability to allow each site to use its own theme and therefore have its own identity. I have in the past had a main news site with separate sites for audio content and for video content, and a site to sell things on. Running a multisite for this purpose is perfect as it allows you to select appropriate themes for the types of the content. For example, yourdomain.com/video could have a specific theme for displaying and organising video content well, which could be different from yourdomain.com/buy, which could have an *ecommerce* theme set up with a shopping cart that can take payments. And because they are all on the same domain you can easily share posts, users and newsletters, making everything streamlined. It's a way of handling a brand with many different aspects/products.

It is important before we go through the steps for activating a multisite that we clear up a few terms.

The three most important terms that you will hear when dealing with multisites are 'network', 'site' and 'blog ID'. The network is the entire multisite installation (the main domain and all the other subdomains/subdirectories). A 'site' refers to a single website on the network and the blog ID is the unique number assigned to each single website (don't be confused by the term 'blog' – it just means 'site').

If you do not see the Network Setup option under Tools go and check the code in the config file. In particular, compare the single quotation marks with the others in the code. They should be straight and not curly – if they are the wrong quotation marks the file will not work. Either copy and paste the correct ones from elsewhere in the code or go and change how your computer is set up so that you use straight quotation marks. For example, if you are on a Mac, go to System Preferences/Keyboard/Text and then make sure you have selected the straight quotation marks (Figure 3.11).

1. Enabling the multisite features is straightforward (Figure 3.9). First, find your wp-config file and add the following code to it:

   Define ('WP_ALLOW_MULTISITE', true);
   It should be pasted just above the line
   /* That's all, stop editing! Happy Blogging.*/

   Log out of your site and log back in again – you should see a change in your dashboard: under Tools there should be the option for Network Setup (Figure 3.10).

   Tip: remember to make a copy of your config file before you start making changes, and keep it safe. I use TextEdit on a Mac to save code files.

2. **Go to your WordPress dashboard**, select all your plugins and deactivate them.

3. **Click Network Setup** under Tools on your WordPress dashboard.

4. **Fill in the network details** (you can change these later). You will also get to choose how your multisite is going to be organised – whether it will use subdomains (http://newsite.yourdomain.com) or subdirectories (http://yourdomain.com/newsite). My preference is subdirectories as I like all the sites to start off with the root (i.e. yourdomain.com). However, if you are trying to change an existing site into a multisite you won't be given this option. You only get the choice if it is a new WordPress install. If it is an existing site, then your

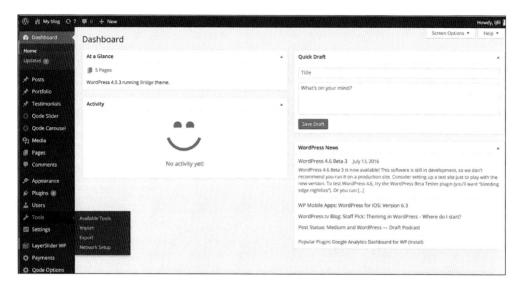

Figure 3.10 Network tools.

Figure 3.11 Change the settings from curly to straight quotations on your Mac.

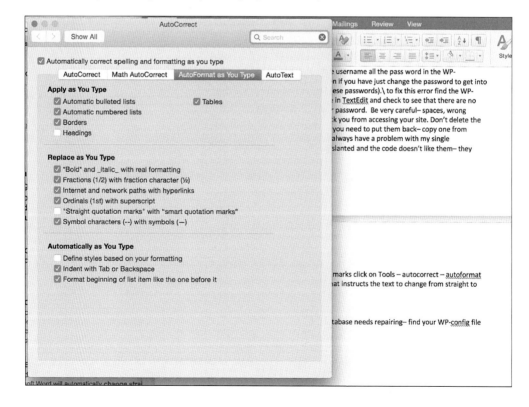

```
                              .htaccess — Not Saved

# BEGIN WordPress

RewriteEngine On
RewriteBase /
RewriteRule ^index\.php$ - [L]

# add a trailing slash to /wp-admin
RewriteRule ^wp-admin$ wp-admin/ [R=301,L]

RewriteCond %{REQUEST_FILENAME} -f [OR]
RewriteCond %{REQUEST_FILENAME} -d
RewriteRule ^ - [L]
RewriteRule ^(wp-(content|admin|includes).*) $1 [L]
RewriteRule ^(.*\.php)$ $1 [L]
RewriteRule . index.php [L]

# END WordPress
```

Figure 3.12 Add this code to your .htaccess file.

Figure 3.13 Create a blogs directory in your wp-content folder.

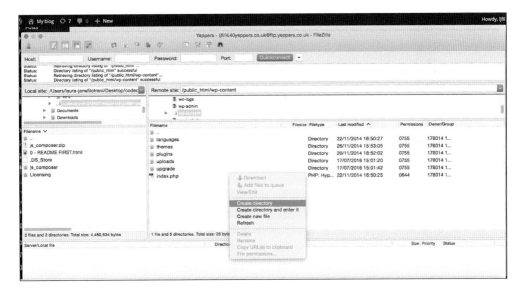

multisite will use subdomains by default newsite.yourdomain.com.

5. **Paste the code over the existing code** in your .htaccess file (Figure 3.12) above the line /* That's all, stop editing! Happy Blogging.*/

6. **Create a blogs directory** in your wp-content folder (Figure 3.13). Add a new directory called blogs.dir (Figure 3.14).
   Log out and log back in to your site.

7. It is easy to see whether you have been successful in creating your multisite. You should see a difference to the dashboard. You should see My Sites on the admin bar and if you hover over there you should get a drop-down menu with Network Admin.

Now you are ready to go. You essentially have two separate areas to deal with, with two separate dashboards – one for the main site and another for the network. In the network dashboard you can create new sites, add users and upload

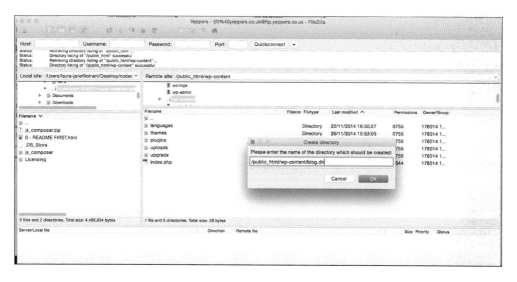

Figure 3.14 Call the directory blogs.dir.

themes and plugins. You can also control the settings for all the sites – some of these settings can be site-specific and some can be network-wide, or all can be network-wide, as you please.

How you run the network is up to you, but just be careful before you give lots of users the ability to create new sites and add new users, and be careful whether you enable admin menus for the plugins on each site, which essentially would give admins of each site the ability to make changes to the plugin files code.

In my experience, it is wise to keep fairly tight control over new elements being added to a multisite without first being approved by the super admin. Allowing changes to plugins, for example, could potentially open your network up to hacks

> If you cannot see your new site – or rather, when you try to click on to the dashboard for the new site you get an error message saying 'Site not found', then unless you have made a mistake in the steps (check this first) it is more than likely that you will have to enable wildcard subdomains on your host.

and malicious activity – and in the worst-case scenarios a virus which will wipe your entire network. This has happened to me, so be warned.

8. **Add a new site.** This is self-explanatory, really – just be careful with the site address because you won't be able to change this if you make a mistake. Put in the contact email for the person who is going to be in the admin role for this site, if it isn't you.

    If you are using Tsohost it is very easy – just go to the cloud-hosting dashboard for your site and click on Manage Site. In the file manager you will see Wildcard Vhosts in the Advanced Management section. Click in there and then enable Wildcard Vhosts (Figure 3.15). This will automatically generate a new report in your *Domain Name System* (DNS) which will allow your new sites to be found (Figure 3.16).

Figure 3.15 If you get an error message when you are trying to create a new site you may have to enable Wildcards on your host.

Figure 3.16 Enabling Wildcards will generate a DNS for your new site.

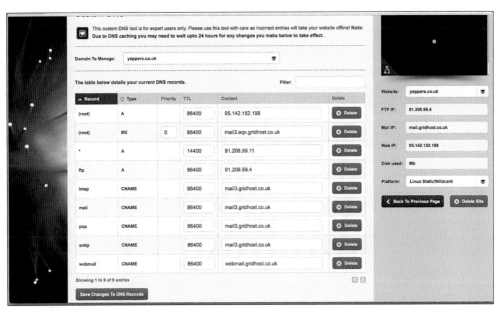

You should now be able to access all the new sites you create on your network.

Multisite themes

You can upload as many themes as you like and make them active across the whole network or you can restrict specific theme use to individual sites. To make a theme available across the network is very simple. Just upload the theme in the usual way (see page 30 for basic installation help) through the network dashboard and then click Network Enable. This will allow the theme to be accessed and used from any single site's dashboard.

If you want to activate a theme for just a single site but not make it available across the network (perhaps you don't want any sites looking similar) you need to something slightly different.

1. Go to Sites from the drop-down Network Admin menu.
2. Click on Edit Site.
3. Enable the theme you want to use.
4. Activate the theme from the site dashboard.

We'll look at some themes built for multisite networks shortly.

Multisite plugins

There are a number of plugins which are handy to have for managing multisites that I will flag up in Chapter 5. All I want to say about plugins at this point is that before you activate any, do a search to make sure they are compatible with multisite installs. Tip: some plugins aren't and can potentially break a network. Plugins, like themes, can be network-activated or activated at site level under the standard plugins menu on the individual site dashboard.

Multisite users

One of the major differences between managing a standard WordPress site and a multisite is the way in which users and roles are affected. On a multisite each single site in the network can have its own set of users – these users can be given access to a number of sites should this be required and they can have different roles on different sites.

The super admin is the only one who can see all users and access all sites by default. Depending on what you decide, you can give permission or restrict the ability for admins of individual sites to create new users.

The standard user roles available for you to choose from on the standard WordPress install are quite limiting. But luckily there are plugins to solve this. I'll be exploring these plugins in the section on users (see page 158).

For now, I think this is enough information about multisites to get you going.

THEMES (.COM AND .ORG)

In this section I am going to cover selecting and activating themes on both .com and .org and also buying and uploading commercial themes specifically for .org. The process for activating a theme, however, is the same for both platforms.

What is a theme?

A theme dictates how a site works and how it looks. It is essentially the face of your website – what the public sees and interacts with; the front end as opposed to the back end, which is what you use WordPress to control.

A theme is not just about how the site looks, however, it is responsible for the whole user experience (UX), so it is very important that you pick a theme that is suitable for the content you are going to be producing. Some themes are organised in a way which is more suitable for video content, for example, while others are better for displaying images or data, or text. When you begin to look for your theme, this is what you need to keep in mind – the function. What do you want your site to do? Everything else – the colours, the fonts, the elements – can be changed.

Each theme has a number of different files – some PHP files, some CSS files and some JavaScript files.

If you are using .org you can find the theme files in the wp-content folder (Figure 3.17).

Each WordPress install comes with default themes for you to use – this is the same for both .com and .org (Figure 3.18).

Before we consider some points regarding choosing the right theme for you, let's look at how to upload and activate a theme, both on a free .com site and a self-hosted .org site (Figure 3.19).

Activating a theme on a free .com site

1. **Go to your site dashboard and click on Appearance/Themes.** (For help with logging into your WordPress dashboard, see page 45.)

Figure 3.17 Your theme files are stored in the wp-content folder.

Figure 3.18 Every WordPress install comes with default themes.

There are hundreds if not thousands of themes to choose from – some free and some that you have to pay for (called Premium). The free themes are the most basic and will not allow you much control – things that you will be able to change will be pretty limited. My advice is to have a play around with a number of different themes before spending any money on a Premium theme. You need to understand what you like and what you don't like before making your choice.

You can filter available themes with keyword searches. Try putting in the word 'news'.

2. **Look at the demo** of the theme before activating – this will show you how your site will look with that theme activated.

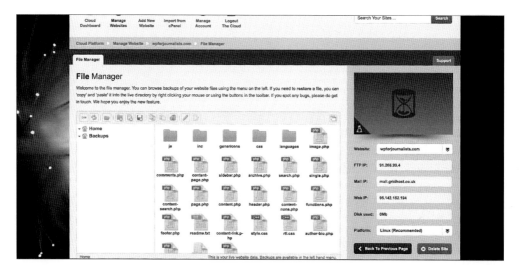

Figure 3.19 Your theme folder contains many files.

3. **Activate theme.** Once you have picked one you like the look of and have had a play around with the demo, click Activate Theme.

4. **Check that your chosen theme is active** – when you click Themes you should see a box saying 'current theme'.

5. **Customize your theme.** Depending on which theme you have selected you will have the options to change colours and backgrounds; add your own logo, menus and widgets; and create/use page templates. (All the different settings are explored on page 46.)

> As so many people access website content via their smart phones, check what your site will look like on a tablet, mobile or desktop by clicking the icons at the bottom of the Customize bar.

Uploading a theme via FTP

Once you have set up your FTP account this is a simple process. You just have to drag and drop your theme folders – unzipped – from your desktop into the wp-content/theme folder. Simple. What's not quite so simple is setting up your FTP account. Go to page 38 for help.

Once you have bought, uploaded and activated your theme you will see a number of new plugins will have been automatically added on your dashboard – or you may be asked to install and activate some in order for the theme to work properly. Go ahead and do this. Once you have all the plugins activated you are now ready to customize your theme. You will find all the options under Theme/Settings on your dashboard.

Help with choosing a commercial theme (.org)

There are a number of places that you can buy WordPress themes from online. I use themeforest.net, which is owned by Australian company Envato, so I will use this platform to illustrate my examples, but the tips and advice given can be applied to whichever ecommerce platform you choose to buy from. Just a note about Envato: I use it because everything that is on its site has been reviewed and checked by its

WALKTHROUGH▶

Installing a theme on a self-hosted site (.org)

This can be a little trickier than activating a theme on a free .com site – not least because you have to upload the theme yourself. Once uploaded, the steps for activating it are the same for the free .com sites.

Let's assume you have chosen and bought your theme and it is currently sitting on your desktop. There are two ways of getting that theme onto your WordPress site. You can upload the theme via the WordPress dashboard – this generally works, unless the files are really large, in which case the process will time out. If the process does time out, you will need to use the second method of uploading a theme – via an FTP server. (See page 38 for help with setting up your FTP.)

First, here's how to upload the theme via the WordPress dashboard.

1 Download your chosen theme on to your desktop – it will download as a zip file (Figure 3.20).

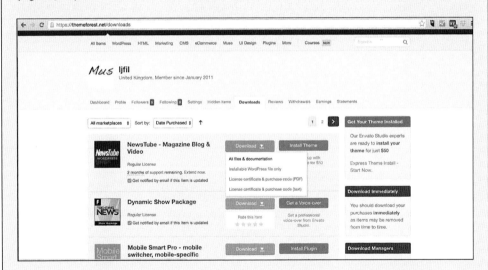

Figure 3.20 Download your theme to your desktop.

Make sure you download all files and documentation from the platform where you have bought the theme onto your desktop and not just a folder that says 'Installable WordPress files only'. This is because all the instructions and any other information you may need will not be included in the installable WordPress files.

In particular, amongst the files that you need to keep safe when you purchase a commercial theme (and a plugin) are the licence certificate and the purchase code. You will need these if you can't get your theme/plugin to work and also for installing/ downloading the latest versions. These files prove that you paid for them and you have the right licence to use them, so keep them safe.

2 Locate the file on your computer and unpack the zip file by clicking on it.

3 Find the zip folder. Open the unpacked folder and find the theme zip folder inside. This is the folder you will need to upload on WordPress. Not all theme zip folders are in the same place so you may have to click on each folder to find it.

You may notice there are other theme files labelled 'child'. I am not going to cover using *child themes* in this book but essentially a child theme inherits all the functionality and styling of the *parent theme* – the main theme, which is what you are using – but you can make adjustments so that it looks and operates slightly differently. There can be many instances when a developer may require this option but we are sticking with the main theme here, the 'parent' theme. So leave anything with the word 'child' attached alone.

4 Drag the parent theme zip folder onto your desktop. This is purely so that you can easily find the file. *Don't unzip it.* (This is one of the main differences between uploading a theme via the WordPress dashboard and using FTP. You always upload a zip file on WordPress but you must upack it first – unzip it – before uploading it via FTP.)

5 Go to your WordPress dashboard and click Appearances/Themes and Add New.

6 Upload the theme – choose the theme zip file and click Install Now. This process should not take longer than 20 or 30 seconds (Figure 3.21).

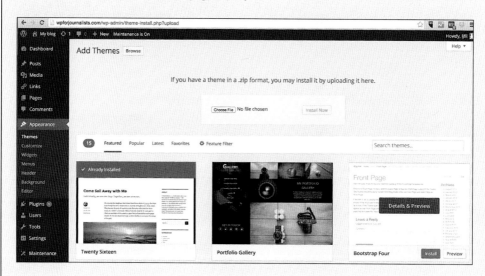

Figure 3.21 Uploading the theme.

Sometimes the theme files are too large for the automatic upload and will cause WordPress to time out. If this happens you will have to upload your theme file via your FTP server (see page 43).

If you have been successful, you will get the option to activate or live preview your theme.

tech teams and its customer support is excellent.

What to look for when choosing a theme

There are a couple of things that you should pay attention to when choosing your theme beyond what it looks like and its functionality.

Alex Price of 93digital says:

Look for a theme that fits the style of design you are looking for in your website. Following that, make sure it is of a high quality. Has the theme author produced lots of other themes? Does this theme have a good reviews? Are there lots of comments suggesting some things don't work?

■ **Does it offer *demo/dummy content*?**
Having dummy content will make your life a whole lot easier as it will mean when you activate your theme you will be given the option to populate the site so that it looks exactly like the demo version on Themeforest. So, if you are able to upload the creator's dummy content your site will show dummy posts, images, headlines, videos – all of the content on the demo version which you will have seen when you bought the theme. All you have to do then is save your own content on top on theirs. If you buy a theme without dummy content, you will have no structure at all when you activate the theme and you will have to build the whole thing from scratch. You will essentially just have a skeleton site. It is much easier to learn how a theme works from a demo than from the instructions.

All themes have their own peculiarities and will work slightly differently from each other. However, you will find that once you start to learn one theme, picking up how another works will become easier and easier.

■ **Is it well documented?** Does the theme come with good, clear instructions? Spend some time reading through the comments and reviews of a theme before buying it to see how responsive the support team is. This will give you a good indication of how well documented the theme is. Also check out its support system. You will need help at some point so it's always best to pick a theme from a developer who has a good support system and excellent ratings. This is particularly true when you are starting out.
The theme will come with instructions (documentation), usually located in the theme folder. They are usually an HTML file and they could be in a documents folder or a licence folder or just floating in the main theme folder. Quite often the file is called readme.html. This file will have all the instructions, from uploading the theme through to creating the home page, creating galleries and all the other different features your theme offers. Be warned – some instructions are better than others! If you get stuck you can email the developers of the theme directly – this is why it's best to pick a theme which offers great customer support.

■ **Is the theme responsive?** This means will the theme adapt to different platforms automatically, i.e. mobile, desktop and tablet? It is very unusual nowadays for a theme not to be responsive, but it's always best to check in the theme features

> **Do not use the images supplied in the demo/dummy content on your own site. You do not have permission for these images – they are purely for demonstration. You must replace any images with your own before going live (that goes for any video and audio content too).**

listed on the ecommerce site where you are buying the theme from.

- **Is the theme compatible with most browsers?** The browsers you definitely want listed are Internet Explorer, Chrome, Firefox and Safari as a minimum.

> On Themeforest click on the live preview of the theme to see what your site would look like.

Some questions to ask yourself when choosing a theme for your website:

- **Menus** Do you want your menu bar running across the top of your site or down the left or right? Do you want the option of a mega menu (preview content) or drop-downs or for the menu to be hidden?
- **Logos** Where do you want your logo to appear – left, centre or right on the *header*?
- **Boxed versus full width** Do you want your site to be contained within a box on a background or do you want to run your site across the full width of the screen? (Most themes will offer the chance to choose either.)
- **Categories** Do you want to have icons displayed with your categories or instead of words? Or perhaps you would like colour bars.
- **Adverts** Do you want to run header adverts or boxed adverts throughout your site, on your posts and in your *sidebars*?
- **Sidebars** Do you want sidebars to run on the left, on the right or on both sides?
- **Function** Do you want to write reviews? See stuff? Use data, graphs and pie charts, run polls, have a rating system, run forums and newsletters? Are you going to have an events page? Contributors page? Shop? Are you going to offer membership? Whatever you want your site to do, look to see whether the theme offers you special functions and templates in order for you to achieve what you want.

- **Images** Will you need to have galleries? Big images, small images, slideshows?
- **Sound** Do you want music to play when a visitor hits your homepage? Do you want to be able to turn this function on or off? Do you want a player on the homepage for your audio content? Do you want to be connected directly with SoundCloud?
- **Videos** Do you want to play live streamed content? Do you need to organise your video content into channels? Do you want visitors to your site to be able to upload video content? Do you want to be connected to YouTube?

Some example themes

There are thousands of themes to choose from, so asking yourself the questions listed above will help you try to give your search some kind of structure. Be warned: trying to find the 'perfect' theme is very time-consuming at the beginning and you will waste hours flicking through theme after theme. So try to be focused and set yourself a time limit – don't be indecisive, and remember you can change your theme whenever you like – nothing is set in stone.

Before I give you a few example themes to get you going I want to talk you through my thoughts regarding one of the themes I use. Hopefully this will give you some idea about what to look for.

The theme I am going to talk about is NewsTube – I chose this theme to use on the journalism student site for London South Bank University, journalism.london (Figure 3.22). The theme is by developer Cactus Themes and has been on the market since July 2015. Here is my reasoning for picking this theme.

I picked NewsTube primarily because I was looking for a theme that handled organising video content well. This theme organises video content into channels and playlists.

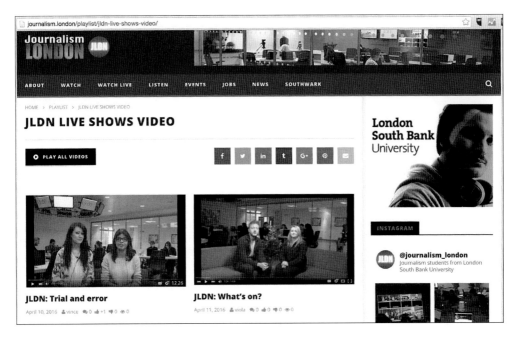

Figure 3.22 Choose a theme that suits the content you are planning to create.

While you can display video content on any WordPress site, if you are going to be using a lot of video content it is good to look for a theme that has taken this function into consideration and built templates into the code so that you don't have to find lots of extra plugins in order to achieve the effect you want.

I also like the number of page/post templates available. The *body text* is displayed clearly – good spacing between the headline and the body – and I really like the social share band under the headline which gives the option to like/dislike the post. It also has a 'more content' drop-down which pulls in similar posts. Now, while all of these elements can be added into any theme by plugins, it is good to find a theme with these elements built in because the more plugins/widgets you have to add on, the greater stress you are placing on

> Remember, you need to continually update your theme with each new WordPress install. You only pay for the theme once – all future updates should be included in this initial payment. Be wary of themes that do not guarantee this.

your site in terms of page load times. Speed is of the essence in keeping a visitor on your site, so you want to try and minimise anything that will cause unnecessary lagging.

The theme also has a 'do not miss' pop-up to encourage visitors to stay on the site.

I also like the ability to colour code the categories, and lastly I like having a news ticker built into the header.

All in all, for a multimedia news site, this theme has everything and it is well documented and very well supported by the developer.

My 2017 top fives (not exclusive – just for guidance)

For news (text-heavy sites)

■ **Grand News** developed by ThemeGoods
■ **NewsMag** developed by tagDiv

WALKTHROUGH▶

Setting up an FTP account

The first thing you need to do is find an FTP server to download onto your computer. I use Filezilla; it's one of the oldest and easiest to use, so I am going to use this as my example. But like all the examples in this book, it is only my preference – you can use another tool if you like. They all follow the same principles, so if you can follow how Filezilla works, you will be able to set up another server quite easily (Figure 3.23).

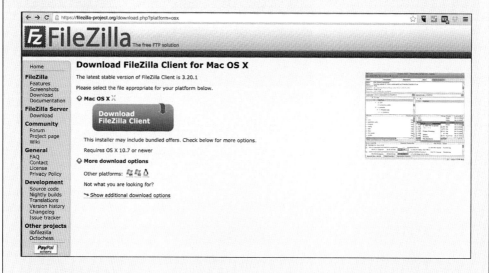

Figure 3.23 There are other FTP servers to choose from besides Filezilla – some, like Cyber Duck, are on Macs by default.

1 Google 'Filezilla Mac download' (or Windows, depending what machine you are using). Do not click on the green button saying Download because this is a bundle download and includes bits and pieces you don't need. Instead, click on Show Additional Download Options and select either Mac OSX or Windows (Figure 3.24).

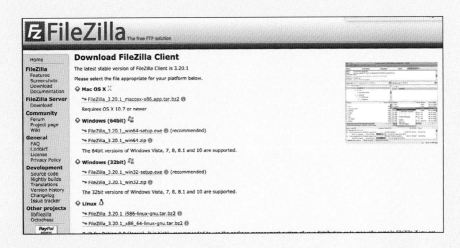

Figure 3.24 Downloading Filezilla.

2 Unpack the zip file.
3 Install Filezilla.

> You may find on a Mac that you are unable to install the file because it comes from an 'unidentified developer'. If you get this message you need to go to your System Preferences on your Mac, and in Security check the the box allowing apps to be downloaded from anywhere. Come back and change this back to Mac App Store and Identified Developers once you have installed Filezilla.

4 Open Filezilla.
What you should be looking at is a screen with local files on the left and remote files on the right (you won't have any files in the remote screen yet as we haven't connected you to anything). Find your desktop under Users in the box under Local Site. Click on it and all your files that you have on your desktop should appear in the box below. Before we can connect to the server on the right we need to create an SFTP account for your website (Figure 3.25).

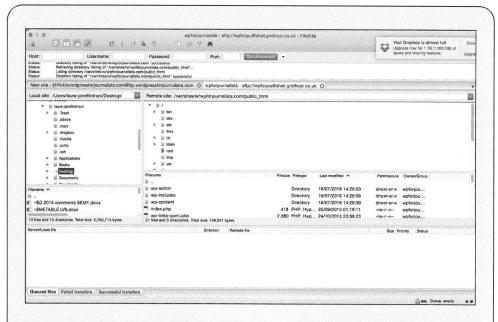

Figure 3.25 Filezilla shows your desktop.

5 On Tsohost go to your cloud-hosting dashboard and click Manage Website and then Secure Shell in Advanced Management Tools (Figure 3.26).

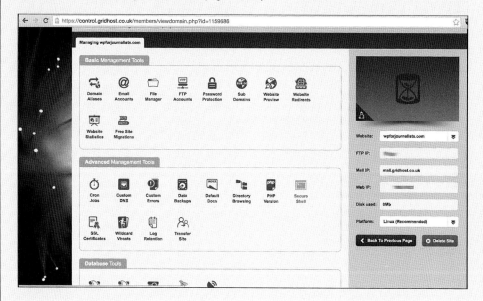

Figure 3.26 Use Secure Shell to keep your files as safe as possible.

6 Activate SSH.
Now you will have the SSH Server, the SSH Username and the SSH Password, which will allow you to connect to Filezilla.
7 On Filezilla, click on Site Manager (Figures 3.27 and 3.28).

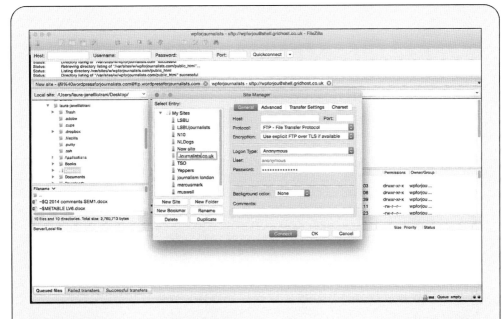

Figure 3.27 The dashboard on Filezilla can seem a little confusing at first but it won't take you long before you know what you are doing and add a new site.

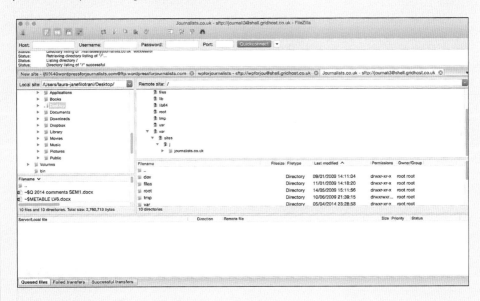

Figure 3.28 Adding a new site.

8 Add in the following information from Tsohost:

Host: SSH Server
  Protocol: SFTP-SSH
  Logon type: normal

User: SSH Username
Password: SSH Password

Hit Connect.

If you can't connect and are getting a time-out message, double-check you haven't made any typos in the information.

9 You will now see your website files in the right-hand box – they are located in the folder var/sites. Click on your site in the top-right box. Click on public_html and you will see all your WordPress files (as explained on page 20).

10 You are now ready to transfer files from your computer onto your website and vice versa.

- **TopNews** developed by MVPThemes
- **Flexmag** developed by MVPThemes
- **Multinews** developed by Memizat

For video/audio content

- **Snaptube** developed by Cohhe
- **Right Now WP** developed by RenkliBeyaz
- **Soundwave** developed by Wizedesign
- **OneVideo** developed by Upcode
- **VideoPro** developed by Cactus Themes

For photography

- **Joker** developed by mad_velikorodnov
- **Kloe** developed by Select Themes

For events

- **Beaton** developed by Wizedesign
- **Soccer Club** developed by PixFill
- **Ironband** developed by Irontemplates

If you do give a developer access, make sure you delete the temporary FTP account as soon as you have finished using it. Don't leave it open.

Use SFTP (SSH), Secure File Transfer Protocol.

For reviews

- **Gameszone** developed by Themefuse
- **Bucket** developed by pixelgrade

For social/forums

- **UnitedCommunity** developed by Diabolique

For multisites (main domain)

- **Benaam** developed by Scriptsbundle

FTP

What is FTP and why do you need it?

As already mentioned on page 33, having an FTP account is very helpful when uploading themes, amongst other things. FTP is a way for you to easily transfer files from your local computer to the server where all your WordPress files are stored. In other words, an FTP server links your computer to Tsohost.

WALKTHROUGH▶

Uploading a theme via SFTP

Uploading a theme via SFTP involves mostly the same process as using the automatic upload on WordPress, with the main difference being you need to upload the unpacked file, not the zip file.

1 Download your chosen theme onto your desktop and unzip it by clicking on it.
2 Open the Theme folder and find the theme zip inside it. Unpack this file and drag the unpacked folder on to your desktop so that you can locate it easily.
3 On Filezilla locate the Unpacked Theme folder on your desktop in the left-hand Local Files box.
4 On Filezilla open the wp-content folder in the right-hand server folders (in public_html) (Figure 3.29).

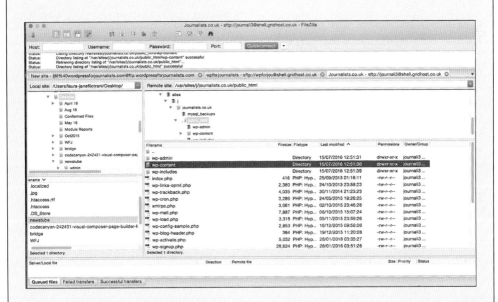

Figure 3.29 Find your theme files in the wp-content folder.

You should now see the folders listed for languages, uploads, plugins and themes and the index.php file.

1 On Filezilla drag the Theme folder from the left-hand box and dump it into the public_html/wp-content/themes folder.
2 You will now see the files transferring in the window at the bottom of the screen on Filezilla. The direction of the transfer is local to server (Figure 3.30).

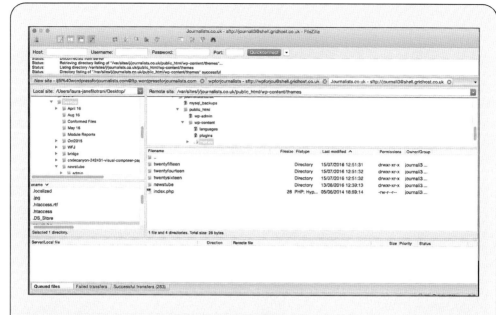

Figure 3.30 You should see your theme in the theme folder.

3 All you need to do now is log in to your website and activate the theme from your dashboard under Appearance/Themes.

You're ready to go!

While you can do all of this via your host, you may well need to give someone (a developer, for example) access to your files without giving them access to your hosting account, and this is where you can do this – set them up with a temporary FTP account and they will be able to see the files without seeing your hosting information.

Giving access to a developer is not the only reason for using an FTP account. I find it much easier to manage file transfers in this way so I always use an FTP when I am moving things around. I should make it clear, though, that as the main user of the account I use SFTP, which stands for Secure File Transfer Protocol, as it is much more secure than a simple FTP account, which 'talks' in plain English (i.e. plain.txt) as opposed to using binary code as SFTP does. This makes SFTP much harder to hack, so please do use SFTP if you can and keep the FTP for temporary access for developers.

REFERENCES

1　Lail, J. (2017). Consumer experience director for the *Knoxville News Sentinel* – interviewed by LJ Filotrani.

2　Price, Alex (2017). Founder of 93digital – interviewed by LJ Filotrani.

CHAPTER 4

The WordPress dashboard

In this section, we will look at how to log on to your website, then we'll look at all the options available to you on your WordPress dashboard, starting with the settings. This is followed by a look at how to create posts and pages, and how to use *categories* and *tags* to organise your content. This is followed by a section on Appearance and all the various elements that come under it, including themes, widgets and menus. Then we'll look at the media library – how to upload and use images – and finally we'll cover users.

I am going to take you through the set-up for a basic working site. There will be options that we come across that you can come back to in your own time when and if you need to, but everything you need to have a fully functioning site is covered in this section.

The dashboard for both the free .com sites and the self-hosted sites .org is essentially the same bar two fundamental areas: themes and plugins. On the free sites you cannot add new themes or plugins (and you cannot access the code files for the plugins and themes already uploaded). Where possible I have indicated whether the information is for .com sites or .org sites or for both.

Logging on to your .com site

You can do this in three ways:

- **Method 1** Go to www.wordpress.com and log in.

- **Method 2** Go to your actual site (e.g. http://ljfilotrani.wordpress.com) and click Login from the meta widget on the homepage.
- **Method 3** Type in your URL and add either '/wp-admin' or '/wp-login.php' (e.g. http://ljfilotrani.wordpress.com/wp-admin).

The last method is my preferred method as this will always bring you to the log-in page – even if for some reason your homepage is down – and it is the method you use for logging in to your self-hosted site; for example, wpforjournalists.co.uk/wp-admin

If you sign in using Method 1 you will be taken to an area which shows content from other blogs. To find your site you need to click on the My Site tab located in the top left-hand corner of your screen. To view what your site looks like on the front end, click on the name of your site – just underneath the My Site tab (Figure 4.1).

While you can access all the settings from this view, I advise you to work from the dashboard, which is the same in style and layout as that of the self-hosted .org sites, making the transition from one to the other much easier. To access the dashboard, once you have signed in add 'wp-admin' onto your URL – for example, yourdomain.co.uk/wp.admin. This will bring up the dashboard.

Flicking between the front end and the back end is not as easy from the free dashboard as it is from the self-hosted sites, so I suggest you open a second window and paste the URL

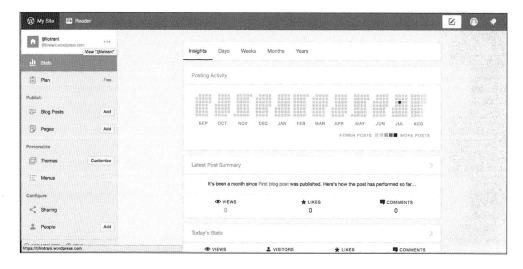

Figure 4.1 To view your site click on the name underneath My site tab.

(domain) in there so that you can see the front end (the view your visitors see).

Logging on to your .org site

To log in to your self-hosted site simply add '/wp-admin' or '/wp-login.php' at the end of your domain; for example, yourdomain.com/wp-admin. Once signed in you will immediately be taken to your dashboard. Switching to the front end is easy – just click on the drop-down under My Blog to visit your site (Figure 4.2).

SETTINGS

In settings, you are given options that control how your site functions. These include: Settings/General, which covers things such as naming your site, and admin emails; Settings/Writing; Settings/Reading; Settings/Media; Settings/Discussion and lastly Settings/Permalinks. You will find these on the left-hand menu bar (Figure 4.3).

Settings/General (.com and .org)

This is the area where you can rename your site and give it a tag line.

The title of your site is obviously important because it is the first thing people see in a search engine results page (SERP). The site title

of any post or page is also appended to the end of the post headline. So it is important for you to put the right name in Settings/General.

The title can, however, be different to the domain name – for example, a popular tourist site for Finland is called This is Finland (with the tag line 'Things you should and shouldn't know') but the domain name is finland.fi, and the New York Times Company site has a domain name of nytco.com.

The tag line might take you a little longer to come up with. It should really sum up what visitors to your site can expect. It should set the tone for the site and also it should ideally include two or three main keywords which will help your site be found by search engines. Ideally, separate these keywords by commas so they are treated individually. You can change these later, so don't spend too much time on this. As a good rule of thumb your site title and your tag line combined should be no more than 70 characters. Here are a few example tag lines:

- Techcrunch.com – The latest technology, news and information on startups.
- Observer.com – News, politics, culture, art, style, real estate, movie reviews, TV recaps.

On the free site that's all you need to change in General Settings.

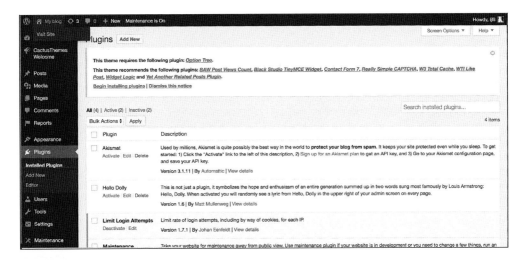

Figure 4.2 Switching to the front end on a self-hosted site is easy – just click on the drop-down under My blog.

Figure 4.3 Settings control how some basic functions work on your site.

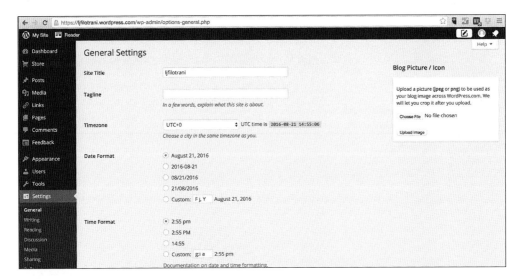

(.org)

On the self-hosted sites there are a couple of other things to enter. Leave the WordPress and site addresses and add in the email of the person looking after the site as the admin email.

In terms of membership, my advice is to leave this box unchecked until you are up and running as you don't want lots of spammers being able to create user accounts.

Settings/Writing (Figure 4.4)

On the self-hosted .org sites, leave the settings in Writing alone for now. On the free .com sites, check the boxes to enable testimonials if you like, and enable portfolio projects. Leave Posts by Email alone for now.

Settings/Reading (Figure 4.5)

The most important option in this section is whether to have a static front page or whether

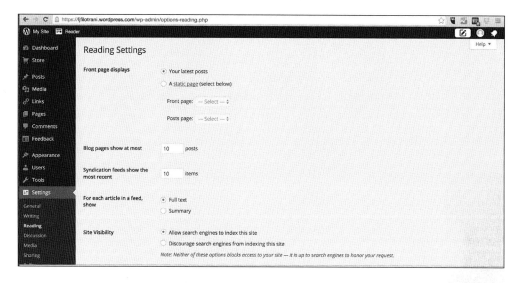

Figure 4.4 On a self-hosted site you can leaving the settings in Writing alone for now.

Figure 4.5 Control how your front page displays in Reading Settings.

to simply display your most recent posts. We will be discussing front pages in the next section, but for now just keep it checked on your latest posts.

Make sure you allow search engines to find your site, and check the box that shows just the summary in a *feed* rather than the full text.

There are other options for you to play around with – come back to these once you are up and running.

Settings/Discussion

All of these options are for you to decide for yourself – the only thing I want to point out is that if you want to turn comments off across the site, this is where you do it.

Settings/Media

Again, come back to this once you know what you are doing – you don't really need to change anything yet.

For the rest of the settings on the free site, explore at your leisure – we will be coming back to some of these sections later on. On the self-hosted .org site, the last thing you need to do is change the permalinks.

Settings/Permalinks (.org) (Figure 4.6)

A permalink is a URL created when you publish a post. I always use, for example, domainname.com/year/month/post_title – here's an example post on journalism.london to illustrate the permalink format I prefer: http://journalism.london/2017/06/win-oscars-best-picture

So if you want to follow my lead, check the box for Month and Name and click Save.

> If you ever get a 404 error message on the front end saying a post can't be found, try resaving the permalink option.

Other settings

There are other things to explore and experiment within the settings which you don't need to decide on right at the beginning – you will find yourself continually coming back to this area as you progress. For now, though, you have everything set up and you are ready to start populating your site with content and organising it in a way that will help it be found by visitors.

POSTS AND PAGES, CATEGORIES AND TAGS

Your whole WordPress site is made up of posts and pages. No matter what content you create, you will be required to create a new post or a new page. The way you organise all of that content so that it can be found by visitors is by using categories and tags. In this section we'll look at how to create posts and pages, how to get content onto those posts and how to create the filing system by creating categories and tags.

Figure 4.6 A permalink is created when you publish a new post or page.

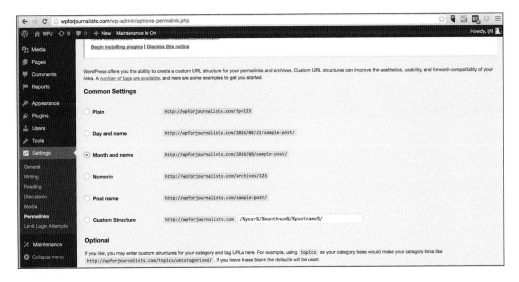

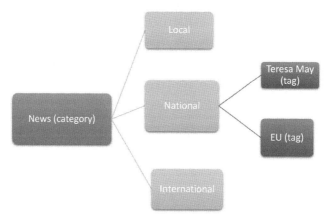

Figure 4.7 Categories and tags are the way in which you organise your content.

Figure 4.8 You can create new categories and tags under Posts.

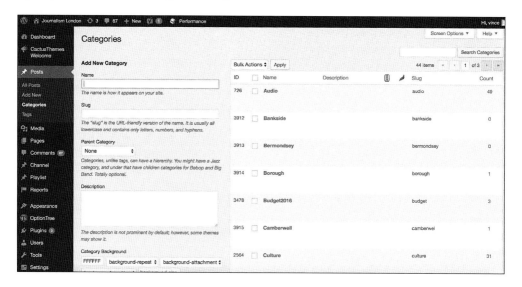

Some definitions first

Pages are for your static content, i.e. content that isn't going to be continually updated – an 'About' page, for example, or a page with terms and conditions for your site. Pages are also where you can create templates for 'fronts' – so you can create a homepage or a category page for video content, for example. Depending on which theme you are using you will find a number of different page templates for you to use. This is one of the considerations when choosing a commercial theme – look at what page templates it offers.

Posts

Posts are where your content is going to be created. Every post will be an article or a video or a piece of audio – each will have a headline, body text and a feature image, and be dated. Each post will be given a category or categories and a number of tags.

Categories and tags

Categories and tags are the way in which you organise the content of your website and a way for your content to be found through keywords from search engines. Categories are your top-level sections. For example, I might want to organise my content into the following categories:

- News
- Reviews
- Video
- Audio

When you are writing headlines, think about the keywords that will enable your post to be found if someone is searching. Use these keywords in your headline. Writing online is all about SEO, so don't be too clever with your head-lines. Say it like it is. (See page 76 for more help with SEO.)

I might then want to break these areas up into sub-categories such as:

- News – local, national, international
- Reviews – theatre, literature, music
- Video – films, factual, explainers
- Audio – live, slideshows, interviews, music

Tags are the keywords attached to an individual post – these can be automatically generated through a plugin (see page 78). So, for example, using the categories listed above, an article called 'Brexit – the best or worst decision for the UK?' would naturally fit in the top-level category News and then the sub-category National but it would also generate tags such as *UK, Cameron, Teresa May* and *EU*. Usually a piece of content will generate around 5–10 tags. These tags can then be used to further organise your con-tent – so you could, if you like, have a section on your website that pulls in all of the articles which mention Cameron or the EU (Figure 4.7).

You can create new categories or tags on the posts and pages you create, or you can add them in the sections under Posts on the left-hand menu (Figure 4.8).

Anatomy of a post/page (Figure 4.9)

The process for creating posts is the same as for pages. Go to your dashboard and click on All Posts and then Add New.

1. **'Enter title here'** is where you put your headline. Don't use punctuation – and don't cap up every letter; it will look as if you are shouting. Depending on your *house style* you might cap up every word, such as 'This Is My Head-line' (this is called 'title case'). My prefer-ence is to just cap up the first word, so it would be 'This is my headline' (this is called 'sentence case'). Obviously, you must cap up proper nouns, though be care-ful as there are exceptions; for example, 'iPhone' and 'eBay'. Initialisms are usually capped – for example, 'BBC', and contrac-tions such as 'SciFi' (science fiction). Don't use exclamation marks – HTML doesn't like them – and no ampersands!

   As soon as you write your headline and click into the body text on your post, the permalink for the post will be created. You can edit out any unnecessary words, leaving the keywords.

2. **Body Text** This where you write your post content.

3. **Visual/Text** There are two views for the body text – the visual view and the text view, which shows the HTML (the code that tells the site how the content is going to be displayed). Get used to click-ing backwards and forwards between the two tabs Text and Visual so you can see what code is being used to make changes to the formatting. You can also add

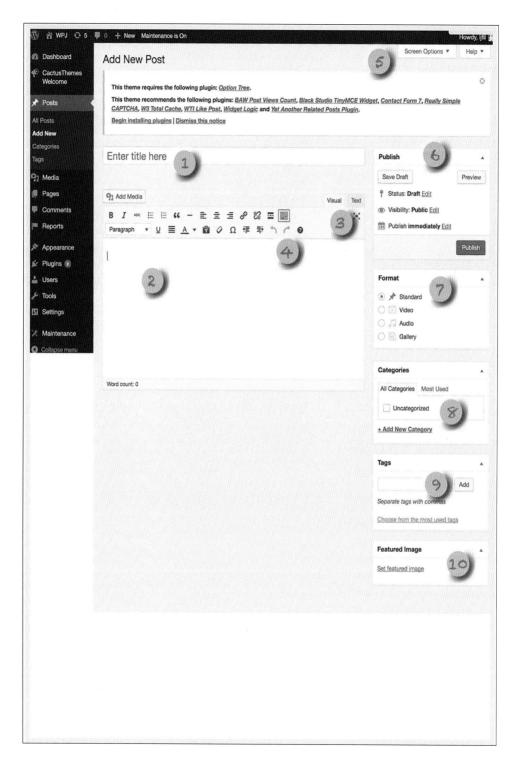

Figure 4.9 Anatomy of a page/post.

HTML code directly into the Text tab to change the way your post looks.

Try out some HTML code for yourself on w3schools.com. (See page 113 for more help with HTML.)

If you are embedding any video or audio content you must paste the embed code into the Text tab or it won't work. This goes for any HTML – you must always make sure you are pasting it into the Text tab.

4. **Toolbar** This is for formatting your content. It is very simple to use and very similar to the tools you use when you create a standard Word document. If you can only see one line on your toolbar, click on the last icon (called the 'kitchen sink') and this will reveal the second line.

I am not going to go through all the tools – you should explore them for yourself – but I will highlight a few of the most important.

On the top line of the toolbar

Paragraph
This controls the size of the text, from Headline 1 (H1) down to text with no formatting. Usually the headline you put in the headline box will be H1, so you should keep the rest of the text on the page/post smaller. The same rules of design apply online as in print. Think about the page hierarchy and format your text in order of importance – bigger and bolder for the standfirst, for example. The exact size and style of these headlines will be dictated by your theme, so you will have to experiment to find the right look for your site. All heading sizes are parsed by Google, which can help with SEO.

> You can override the presets for all the headline sizes and styles by changing the code under Appearance/Editor and finding the style.css page. (See page 113 for more help with CSS.)

> If you are hyperlinking people/work/events, find a contact email and send them the URL of your post. This will encourage the possibility of a back link and increase the likelihood of your content being found and read.

Hyperlinks
An incredibly important part of writing text online is hyperlinking. One of the fundamental jobs for journalists is to provide extra information for a post – good-quality links show research and can afford credibility to the article. Any stat or report mentioned in a post should be hyperlinked back to the original – not another article, if possible, but to the actual source. For anyone who is named, try and find their own website or something they have written which adds further insight to your own post. Any locations, places of interest or events should all be hyperlinked.

The purpose of hyperlinks is twofold: first, to provide extra information, context and validity to the post and second, to connect your post with other sites on the web – increasing the chance of visibility. Someone linking to your site from theirs creates a *back link* – all good SEO.

To create a link, open up another window, find the web page you want to reference and copy the URL. Go back to your post on your website and highlight the keywords you want to link on your site. Click on the hyperlink icon, then paste the URL you have just copied and save. Check that it has worked by previewing your post.

Do not hyperlink instructions such as 'For more information click here' – you should be hyperlinking keywords. So, for example, if you have written about a league table for secondary schools, hyperlink the whole phrase 'league table for secondary schools'. By hyperlinking the phrase you are increasing SEO on these keywords – as opposed to hyperlinking 'click here' (no one is going to be searching for content using the words 'click here').

'Read More' tag

This is used when you want to cut your post down to just a few lines of text (excerpt) that show on your front page or on an archive page (a page which pulls content with the same category or tag). To use the More tag put the cursor after the last word you want to appear (usually three or four lines of text) and click the More tag.

> If you are pasting text from another source, for example Word, clear all formatting and bring it in as plain text. I use the Mac application TextEdit to do this.

Many themes will automatically create excerpts for you, but if yours doesn't this is the way to do it easily. The other way of creating an excerpt is by using the WordPress excerpt box – see number 5 on page anatomy.

Clear Formatting

If your text is not formatting properly, try highlighting it and clicking Clear Formatting. This is particularly useful if you are pasting text from another source. (You should also have a look on the Text tab to see what's going on with the HTML.)

5. **Screen Options** Click on the arrow to reveal more WordPress functions which may be hidden. For example, by default the excerpt box is hidden.
6. **Publish** This is how you publish your post or save it as a draft. You can also keep your published post private – visible only to the users who are logged into your site. You can also schedule the publishing date. This is very useful if, for example, you wanted to upload a number of articles on one day but wanted to spread publishing them across the week in order to maximise coverage.
7. **Format** This is how your post will display depending on your theme – there will be different elements offered depending on which format you choose and on your theme. Experiment.
8. **Categories** This is how you assign a post to a category. You can select from categories you have already created (see earlier in this chapter) or you can add a new one from here.
9. **Tags** Create new tags or choose from most popular ones on your site (or use a plugin that automatically generates tags for you – see Chapter 6 on essential plugins).
10. **Featured image** Add your featured image here. Depending on your theme your featured image may or may not appear on your post. If it does and you don't want it to, check your theme for ways of switching this function off. You should always have a featured image, as these images are used mostly by sliders and always by archive pages as thumbnails to appear alongside the excerpt of your post. Some themes are better than others at handling featured images – if you are having difficulty with the sizes, check your theme instructions for help or look for a plugin that will force a resize to accommodate your theme.

APPEARANCE (FIGURE 4.10)

On your dashboard Appearance houses many of the functions that you will be using regularly – Themes, Customize, Widgets, Menus, Editor (you may have a few more tabs depending on the theme you are using. You can see by my example that I have Page Builder as well).

There are some differences to note between the free sites and the self-hosted sites – the most important of which is the Editor tab. You don't get an Editor tab on the free sites – this is because you do not have access to the code. On a self-hosted site this area is where you can amend core files directly from the dashboard.

We've already looked at themes in a previous section in this chapter so let's move to Customize. This is a standard WordPress function that allows you to change many aspects of your site from the front end. What options you are given will depend on the theme you have activated. I tend not to make changes to my sites through Customize but rather through the theme settings instead.

Widgets

What is a widget? A widget is a piece of code that adds extra functionality to your site. They can be added easily into areas on your website called sidebars, *footers* and headers. This is one of the things you should consider when choosing your theme: where are your widget-ready areas? You should always choose a theme that offers you widget areas – this will give you ongoing flexibility and will allow you to continue to develop your site. WordPress by default comes with several widgets, including Categories, Tag Cloud, Calendar, Search and Recent Posts.

Widgets are very easy to activate – just drag the widget you want to use into a sidebar area by clicking, dragging and dropping. Each widget will have individual settings to modify. Once you have selected your widgets, simply click Save and go and check on the front end to see whether the widget has activated properly in the place you

expected it to (Figure 4.11). Many themes have their own widgets and so do plugins.

On the front end, the sidebar runs down the right side of a page by default. Your theme might allow you to switch it to the left or to have two sidebars, one on each side. Likewise, your header and footer area may or may not be widget-ready areas. This will depend on your theme. We will have a look at the standard widgets in the next chapter on plugins.

Menus

This is where the navigation for your site is controlled (Figure 4.12).

Depending on your theme your main menu may run across the top of your site like in my example (Figure 4.13) or be hidden behind a tab or run down the left side of the screen.

In my example I have got: Home, Blog, External Page, Work, About. These buttons are the way you allow a visitor to navigate through your site, and as such are very important so that your content is found. Think carefully about how you want to organise your content.

Figure 4.10 Appearance houses many of the functions you will use most regularly.

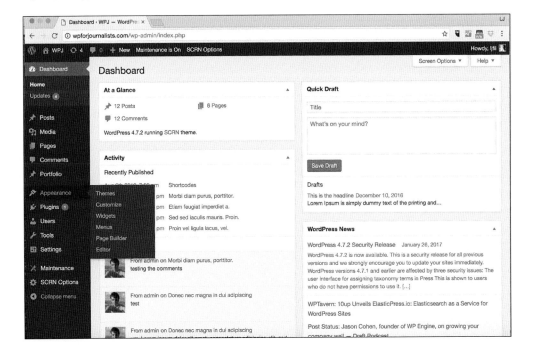

Figure 4.11 Many themes have their own widgets which you can add to your sidebars.

Figure 4.12 Your menu is how a visitor will navigate through your site.

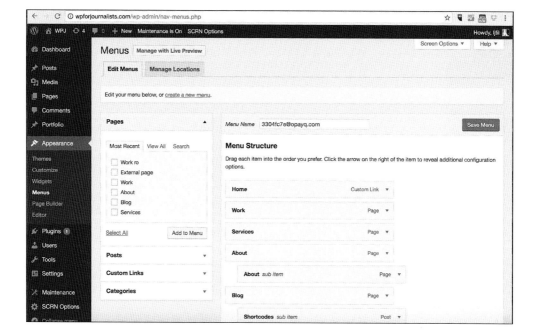

Figure 4.13 A menu can run across the top of your site or down the side or be hidden behind a tab.

To create a menu

1. Click Create a New Menu – give it the name 'Primary' if it is your main menu.
2. Select what you want to add to your menu from the left-hand column. You can add a button for a particular page such as your About page, or for a particular post that you want to highlight or a category. You can also add a custom link. This means you can create a button to an external site if you like or you can create a link to your homepage.

To create a button to your homepage, select Create Custom Link and paste in the URL to your front page, then name it 'Home' (Figure 4.14).

Figure 4.14 Create a button to your homepage with the custom link.

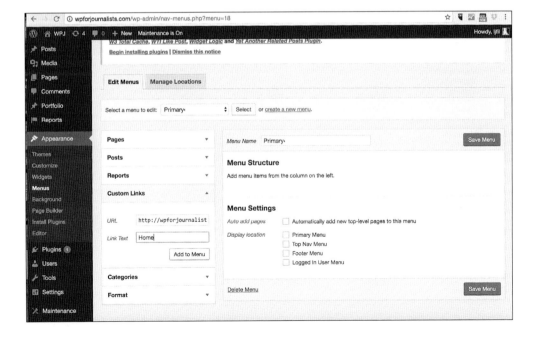

1. Once you have added all the buttons you want, click Save Menu.
2. Now you have to activate the menu you have just created. To do this, click on Manage Locations (Figure 4.16). You can see by my example that this theme allows for four menus – you may just have one. Select the menu you have just created and click Save. Now go and check that the menu has appeared on the front end.

> You can create dropdowns on your menus by dragging a button to the right (Figure 4.15).

safe before you make changes, just in case you break the site with some faulty code. Then if you do break the site you can always go back and paste the original code over the faulty code. If you have broken the site so that you can't access the dashboard, don't panic! Simply locate the file you made changes to via the FTP server (see page 38 for help with setting up an FTP account) and paste the original code back into the file.

Editor (.org)

The WordPress built-in editor allows you to edit theme files directly from your browser – you can edit the theme files in Appearance and the plugin files in Plugins (Figure 4.17).

The files that you can edit are PHP and CSS files. Just be very careful with making any changes in here. Always copy the original file and keep it

THE MEDIA LIBRARY

The media library is where you upload all your images. You can upload audio and video content too, but generally speaking this is not advisable. Audio and video files are large – they take up a lot of space and need a lot of memory to make them load quickly and smoothly. When you want to include video and audio content it is much better to house the file on a third-party

Figure 4.15 Create dropdowns on your menu by dragging the buttons to the right.

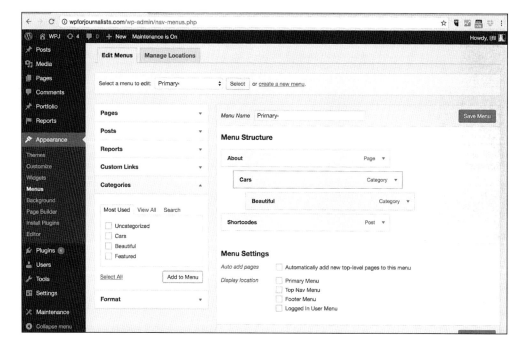

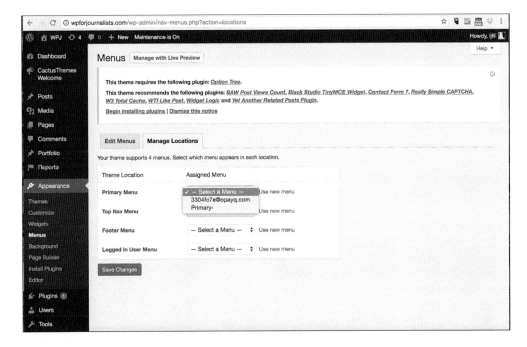

Figure 4.16 Don't forget to activate your menu in Manage Locations.

Figure 4.17 You can edit the theme and plugin files directly from your dashboard but be careful to save a copy of the code first.

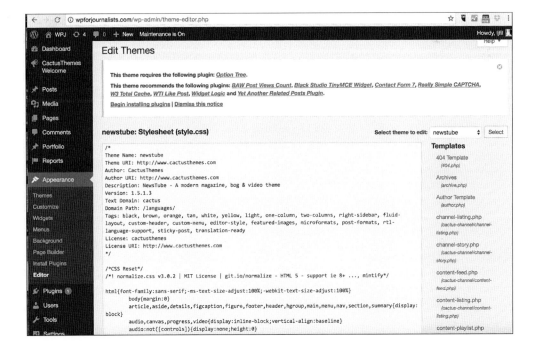

platform such as YouTube and SoundCloud and then embed their players rather than uploading your video and audio files directly to your media library. You will find more help with this in Chapter 7.

So for now we will concentrate on the main functionality of the media library: to serve images to your site.

You should already have some images in your media library, particularly if you have uploaded dummy content for a commercial theme.

1. To add a new image click Add New. Select a file from your computer – you can only upload JPEGs and PNGs; you cannot upload TIFFs, so if you get an error message check what kind of file you have tried to upload.

2. Click Edit and you will see that the permalink for your image is created with the name of the image file. If you have named your image file correctly, then the headline/permalink should have keywords in it. If you haven't, you can change the permalink from the image post by clicking edit.

If you do change the permalink, click the update button on the right of the screen and you will be taken back to the Edit page. If not, click Edit Image.

> **Before you upload your image, make sure you have named the file with keywords that describe the image, and not numbers. This is because you want your image to come up in searches, and it won't if it is just called a random number. So, for example, if you are uploading a picture of London Bridge, make sure the file is called 'London Bridge' and not '01939983710' or some other random collection of digits.**

> **Try not to do any editing or rescaling of your images in WordPress. Do any editing or cropping before you upload your image – this will help with page loading times. Work out what sizes you need on your site and standardise them throughout – this is fundamental for establishing your house style.**

Edit Image

There are a few things you can do from this page, such as adjust the scale of the image (always scale down, never up – otherwise the image will pixelate) and crop the image. You can also flip it from left to right or rotate it. (The buttons for these functions are under the permalink.)

Do not add captions here. I know many will feel that this is wrong, but my advice is you should add captions actually on the post where the image is going to appear rather than in the media library. If you add a caption here, it will essentially be treated as part of the image and will therefore not be searchable.

Add alternative text (alt text). You should add the alt text – usually just the keywords describing the image – because it helps search engines understand what the image is, and if it doesn't load properly, the alt text will appear in its place. Without the alt text there will just be a blank space.

Description

This can be hit and miss because some themes don't display the description. I tend to leave this clear and concentrate on the alt text, which is always displayed and integral for SEO.

A note on sizes and images: generally speaking you are never going to need an image bigger than 1,500 pixels wide. Most screen resolutions are well below this (in fact at the time of writing, worldwide, the most common resolution is 1366×768). This means that you should not be uploading any pictures larger than 1,500 pixels – the bigger the image the longer the load time and the greater the adjustment your site needs to make in order for the image to display properly. For example, if you upload a pic that is 4,000 pixels wide your site needs to work quite hard to resize that image to fit your theme. So the advice is, do your resizing in Photoshop before uploading your images.

USERS (.ORG)

Note: on .com you can only invite users.
This is where you can add users to your website. There are a number of default roles that you can assign a user. These roles are different levels of commissions. We'll look at them shortly but first this is how you create a user.

Add New User

Pick a username that you are happy to have seen by your visitors. This cannot be changed. I would stick to first names or, if you wanted something more impersonal, you could give them role usernames; for example: Editor, Features Editor, or Fashion Editor.
Put in the email address where you want mail from the site to be sent.
You can miss out First Name and Last Name as most themes do not display this information.
'Website' should be a different site to the one you are on if you want to add this information. Again this is not vital as most themes don't display this information as standard (later I will be talking about a plugin that you can install that displays user profiles).

Password

If you put in a weak password you will be asked to confirm the use of it. Please try to use complex passwords – the easier the password

is, the easier it is to be hacked, potentially causing all sorts of issues. Ensuring strong passwords becomes particularly important when you have a number of users contributing to your site.

Role

The default roles in WordPress are: Subscriber, Contributor, Author, Editor, and Administrator.

- A **Subscriber** can only read the posts.
- A **Contributor** can add new posts and edit their own posts but cannot publish them and they cannot upload any images or embed anything. They cannot edit anyone else's posts and they cannot create pages or delete anything.
- An **Author** has the same permissions as the Contributor and can also publish their own posts and delete them.
- An **Editor** has full control over the content on the site – they can add and edit and publish any content. They can also create pages and delete posts.
- **Admin** – this role gives a user complete control over everything. This means they can add and remove plugins, change themes and add and delete user accounts. Be careful who you give admin access to as they are essentially the same as the site owner.

You can edit any user profile by bringing up the list of all users and clicking on Edit.
In the Edit section you can change the password and add some biographical info about the user. The user profile pic will be attached to their email account by default – if you want to add a different picture you need to add a plugin, which we will cover in the next chapter.
You can also change a user role from here.

CHAPTER 5

Plugins

This chapter follows on from the chapter explaining the different elements on a Word-Press dashboard, so if you haven't already set your site up and followed the instructions in Chapters 3 and 4, then you should go back and do that before tackling plugins.

I am assuming, therefore, that your site is up and running – that you have changed all the settings to suit, that you have chosen, uploaded and activated a theme and you know how to create posts and pages and upload images. I am also assuming you have had a go at activating widgets.

This chapter covers a huge area. The plugins are organised into different sections so that you can see which are used for which specific functionality. If you are on a .com site, then the first section on standard plugins is for you. The rest of the chapter is dedicated to plugins that you have to upload yourself, so is directed to those of you on .org.

■   **Standard plugins** The first section covers the basic standard plugins that come acti-vated by default on a .com site. (Page 63.)

■   **Essential plugins** This section covers essential plugins – those that I have found most useful when creating sites. They are my choices – you will find as you become more proficient that you will discover your own essentials, so use these as a guide. (Page 67.)

■   **Performance plugins** This section covers plugins that help your site work faster and

smoother. These are called performance plugins. (Page 73.)

■   **SEO plugins** SEO is a fundamental area for the success of any website. In this section you will find an explanation of what this is and suggested plugins to help you achieve the best results for getting traffic (visitors) to your site. (Page 76.)

■   **Security plugins** The chapter then covers security plugins – tools that will keep your site safe from hackers – and some general advice about good practice. (Page 80.)

■   **Mobile plugins** Then comes a section on mobile as a platform and plugins that will help your site display properly and effi-ciently on smart phones. (Page 82.)

■   **Social media plugins** Last there is a section covering all the essential plugins you need to set up and connect your social media accounts, and advice on managing your social media content. (Page 85.)

First things first: a definition...

PLUGINS

A plugin is a bit of code that can extend the functionality of a standard WordPress install. This is one of the areas which distinguishes a free .com site from a self-hosted .org site. On a free .com site you will only be able to see the plugins already installed and you will only be able to activate/deactivate some of them. You won't be able to add extra plugins. On a self-hosted .org site you are in complete control of the plugins, and there are thousands to choose from.

Activating plugins

All the plugins you have on your site are listed in Plugins/Installed on your dashboard and can be activated and deactivated whenever you like. If you want to add a new plugin, click on Add New. This will bring up the directory of approved WordPress plugins. You can search for the function you want and then view the plugins' details before activating them. Before you install the plugin, it is a good idea to look at any screenshots available to see if it offers what you are looking for, so click on Details. And keep in mind that there are always lots of variations to choose from, so if the one you find doesn't do exactly what you want, keep looking.

To activate a plugin, first click on Install. As soon as it is installed it will appear in the Plugins/Installed list. To activate it, simply click on Activate. Once it is activated, depending on what it is designed for, you may see another tab for the plugin on your left-hand menu on the dashboard. More often than not it will appear under Tools and you will have various options to select and information to fill in. So check to see where these options are as soon as you have activated the plugin. If you can't find the plugin options, go back to Plugins/Installed – find the plugin and click on Settings. This should take you to where the options are.

You should also check in Widgets as quite often a plugin comes with a widget that you can add to your sidebar. This again is dependent

Google 'best WordPress plugins for ...' to help you find what you are looking for, as you won't always find what you need by searching in the plugin directory on your WordPress site. Sometimes you don't really know what words to search for, so a general search on Google will often bring up posts from tech companies and developers listing the most useful/best WordPress plugins. Once you have found one you like, you can go back to the directory on your WordPress site and search by specific name or developer.

on the functionality the plugin is designed for. But always check.

Installing a plugin not in the WordPress directory

Most of the plugins will be in the WordPress directory and so are easy to install. But if you find one that isn't and you need to install it, you should follow the same steps as you would to install a commercial theme via an FTP account but upload to the wp-content/plugins folder. See page 38 for help with this.

Errors

If you activate a plugin and you get a message about missing headers, go back and try activating it again. Usually this sorts this message out. If for some reason it still registers with this error, you should find an alternative plugin. If by activating the plugin you completely break your site – i.e. you find a fatal error message and you cannot get back into your dashboard to delete the plugin – you should go to your FTP account and find the plugin in the wp-content/plugins folder. Delete it from here and your site should go back to working properly.

What follows are lots of different plugins, with explanations of what they are used for and any information helpful for setting them up. If they are complicated I have provided you with step-by-step guidance. We start with the plugins that are installed and activated by default on .com sites.

STANDARD PLUGINS

It must be noted that the plugins you'll find on a free .com site will not offer you much by way of control – they are activated by default, so I will just outline what they do here. At the time of writing the default plugins already active on new install are as shown in Figure 5.1.

Jetpack overview

Jetpack is a collection of plugins that covers many of the functions you can add individually to a .org site. Amongst other things, the collection of plugins looks after your site stats, so that you can see how many visitors you have; it gives you sharing buttons, so your visitors can share content through social media; it optimises your content for search engines; it gives your site protection from hackers; it fixes *malware*; and it can backup your site and restore a site. While you can install Jetpack on both the free .com sites and the .org sites, on a free .com site you have no control over this functionality and you have no choices about whether to use it or not. It is installed and activated by default.

Stats

One of the functions offered by Jetpack is a plugin showing your site stats. The plugin keeps track of your posting activity, and visitor activity, giving a breakdown of stats for popular tags and categories, *page views* and number of visitors. You can also see your views by country and also by referrer – this means what site (where) they have come to your site from.

For the majority of you just starting out, this is more than enough information, but to really drill down on the activity and to understand exactly which content is driving traffic, you will need a more sophisticated analytics packages such as Google Analytics (see page 160 for help with this).

> A page view is counted when a visitor loads a related page. A visitor is counted when we see a user or browser for the first time in a period (day, week, month).

Social Media and Publicise and Likes

These plugins add share buttons to your posts automatically. You can select which buttons appear on your posts in Settings (Figure 5.2). You can also connect your own social media accounts here so that when you post something it is shared with your other platforms (these all have widgets – look under Appearance/Widgets for them).

Email Subscriptions

This plugin allows people to sign up for notifications of when you have new content on your site. The plugin has a widget that you can drop into your sidebar (look under Appearance/Widgets for this).

Related Posts

This plugin will pull up other content that is similar to the post a visitor is viewing to encourage them to go from one post to another – and keep them on your site.

Akismet (spam filter)

A spam filter is essential on your site. Otherwise, you'll get hundreds of comments a week generated by bots – these automatically generated comments are used to embed back links to other sites. Getting a back link to your site on someone else's pushes up your Google ranking and in essence means your site becomes more visible in searches. Companies pay for marketing companies to spam thousands of sites in one go.

The Akismet plugin is activated by default. It's free – but you have to create a user account for it to work and is one of the best plugins on the market. For more control, and on a self-hosted .org site, you will have to pay a monthly fee which, at the time of writing, was about $5 a month.

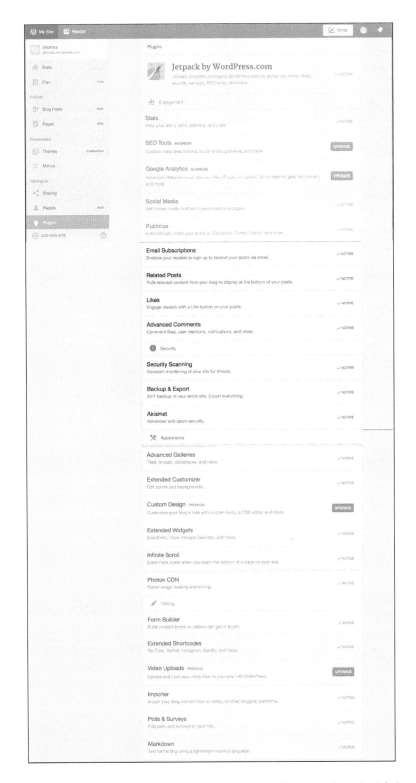

Figure 5.1 A standard WordPress install on .com comes with a number of activated plugins by default.

Form Builder

Use this to build contact forms.
To add a contact form, click on Pages/Add
New. On the toolbar click the symbol with the +
in a circle and you'll be given the option to add
a contact form. Once you click on Add Contact
Form you'll be able to add or delete from the
four predefined fields. By default, the contact
form asks for name, email and website and
there's a text box for comments. You can edit,
delete or add more fields to the form – here are
a few extras that you can add:

- **Check box** This will allow a user to tick a
  box to make a choice.
- **Drop-down** You can create a drop-down of
  different options for your user to select.
- **Radio buttons** Similar to the checkbox.
- **Text area** You can add a box so people can
  write the description of something, for
  example.
- **Web address** This requires a URL.

Once you have added your contact form to your
page, click the Text tab to have a look at the
code. You will see that the labels are enclosed
in square brackets – this is called a shortcode.
Here's an example of the code on a standard
default contacts page:

> [contact-form][contact-field label="Name"
> type="name" required="1"/][contact-field
> label="Email" type="email" required="1"/]
> [contact-field label="Website" type="url"/]
> [contact-field label="Comment" type="tex-
> tarea" required="1"/][/contact-form]

You can also make it so that
some information is required;
for example, someone's email
address. If you make a field
required, the person will not be
able to send a form until that
information is entered.

Do not use these contact
forms for sensitive information
as they are not secure.

> If you're finding it dif-
> ficult to find the dash-
> board, just put your
> URL in the browser
> with /wp-admin – for
> example, ljfilotrani.
> wordpress.com/wp-
> admin

Polls and surveys

Polls can be a way of encouraging interactivity
with your site. There are many plugins that
offer this functionality but the default on
WordPress.com is run by third-party company
Polldaddy. In order to run polls on your site
you must first create an account with Polldaddy. (You will be guided to do this through
the settings on the dashboard on your site.)

Go to polldaddy.com and create a new
account. This will automatically connect with
your WordPress account if you're signed in to
your website. Polldaddy offers premium functionality which you pay for but you can get a
simple poll on your site for free. You create new
polls on polldaddy.com, then copy the shortcode
and paste this into a new post on your site.

So first, on polldaddy.com, create a new
poll. You will be given a number of choices
about what your poll will look like on your
site in terms of size and colours and format.
When you're happy with your poll, hit Create
and this will generate a WordPress shortcode.
Copy this code and go back to your Word-
Press site. Create a new post and paste this
code into the newly created post (give the post
a headline which relates to the poll). Remember to paste the shortcode into the Text tab
on your new post. The results of the poll will
be collated and available to view on polldaddy.
com. Have a go.

In 2015 BuzzSumo data showed that on
average a quiz is shared 1,900 times, with
some quizzes (for example, 'What colour is
your aura') reaching nearly 4 million shares.[1]

Backups and export

WordPress.com says it backs
up a site automatically but
because you do not have
access to files, of what use
this particular functionality is
to you on a .com site is ques-
tionable. To be able to fully
backup your site you need to
be running a self-hosted site

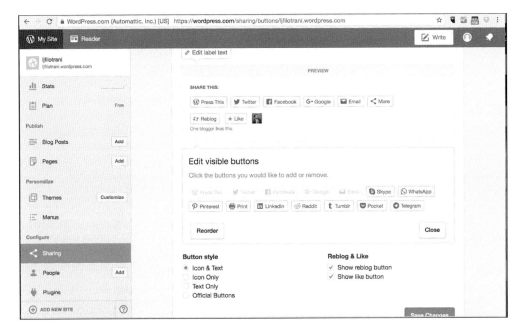

Figure 5.2 You can select which social media platforms to share posts with.

on WordPress.org. (See page 81 for backup plugins.)

What .com sites do offer is the option to export your posts and pages. In order to do this, select Export under Settings and Tools. You must first click Start Export and then select All Content and hit Download Export File. The file will be saved as an XML file which you can then import to another site by using the same process but selecting Import instead of Export. It is a good idea to get into the habit of exporting your content regularly if you are on a free .com site, just in case.

> At 93digital our general rule of thumb is to keep the use of plugins limited, as the fewer that your site relies on, the less chance of some kind of plugin 'clash' that results in some unwanted behaviour. Plugins like Yoast SEO are great for SEO and used on millions of sites, and we find Gravity Forms is used on lots of sites as a great and easy way of building forms. Advanced Custom Fields is also a great plugin for more advanced WordPress development.[2]
>
> Alex Price

ESSENTIAL PLUGINS

There are thousands of plugins to choose from and throughout the rest of this book I'll discuss many plugins suitable for particular functions. In this section, however, I want to cover a few essentials that will make your life easier and your site more effective.

As already stated, these are my essentials – plugins that I have found through experience to be useful. They are not meant to be an exclusive list, but more of a guide. You will add to this list as your site grows and there will no doubt be functions that you need that I don't and so you will require a different set of essential plugins.

Switch Users – developer John Blackourn

This is a plugin that is essential if you have more than one user account – and is an absolute must if you are running a multisite as it allows you to switch into any user account so that you can see what they can see, without having to log out and log back in as them. This is particularly useful if you want to check that they have the right access rights, and it is also useful if they are having trouble posting content. You can troubleshoot these issues by switching easily between users.

Avatar Manager – developer Caitlin Dogaru

This is an essential plugin because it allows your users to upload their own profile picture locally to your site instead of forcing them to use the default avatar generator, Gravitar. (If a user has registered on your site with a Gmail account, the profile picture from this email account will automatically be used as their user profile.)

WP Mega Menu – developer mythemeshop

A mega menu allows you to add pictures, icons and embedded content into your menu. There are various free plugins available but I really like WP Mega Menu, which is a premium plugin and costs around $30. It adds more navigation options for users and is really customizable, so you can change how the menu looks, and the code is SEO-friendly. You control all the settings for your menu under Appearance/Menus and also categories and tags.

One thing to note is that many commercial themes offer a mega menu built in, so this plugin wouldn't be needed if you choose your theme wisely.

Disable Comments – developer Somir Shah

WordPress lets you selectively disable comments on posts by default but if you want to override this function site-wide, this is the plugin you need. This is a particularly useful plugin for multisites – it will disable comments on every site.

Just a word about comments. I would urge you to use caution when thinking about allowing them – you'll be spammed relentlessly and having your site open to comments means you will have to be constantly vigilant. There are of course benefits to allowing comments – being able to directly communicate with your visitors, for example – and the comments can also be a good gauge of interest in your content. However, they can also be inappropriate, vicious and random. A post with hundreds of comments

may seem attractive, but the more comments you get, in reality the less value they are to you, as it is unlikely that you are or anyone else will be able to read them all.

Since the audience has been able to enter into a dialogue with journalists directly through comments sections on papers online, news organisations have been in a constant battle to moderate those conversations. While engagement is obviously a good thing and open discussion is incredibly valuable to journalists, abuse, hate and fake news are not. Policing these comments sections can be incredibly resource-heavy. So much so that in 2015 a number of high-profile publications such as Recode, Reuters, *Popular Science, The Week*, Mic, The Verge and *USA Today*'s FTW all shut off their comments. More news organisations followed – NPR closed off its comments section in August 2016, and in early 2017 Google launched a new tool to try and combat abusive comments to allow news organisations to keep this area of engagement with readers open. The software, called Perspective (www.perspectiveapi.com), is currently being trialled by a range of news organisations, including the *New York Times*, the *Guardian* and the *Economist*.

Neiman Reports published an article in early 2017 looking at the future of the comments section – it's worth a read.[3]

To some extent the ability for a reader to comment on a post has been superseded by the number of social media outlets available which allow for direct communication with a publisher or a specific journalist.

But, if you are going to allow comments, you need to decide about moderation. Are you going to check each comment before it is allowed to be published (pre-moderation), or are you going to allow it to be published first and then take it down if it is offensive (post-moderation)?

Auto tag generator

An auto tagging plugin is essential as you will forget to add tags manually to posts and pages. The only thing to be careful of is that some plugins create too many tags, many of which are not useful, so you will have to regularly check and delete these. I use WP Full Auto Tags Manager,[4] which is very easy to use and will also tag old posts (Figure 5.3).

Contact Form 7 – developer Takayuki Miyoshi

Using contact forms can be tricky – there are often issues with email addresses and forms sent not being received – so in truth I tend to not use them unless they come built in with the theme. If I just want to allow visitors to get in touch with me, I use a button which will bring up a direct email. This is partly born out of my preferences as a user – I don't like built-in contact forms because I am never really that confident the form will get read (more often than not they end up in the site admin's spam folder). I much prefer being able to email someone directly, and will always search for a contact email when I am on a site, instead of using a form. So for this reason, when I'm building my sites I put contact buttons everywhere that allow visitors to send a direct email.

If you really want to use a contact form, probably the most popular free plugin is Contact Form 7 (and actually it is often the one that comes built into themes). With Contact Form 7, you can create multiple forms and customize them (Figure 5.4). It works with shortcodes: you create a form and it generates a shortcode which you then copy and paste into a new post/page. Remember to paste the code into the Text view rather than the Visual view. The form will be sent to the email address you have added in Settings/General.

If you want something more sophisticated, such as linking the forms to PayPal, then one of the best premium plugins is Gravity Forms.

However, if you want something that will gather information for you – in a way that you can analyse – I would advise using a third-party site such as Typeform. This is an excellent platform for gathering data about your visitors. You create the forms on the platform typeform.com and then it handles all the sending and receiving of information. You have access to a dashboard on typeform.com which will show you the data gathered and some analytics on behaviour. You simply create your form (there are both free and premium templates to choose from) and when you are happy, you select Share, copy and paste the embed code onto a WordPress page on your site, and that's it. Easy.

Figure 5.3 An auto tag generator is a good idea so that you don't have to spend time thinking about tags for individual posts.

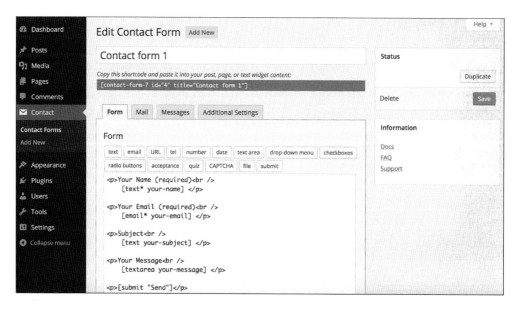

Figure 5.4 You can create multiple forms with Contact Form 7.

Black Studio Tiny MCE – developer Black Studio

This is a fantastic plugin for customizing a text widget – without it you'll need to know HTML. It is very easy to use: just activate it, go to Appearance/Widgets and then drag and drop it onto the sidebar you want to add something to. Then you can quickly embed linkable pictures, text, anything really (Figure 5.5).

Yet Another Related Posts Plugin (YARPP) – developer Adknowledge

There are many variations of this plugin but I like this one best. This plugin offers up related content to your posts based on tags, categories and custom post types. It's a good way to promote other content on your site and keep your visitors exploring what you have to offer. It's very easy to use – just activate the plugin and then choose how you want the related content to be displayed in Settings/YARPP (Figures 5.6 and 5.7).

MailPoet Newsletter – developer Mail Poet

If you're planning on gathering a group of subscribers, sending out a weekly or monthly newsletter is one of the best ways keeping in touch with them and the way to directly market yourself. MailPoet is one of the best plugins available for this purpose. With this plugin you can create newsletters from templates directly on your site, dragging and dropping hyperlinked content and then emailing your subscribers from your website.

The plugin allows you to see who has clicked on your links and which links are generating the most activity. The basic version is free but there are added features available with the Premium version, which is $99 a year (at the time of writing). It is worth paying for the Premium version because you get more template options and more stats on the recipients of the newsletter. You can also integrate the plugin with Google Analytics.

ManageWP – developer Orion

If you have more than one WordPress site – which many people do – this is an essential plugin to manage all those sites from one dashboard. Instead of having to open each site individually, with this plugin[5] you can access them all from one place – allowing you

Figure 5.5 Black Studio Tiny MCE is excellent for customising a widget.

Figure 5.6 YARRP offers up related content to a post for your visitors.

to update all themes/plugins with one click, delete all spam, approve comments and generally keeping an eye on things (Figure 5.8).

You can also create backups and clone sites, which is very useful if you have set up a test site as well as your main site to test out features or to build a whole new launch safely. Once you are happy with the test site (you can set up a sub-domain for this – for example, www.test.wpforjournalists.co.uk. To set up a sub-domain go to Tsohost and in your cloud dashboard click on Manage Your Website and in the Basic Management Tools you can click on Sub-domains and Add New.)

On ManageWP you can clone your test site when you are happy and then paste it over your new site. ManageWP looks after the whole process. (Note: this is a Premium function. The basics are free and then you scale up your membership depending on your use. It's affordable, though, and well worth it if you are building more than one site.)

Maintenance – developer fruitfulcode

It is good practice to take your site down out of view while you are working on it. This is called 'down for maintenance' and there are quite a few plugins available which will show a splash screen instead of just a white page saying 'Down for maintenance'. The one I use by fruitfulcode is very easy to use and allows you to customize your splash screen and add your own logo and description. To install it, activate the plugin then go to your dashboard and Maintenance. From here you can turn Maintenance on and off – when it is on, only users who are logged on will be able to see the content of the site; everyone else will just see the splash screen.

Try it – enable it and then log out of your site. Try to load your domain again and you should see the splash screen. Now log back in and make the page look the way you want. It's all fairly self-explanatory. Whenever you are doing anything lasting more than a few minutes enable this plugin and then your audience won't see you tinkering away.

Bulk Password Reset – developer Ruben Woudsma

I love this plugin (though it hasn't been updated in a while, so perhaps find an alternative – try

> Creating a sub-domain is a useful way of creating a test area so that you don't mess up your live site. You can recreate your live site on the sub-domain – you have to go through the whole process of installing WordPress on your sub-domain (see page 12 for advice on installing Word-Press) as it is essentially a separate site. Keep your sub-domain under Maintenance and then you can test things without worrying about mucking anything up.

Emergency Password Reset by andymoyle or a premium plugin by Young Tech Leads: https://shop.youngtechleads.com/downloads/wordpress-bulk-password-reset).

Being able to reset everyone's password in one go is a very useful function to have if you have a lot of users. The plugin by Woudsma is very easy to use – you can bulk-reset the password for all your users, or for certain roles. If you wanted to change all the passwords for your subscribers, for instance, you can set it to change the password for everyone with this role and then an email will be sent to each user asking them to reset their password. Or you can decide on a password yourself – I usually do this sporadically for all my students. I change the password for all users to one that I have decided on and then send an email out with the new password that advises them to change it themselves when they log on. I do this mostly to ensure that the email notifying them of this change doesn't go straight to their spam folders.

Custom Sidebars – Dynamic Widget Area Manager – developer WPMUdev

This is a very useful plugin: it allows you to create new sidebars and widget areas on your site, allowing you to have specific sidebars for specific pages, posts, category pages, etc. This means you can tailor the widgets you want to appear and tailor the content so that it is appropriate to the content of the page. For example, your website might be about news in London and you may have category pages for each borough. You could create a sidebar for each borough and then drop RSS feeds (see page 118 for help with RSS feeds) with news

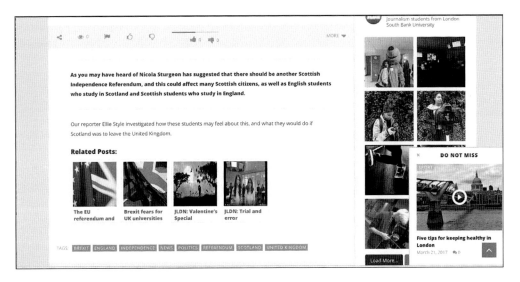

Figure 5.7 Related content with the YARRP plugin.

Figure 5.8 If you have more than one WordPress site, ManageWP is invaluable.

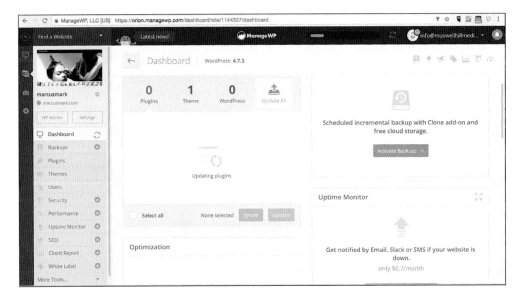

about the individual boroughs instead of having to use one sidebar for everywhere (Figure 5.9).

PERFORMANCE PLUGINS

When developers talk about performance with reference to WordPress, they are talking about page load times – how quickly pages and posts appear when you click on them.

Why is it important? Because speed counts.

According to research from (Google-owned) ad serving company Doubleclick in September 2016, "53% of mobile sites are abandoned if pages take longer than three seconds to load"[6] with desktop users expecting a site to load in just two seconds.

How quickly your site loads isn't just dependent on you; the network a visitor is using to

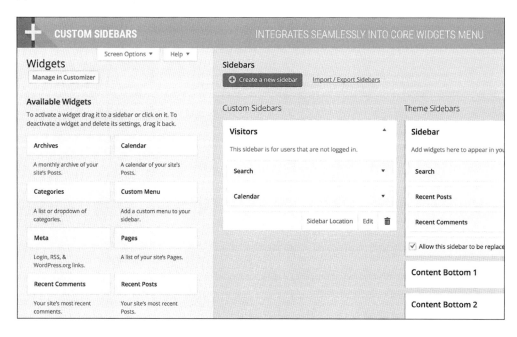

Figure 5.9 Being able to create specific sidebars for specific areas on your site can be very useful.

access your site will have a huge impact on speed, and 3G will serve sites a lot slower than 4G, for example. However, there are things that you can do to make sure your site loads as quickly as possible.

The first is run some diagnostic tests on your site to identify areas that are causing lagging. There are quite a few online tools which will test your site for you: **Google Page Speed, Webpagetest, Dynatrace** – but I use Pingdom.

This tool will give you a performance percentage and page load time and will show you exactly what is slowing your site down, enabling you to address these areas.

It offers a lot of information but what you should concentrate on in the first instance is the performance insights. What you are looking for are A grades for each area.

When you are looking at the results on Pingdom, one of the things you will see is whether there is a particular plugin that is making things sluggish. If you do identify a problem plugin, try and find an alternative or get rid of it completely if you are not really using it.

If you have a low score in a particular area try the following plugins:

W3 Total Cache – developer Frederick Townes

W3 Total Cache will address quite a few of the areas highlighted by Pingdom. One of the quickest ways of increasing the speed is by leveraging browser *caching*. This basically means not loading every single element on your page fresh – for example, a logo is going to be the same each time the site is accessed, so instead of having to download that logo each time a visitor hits one of your pages, a plugin can tell the browser to save the logo and use the saved version instead. This may seem like an insignificant feature but when you consider how many different elements a page consists of, having a plugin that only needs to download fresh content will make a huge difference to how much time a page takes to load.

After you've activated the plugin the first thing you should do is run a compatibility check to make sure the plugin is going to work properly. Before you make any changes to the settings go back to Pingdom and run another speed check to see whether just by activating W3 Total Cache you have improved the performance of your site. If you have jumped up to an A grade, change nothing on the plugin.

If there has been no change to the performance grades on Pingdom, you will need to make adjustments to the settings on W3 Total Cache. Search online for optimum settings for this plugin and then work your way through, changing one setting a time on W3 Total Cache and checking at each stage to see whether you are improving or making things worse on Pingdom. As a first step, though, the default settings should be fine.

Tip: remember that if your site is slow to load this could be to do with your internet connection rather than the site.

A word of warning: W3 Total Cache isn't compatible with all plugins, so if your site goes down once you have activated it and changed the settings, go into your FTP server and delete this plugin. The other two alternatives I have used successfully are **WP Super Cache** (developer Automattic) and **WP Fastest Cache** (developer Emre Vona).

Smush – developer WPMU DEV

One of the biggest issues with page loading is image size. So many people don't bother to resize their images before uploading them – they upload ridiculously large files, forcing the server to work hard to resize images to the correct size. If you're not going to be disciplined about resizing images you need a plugin to do this for you. One of the best is Smush.

This plugin will resize, optimise and compress all your images. You can set the maximum width and height of all images – anything above 2,048 pixels in either width or height is huge and not recommended. Remember: the bigger the file the more time it will take to load (Figure 5.10).

Other factors that can affect performance on your site are:

■   **Web hosting** If you are on a cheap hosting package in particular, you will be on a shared server, which essentially means your site will be competing with other sites for space. My advice is to start with a cheap package but look to increase the money you are spending on your host as your site grows, and definitely adjust your spend if you are finding things slow (you may experience slowness at different times of the day

Figure 5.10   Smush is a good plugin for keeping a check on your image sizes.

when there is a spike in activity on your shared server).

- Plugins Some plugins don't work well with others and this can cause your site to slow down. If you are experiencing sluggishness on your site, deactivate all your plugins and then reactivate them one by one, taking note of any changes in functionality. This will isolate any plugins which are causing issues. If you find one that is affecting your site, get rid of it and find an alternative.

- Old versions of WordPress Running an out-of-date version of WordPress is a big no-no – particularly as it opens your site up to a potential hack – but it will also make a site run slower, so make sure you are always running the latest version (this goes for plugins and themes – everything needs to be up to date).

- Excerpts Make sure you are using excerpts on archive pages and your home-page instead of forcing your site to load the full content of every post (see page 76 for instructions on how to do this). Change your settings to serve excerpts to any RSS feed as well – you do this on your WordPress dashboard in Settings/Reading. Check the box for each article in a feed show summary.

- Video and audio files Don't upload video or audio files into your media library – use a third-party site to host these files, such as **YouTube**, **Vimeo**, **SoundCloud or Audioboom** and then simply embed their respective players.

SEO PLUGINS

What is search engine optimisation?

SEO is the way you improve your website so that it shows up in searches and therefore increases your traffic (visitors). It is a massive area and I'm only going to cover the basics here. If you are serious about this area you can make a career out of it – the search engine industry is estimated to be worth

more than $65 billion (Borrell Associates 2016).[7]

I suppose the first thing to clarify is the term 'search engine'. An example of a search engine is Google, Bing or Yahoo. How people find your site is dependent on the search engines pulling up your domain when someone puts in a search word (the words people search with). How these words match your site forms the basis of SEO: "Search engines have two major functions: crawling and building an index, and providing search users with a ranked list of the websites they've determined are the most relevent."[8]

How these search engines determine which sites to rank highly is down to setting rules/equations known as *algorithms*. When a user puts in a search term, the search engine will use an algorithm (a computer process) in order to decide which sites best matches the search and will rank them in order, using various determining factors such as trustworthiness, reputation and authority. This is a complex process and not easy to understand. Google, for example, relies on more than 200 unique clues to process a search. These clues could be keywords on your website or the freshness of your content, or they could be based on location. How these algorithms work is continually changing and being updated, so trying to guess what the search engines are looking for is nigh-on impossible. Google gets over 100 billion searches a month.[9]

When you consider that at the time of writing there were more than 1 billion websites online (internetlivestats.com),[10] coupled with the fact that most people only look at the first couple of pages returned in a search, getting your site on the first page of results is highly unlikely. Research in 2009 found that 91% of searchers do not even go past page one of the search results.[11]

So, unless you are a major player with some serious financial backing, or you have a very particular niche, longevity and a good reputation, your aim should not be about getting on that first page of search results. Your aim should not even involve the quantity of visitors to your site. Your aim should be the quality of your visitors. It is who is visiting, not how many, that is important (most of your visitors are going to find you through direct links and not through organic search anyway).

However, there are things you should be doing to give yourself the best chance of being found, and one of the first is making sure your website is mobile-friendly. Google rolled out its mobile-first index in 2016,[12] meaning it is now using the mobile version of a website as the primary search engine. We'll look in more detail at mobile later in this chapter. For now, I want to concentrate on a few areas that you can affect in order to optimise your site.

- Install an SEO plugin.
- Optimise images – add descriptive *alt tags* and filenames.
- Create an XML *site map*.
- Add a robots.txt file.
- Connect social media accounts.
- Install Google Analytics.
- Ensure your site is responsive.
- Build internal and external links.

Install an SEO plugin

Probably the most popular SEO plugin is Yoast (developer Team Yoast). Easy to install, this plugin gives you many elements integral to SEO – one of the best is the page analysis it offers (Figure 5.11).

The plugin gives you a breakdown of everything on a page, awarding good practice with green bullets. It is very easy to see where you need to make improvements – the goal being to score green on every element. One word of warning though: don't be tempted to make things up just to get a green bullet – this is particularly true of your focus keywords.

What is your focus keyword? It is the word you want people to use to find your content in a search. Choosing these words

can be tricky. You need to spend some time researching search terms around the main focus of your site, building up a list of keywords – both single words and phrases – otherwise known as longtail keywords.

Fifty per cent of search queries are four words or longer.[13]

There are many online tools to check the popularity of keywords (try serps.com) and you can also use the tools that come with **Yoast, Google Trends** and **Adwords.**

Setting up Yoast is really easy with the configuration wizard. After you activate the plugin find this wizard in the Plugin Settings on the dashboard under General (Figure 5.12).

I'm not going to go through all of the different elements in a piece of content identified by Yoast, but I just want to highlight how useful the snippet preview is, to see what your content looks like in a search on Google (Figure 5.13).

To find your page analysis: it is usually underneath the body text box when you are editing a page/post.

Diligently adjusting your SEO titles and meta description will give you the best chance of improving your site ranking, but you must be consistent.

Optimise images – add descriptive alt tags and filenames

Make sure all images have alt text and proper filenames. For any image on your site the alt tag should describe what the image is – this is partly for accessibility, as a screen reader will read out the alt tag for visually impaired users. However, the alt tag is also incredibly helpful for searches. This goes for the image filename too. Imagine you have a picture of Prince William at Buckingham Palace. The keywords 'Prince William' and 'Buckingham Palace' are search terms, so an organic search for these terms may pull up your content because you have identified your image with those words. If, however, you uploaded the image file as a random

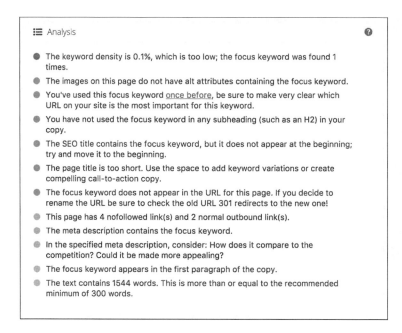

Figure 5.11 One of the most popular plugins showing SEO on a post is Yoast.

Figure 5.12 Use the configuration wizard to set up Yoast on your site.

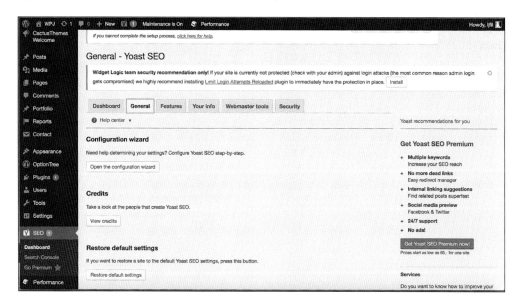

number – '007 0964', for example, and there are no words describing the image in the alt text, there is no way that this image is going to be found in an organic search.

The bottom line is, be disciplined. Every image you upload into your media library needs a proper filename with keywords and an alt tag with a description, again using these keywords.

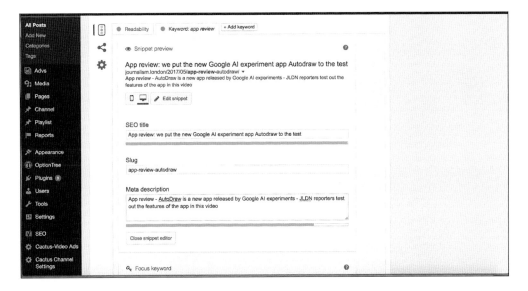

Figure 5.13 The snippet preview with Yoast is very useful to see what your content looks like on a search page.

Create an XML site map

A site map is essentially a list of all the pages/posts that make up your site collated into one document, which allows search engines to crawl your site more effectively. There are many free plugins that will create your site map for you and premium versions of plugins too, such as Yoast.

Try Simple WP Site Map (developer Webbjocke). All you have to do is activate it. There are some settings you can control on the dashboard under Settings/Simple WP Site Map but you don't really have to make any changes at all. Search engines will automatically find the file, so you don't need to do anything other than activate the plugin.

Add a robots.txt file

The robots.txt file is really only important if there are certain areas of your site that you do not want search engines to crawl through, or you are getting huge spikes in traffic from disreputable bots, causing your site to crash. This has happened to me a number of times, and installing a robot.txt file with instructions to block these bots has fixed the issue.

You can easily check if your site has a robots.txt file – there are lots of websites that will run a check for you such as seosite-checkup.com – but really all you need to do is put your domain with /robots.txt in the search bar.

If you have a robots.txt file, the file will show you what the engines have access to. If you want to make any changes, find the text file using your FTP (see Chapter 3 for help with setting up and using an FTP account) and then edit the file, specifying any file or folder you want to block or allow.

If you do not have a robots.txt file and you want one, you can create one very easily from your FTP server. Just create a text file, name it robots.txt and save it in your public_html folder (Figure 5.14).

Connect social media accounts

You should be linking your site to a Facebook, Twitter and LinkedIn account at the very minimum. For more on connecting your social media accounts with your website, see page 85.

Install Google Analytics

There are lots of reasons for verifying your site with Google Analytics – this is covered in detail in Chapter 8.

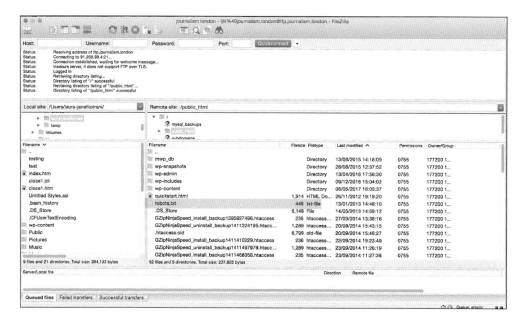

Figure 5.14 Create a robots.txt file via your FTP account.

Ensure your site is responsive

This just means that your website should work on all devices – mobile, tablet and desktop. If you have picked your theme wisely (see page 30 for help with choosing a commercial theme) your site will already be responsive. There are plugins that you can add to fix a theme that isn't responsive, but it is easier all round just to pick another theme.

Build internal and external links

Make sure you are hyperlinking as much as possible – providing extra information for your readers on your content is not just good practice but also a useful way of connecting your content with other sites. Working online is joining a network – you want to be as plugged in as possible to that network. Hyperlink people's names, locations, surveys … anything that can provide extra information to support your content. Do not hyperlink words such as 'Click me'; you should hyperlink anchor text which contains the keywords. For example, if you are writing about a title of a book don't write 'Click here for more information'. Instead, hyperlink

the title of the book. Remember, everything you do should reinforce keywords in order for your content to rank in a search.

You should also remember to link to your own content across your site – providing internal links with keywords also encourages site ranking. And if you can get external sites to link back to your site all the better (these are called back links). So, any time you link to an external site, email them and let them know you are linking to them – they may well link back to you. (At the very least they should be curious enough to visit your site to check the link out. One more visitor for you!)

SECURITY PLUGINS

More than 50 million website users in 2017 were warned that a site they were visiting contained malware, according to Sucuri.[14]

Security is big issue for WordPress sites – most people will say this is because the code is open-source, which makes it a vulnerable platform, but this is not quite true. The real reason for a WordPress site being vulnerable to attacks is mostly down to negligence on behalf of the site owner. It is your responsibility as an owner to take care of your site. Here are a few plugins to help you.

Wordfence – developer Wordfence

Wordfence is one of my essential plugins – it protects your site from unregistered people trying to log in and is a fantastic block to brute-force attacks from bots. It acts as a robust spam filter and will also show you information about your visitors, such as their IP addresses, countries and time spent on site – all live reporting in real time. It also offers you the chance to block users, IP addresses and whole countries from logging on. But the function that I like best is the scanning. This plugin will scan all your WordPress core files, your plugin files and your theme files and compare them to the original files, checking to see if there have been any changes to the code. If there are any changes, the files are flagged up as corrupt and you are given the option to repair the file by overwriting it with the original code, with one click. Super helpful (Figure 5.15).

Limit Login Attempts – developer Joehn Enfeldt[15]

This is one of the most annoying plugins but also one of the most useful. By activating it you can block people attempting to get into your site through trial and error. In Dashboard/Settings/Limit Login, you can choose how many attempts to allow and you can also choose the amount of time to block a user after this limit is reached; for example, 10 minutes. I have said this is one of the most annoying plugins because I have often found myself blocked after three attempts and then had to go and delete the plugin using my FTP account so that I could get back into the site.

Hide My WordPress – developer WPPlugins[16]

This is a great plugin which will hide the /wp-admin URL. You can choose another URL that only you will know in order to access the dashboard. So, for example, you could change the default URL from myWordPresssite.com/wp-admin to myWordPresssite.com/onlyforme

Back up! Back up! Back up!

You must get used to regularly saving your site off-line – preferably on an external hard drive which you keep safe. Depending on how regularly you are posting content you should be doing this once a week or at the very least once a month. Most hosts will keep at least a week's worth of backups which you should be able to download directly and save – but there are a number of plugins that offer you the chance to set up regular backups (you can do this with **ManageWP** – see page 70 for help with this tool). One of the most popular and easiest to use is **Xcloner – Backup and Restore** (developer Liuta Ovidiu).

Once your backup has completed (make sure you are backing up both your WordPress files and your MySQL database), find the file on your server using your FTP account and save the files onto an external hard drive, labelling the files by date. One other thing: it is best to do your backup when you're connected via an ethernet connection – if you are on Wi-Fi and the connection drops for a second, the process will stall and you will most likely have to start again from the beginning.

Disable file editing

If you're going to have a number of users accessing your admin area, it is a good idea to disable the ability to edit your theme files and plugins direct from your dashboard. This functionality is enabled by default. It is, however,

> Make sure all themes and plugins are kept up to date and you are running the latest version of Wordfence – this is your greatest defence against attacks.

> Don't ever use 'admin' as a username, and choose a complex password.

quite easy to disable it by adding a bit of code to your wp-config.php file (see page 13 for instructions of where to find this file).

Here's the code to add:

```
//Disallow file edit
    define ('DISALLOW_FI-
    LE_EDIT', true);
```

And here's where to add the code: just above the line

```
/*That's all, stop editing!
    Happy blogging.*/
```

2-Step Verification –
developer as247[17]

Most people use the same password for multiple accounts online, which can leave a user vulnerable to identity theft. One of the things you can do to combat this is to add a two-step verification plugin. This plugin is very easy to use and allows you to get a verification code sent to your phone when you try and log into your site. I use 2-Step Verification on a number of sites, particularly for my PayPal account. It means that no one can access my sites without having the unique code sent to my phone. Setting up this plugin requires you to first download Google Authenticator, then scan a barcode

> **When you are using a backup plugin and your backup keeps timing out before completing, try excluding the biggest files or splitting your big files into two. Most backup plugins will allow you to specify these big files in the settings.**

and hit Verify. It's very easy – you will find the settings/instructions under Dashboard/User/2-Step Verification on your WordPress site once you have activated the plugin.

THINKING MOBILE

As I have already stated early in this book, mobile should be a major consideration when planning your website. Not only are users now accessing content mostly via their smart phones, their first port of call is a social media feed, which they will then click through to a website. This is why your social media accounts and your website need to be seamlessly integrated, and you should be using a theme which is fully responsive across tablets, smart phones and desktops. I am going to look in more detail at social media in the next section. In this section I want to cover 10 points to optimise your content for smart phones.

1. **Use a responsive theme.** The most important factor is having a responsive theme – there

Figure 5.15 Scanning your site for potential issues is easy with Wordfence.

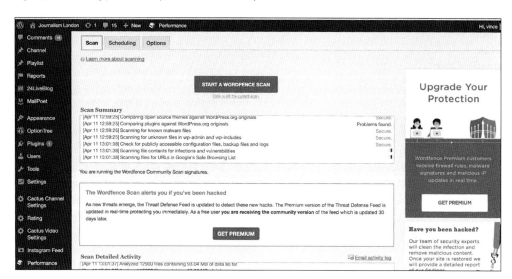

really isn't any excuse now not to have a theme which is built to adapt to whichever device you are accessing it from. It used to be that you had to create a separate mobile version of your website, but this is a very outdated practice now that the commercial themes are so fantastic at adapting your content to suit the device. I have already given you some theme ideas in Chapter 4, but here are a few more that are particularly good on mobile:

Upfront – developer WPmudev

This company is really good, but buying a theme from them requires you to become a member – there is a monthly fee, so this may be a little pricey for students. However, for this monthly fee you do get a whole heap of services as well as themes and plugins and great support, backups and security, which are all worth the money when you are starting out and unsure. There is no tie-in, so you could sign up for a couple of months while you get started, if you can afford to. I recommend its Upfront Issue theme, which is grid-like in style and works really well on mobiles. It is also incredibly intuitive and gives you so much control over the site.

- ■ **BeTheme** – developer muffingroup.
- ■ **X WordPress Theme** – developer Themeco. There are four different styles to choose from. Try Ethos – it's gorgeous.

> **Hackers often hide code in inactive themes giving them a *backdoor* straight into your site, so delete any theme or plugin that you are not using.**

> **The mobile/tablet now outstrips the computer. We have reached the mobile tipping point with a publisher like the BBC reporting that around 70% of traffic now comes from mobile devices.[18] (Figure 5.16.)**

> **The average mobile viewing session on YouTube lasts more than 40 minutes.[19]**

- ■ **SimpleMag** – developer ThemesIndep. Here's an example of a site that is using this theme: thelux-einsider.com

2. **Consider installing AMP.** AMP stands for Accelerated Mobile Pages – an open-source project led by Google – and **AMP for WordPress** (AMP for WP) was developed by Ahmed Kaludi and Mohammed Kaludi.

Forty per cent of users drop off after just three seconds if the content doesn't load.[20] AMP dramatically improves the performance of web pages on mobile sites – page loads are instant. It has been built with a number of different collaborators, including WordPress, and many different publishers and developers. I am not going to go into the details of how it works but needless to say it does work – though it has to be said, unless you are a developer, you are going to lose the look and feel of the desktop version of your website as you are only offered three possible default layouts to choose from on a mobile. If you are OK with this, go ahead.

First, install the default support plugin by Automattic, **AMP.**

Second, install AMP for WP – Accelerated Mobile Pages.

There are a number of things you can do to customize how your pages appear on mobile which you should explore – but bear in mind what I have just said about how your content is going to look.

You should definitely make sure you have changed the menu – click on

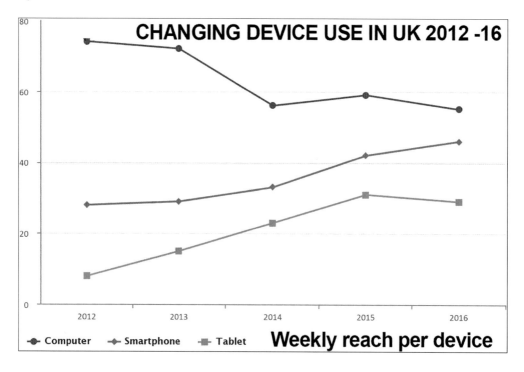

Figure 5.16 Digital News Report (2016) Reuters Institute for the Study of Journalism.

Dashboard/Appearance/Menus and select your menu for AMP Menu in Manage Locations. To check what your site looks like on mobile add /?amp at the end of your website URL; for example, mydomain.com/?amp. You should get the AMP version of your website. You can then go through all the settings to make your site look like you want it to (as much as is allowed).

Make sure you add your logo, have a play around with the design and add your Google Analytics tracker ID. (You can find your tracker ID on your Google Analytics dashboard – click on the Admin wheel in the bottom-right corner and then select Property Settings. For help with setting up Google Analytics, see page 160.)

In 2017, 90% of households in Great Britain had internet access, an increase from 89% in 2016 and 57% in 2006, with 73% of adults using their mobiles/smart phones to get online.[21]

3. **Make sure your menu works on mobile.** Sometimes even with a responsive theme the menu doesn't work so well on a mobile device – buttons don't click and text overlays. This can sometimes be caused by custom code or by the combination of certain plugins. Having a working menu is obviously vital – you will lose your visitors if they can't click on the things they want. If you have installed AMP for WP you can control your mobile menus with that. If you haven't, try **WPMobile Menu** (developer Takanakui).[22]

> Some of the considerations for creating content for mobile are having a responsive site and keeping the file sizes of uploaded content small – particularly images. Martin Ashplant, digital director, metro.co.uk

4. **Keep testing your site to see how mobile-friendly it is.** Google has a free tool online which you can use to test your site: search.google.com/search-console/mobile-friendly.[23] Address any issues it pulls up (Figure 5.17).

5. **Avoid pop ups.** I am not that keen on pop ups anyway, but if you really want to have a pop up make sure you install a pop up plugin that you can turn off for mobile.

6. **Make sure your content is suitable for mobile devices.** Keep your headlines short and make every word count – no more than about 50 characters. Make sure your keywords are at the beginning (keep an eye on which articles are working on Google Analytics, and change keywords if articles are not being found/read).

7. **Reduce the word count for articles on mobile.** Keep your content for mobile short – less than 500 words. Anything longer: keep it for your website. You can restrict the longer articles from showing on mobile with the AMP plugin.

8. **Don't use *clickbait*!** You will get a potential spike but those readers won't come back to you once they realize your headlines aren't appropriate to the actual content.

9. **Create posts with lists.** Numbers in a headline seem to work well. For example: 'Ten things to make sure your content is optimized for mobile'.

10. **Keep your image sizes small.** Don't upload huge images – make sure you resize all your images to the recommended sizes for the theme you are using.

BBC desktop traffic peaks between 12pm and 2pm, while mobile is more stable, with a bump in the morning, starting at 6am, and another in the evening.[24]

CONNECTING YOUR SOCIAL MEDIA

One of the biggest considerations for running an online news and features platform is its connection to social media. The relationship between your WordPress site and your social media accounts is fundamental to the success of your site. In this section we are going to look at how to connect your website with the major players: Facebook, Twitter, LinkedIn, Instagram and Pinterest. (Snapchat is covered in the section on live streaming – see page 140.)

Facebook

So let's begin with the giant, Facebook.

Since its launch in 2004 it has completely dominated the market – in March 2017, Facebook's figure for daily active users was 1.37 billion.[25]

There are a ton of WordPress plugins to experiment with, each offering something slightly different, and some of them can be very tricky to make work. What follows are instructions for creating your Facebook page and connecting this page to your website so that anything you post on your website will automatically appear on your Facebook page, and anything you post on your Facebook page will automatically appear in a feed on your website. If you can get these two working, you'll be pretty much set to tackle any of the others.

There are many steps to follow. You have been warned.

Setting up your Facebook account

You need to give your account name some thought. Chances are you already have a personal account, which is

> Make sure all your social media accounts use the same email address that you have created for your website. One of the things that gets people in a mess is having lots of different accounts all registered to different email addresses. Keep it simple: one email for all accounts.

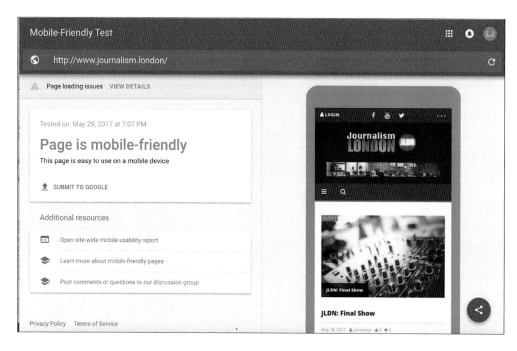

Figure 5.17 Test how well your website displays on mobile at search.google.com/search-console/mobile-friendly

fine, but you will want to adjust your privacy settings when you connect your website to it. Much safer is to create a separate account afresh that will be your professional account. To do this you will have to create a Gmail account with the email account that you are going to use for your website (you should have already done this) (Figure 5.18).

Once you have created your new Gmail account you are ready to set up a Facebook account (Figure 5.19).

Confirm your account and then set up a Facebook page for your website.

Click on the drop-down arrow in the top right of the screen on Facebook and the first option you are given is to create a page.

Choose a section for the page – Company is probably the best, unless you have set up a website about a particular band or venue or product – and then select a category; for example, News.

Put in your website name without the 'www.' – so just WP for Journalists, for example, instead of www.wpforjournalists.com

Click Get Started.

You can now spend some time adding profile pics, descriptions and contact info on your page by clicking on the various boxes. Don't forget to put your website in the About box.

If you click on the Settings tab – on the right, next to the Help tab – you will find lots of options for your page. It is in this area that you can control who has permission to act as an admin to your page. This is a useful tool to share responsibility for the page.

Now you are ready to connect your website with your page. I am warning you, this can be complicated. There are many steps from now until you are through the other side. Be patient and don't skip any steps, and pay attention to what you are doing.

Ready?

Go to your WordPress site and install the plugin **Custom Facebook Feed** (developer Smash Balloon); there are many others to choose from and they all work on pretty much the same basis.

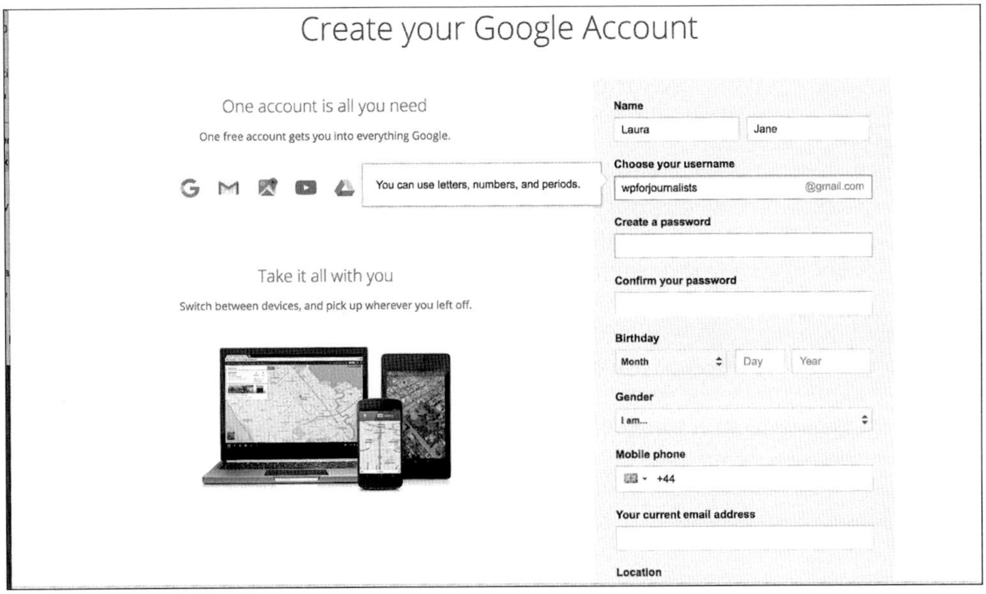

Figure 5.18 Create a Gmail account to use for all your plugins, social media and anything else associated with your website.

Figure 5.19 Create a separate Facebook account to use for your website – don't mix personal and professional.

Activate the plugin and then go to Dashboard/Facebook Feed/Settings.

You will need to add your Facebook Page ID in here.

To find your Facebook Page ID: if you have a Facebook page with a URL like this, www.facebook.com/your_page_name, then the Page ID is just 'your_page_name'. If your page URL is structured like this, www.face book.com/pages/your_page_name/ 123654123654123, then the Page ID is actually the number at the end, so in this case '123654123654123'.

This plugin offers you the chance to enter your own Access Token and says it is recommended to do so. Don't do this now as I'm coming back to this stage with the next plugin anyway. All you really need is the Facebook Page ID for this plugin.

Then there are a few things to change – select Page for 'Is this a page, group or profile', select Page Owner and Other People for 'Show posts on my page by', and change the Localization to English (UK) and the Timezone to (GMT) Greenwich Mean Time. Click Save Changes.

You can have a play around with how the feed is displayed in Facebook Feed/Customize.

When you are happy, create a new page/ post and paste the shortcode '[custom-facebook-feed]' in the Text tab, or you can put it in a widget and drop the feed into your sidebar (Figure 5.20).

OK, now that you have navigated getting a feed from your Facebook page onto your website you need to do this the other way too – so that what you post on your website automatically gets posted on your Facebook page. In order to do this, you need another plugin.

Install **Facebook Auto Publish** (developer xyzscripts.com).

Activate the plugin. You then have a few extra steps to go through before your website content can be posted on your Facebook page. You need to create a Facebook developer account and get an Application ID and an Application Secret:

- Go to developers.facebook.com and click on Log In in the top right of the screen.
- Log in using the account details you have just created your Facebook account with (not the page details).
- Click on Register.
- Accept the Facebook terms and click Next.
- Enter your phone number to confirm your account.

- Facebook will send you a text message containing a confirmation code. Enter it in the box and click Register.
- You're now registered as a Facebook Developer. Click Done.
- Hover over My Apps and then click on Add a New App.
- If prompted, click on Basic Setup.
- Enter your App Name. This can be anything you like. Choose a Category. Click Continue.
- Complete the Security Check and click Submit.
- Your app is now set up. Click on Dashboard to find your app information.
- You will see your App Id and your Application Secret – click the Show button to see the Application Secret.
- Now go to Settings/Basic. Scroll to the bottom and click on the Add Platform link.
- Select Website.
- In the Site URL box enter the URL of your WordPress site; for example, http://www.wpforjournalists.com
- Click Save Changes.
- Make the app 'Live/Public' – go to the App Review.
- Click Make App Public.
- Now you should see a green button next to your app name on the dashboard.

You are ready to connect.

- Go back to your WordPress site and paste in the Application ID and the Application Secret. Click Save. You will be asked to authorize the plugin.
- Click Authorize and you will be taken to your Facebook page and asked to continue posting as ... you, hopefully. Click OK.
- Select the Public option and click OK.
- Click OK on the next box and the authorization should be complete.
- Go back to your WordPress site and you will see in the Plugin Settings that you now have a green bar saying your plugin is authorized.

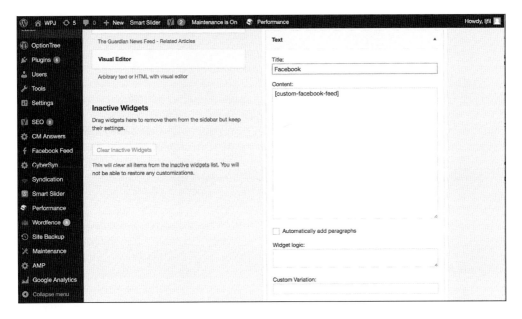

Figure 5.20 You can create a feed from your Facebook page to run in a sidebar.

Make sure the box enabling auto publish to your Facebook account is set to Yes. Then you have various options that you can choose from – for example, do you want all your content to be reposted on Facebook or do you just want a select couple of categories? When you are happy, click Update. You should get a green box saying the update was successful.

You will also see a message asking you to give a back link to the plugin. I always do this, particularly if I am using a plugin for free (I also often donate money to the developer if there is a button to do so. Remember: you are using all their skills and knowledge for free – a back link costs nothing but will improve their Google ratings!)

Create a test post and see whether it appears on your Facebook page. If it does, well done! If it doesn't, commiserations! You are now going to have a few hours trying to work out what you have done wrong.

You can use the publishing tools on Facebook to schedule your posts.

Get involved – facebook.com/ facebookjournalismproject

The three most-used apps by millennials and Generation Z are Facebook, Snapchat and Instagram (which Facebook bought in 2012), and according to Mary Meeker's influential report 2016 Internet Trends, "80 percent of the total time spent on smartphones is spent in just 3 apps".[26]

A great plugin for allowing all your users to sign into your website with their own Facebook account is **Nextend Facebook Connect** (developer Nextendweb).[27] Although this plugin is primarily for Facebook it also has a social media button generator which you can use to allow your users to connect using their Twitter and Google accounts. Simply activate the plugin and go to Dashboard/Settings/ Nextend FB Connect and fill in the Facebook App ID and Secret which you have just created. The buttons will automatically be added to the log-in page but you can also drop buttons in your sidebars by pasting the button codes into a text widget.

Twitter

Like Facebook you should really have a professional Twitter account that you use for your journalism – in fact, you should apply this rule to all your social media accounts.

Twitter is an amazing platform for journalists – it is a great way of building contacts, a direct way to contact people who otherwise would be closed to you, a great search tool for finding news, a good platform for promoting your own content and an excellent tool for keeping an eye on trending topics. Things to be careful of are that it is generally used by a lot of media organisations and journalists, so the views and conversations aren't necessarily representative of society, and there are plenty of instances of fake news so beware of blithely retweeting something – check, check and check the source before passing on the information.

Twitter is also the best for monitoring breaking news – if you want to find out what is happening right now, this should be your first port of call.

Twitter was launched in March 2006 by Jack Dorsey, Evan Williams, Biz Stone and Noah Glass and its growth is phenomenal – it took just three years from the first tweet to reach the billionth tweet and now there are around 6,000 tweets sent per second (figures correct as of June 2017).[28]

On its sixth birthday in 2012 there were 340 million tweets.[29]

Setting up your account is very simple so I am not going to go through the steps. What I am going to cover here is how you get your Twitter feed onto your site and how you can manage this tool so that it works for you.

There are plenty of plugins that will give you a feed on your site but the easiest way (and the most failsafe way) is to create a widget for your Twitter feed and then paste this into a sidebar. You can add any public Twitter timeline.

Click on your Twitter profile and Settings, then Widgets/Create New Widget – you can choose to have a widget displaying your profile or your likes, or a list that you have created or a search using a hashtag.

Click Create Widget and the embed code will be generated. Copy this code and go back to your website. Go to Appearance/Widgets, paste the code into a Text tab and drag that into the sidebar. Click Save. You should now have that search feed in your sidebar. You can also paste the code into a new post/page (make sure you are on the Text tab).

There are quite a few plugins which will handle a number of different social media accounts – for these you need to generate a Twitter API token. Try **Feed Them Social – Facebook, Instagram, Twitter, Vine, Pinterest, etc.** by SlickRemix.

Activate the plugin, and on your dashboard go to Feed Them/Twitter Options.

You now have a few boxes to fill in but first you must go and get a Twitter API token – this is similar to what you have just done with Facebook.

Go to https://apps.twitter.com/app/new and sign in if you haven't already (if you are signed into Twitter with a different account than the one you want the feed from, sign out from it before creating the token – otherwise it will be linked to the wrong account).

Create an application – put the name of your site as the name of the application and add a short description of your site. Then put the full URL in with the http:// and click yes for the T&Cs, then Create Your Twitter Application.

After creating your Twitter Application click on the tab that says Keys and Access Tokens. You have to give access to your Twitter account to use this application. To do this, click the Create My Access Token button at the bottom of the screen.

Copy the Consumer Key (API Key), Consumer Secret, Access Token and Access Token Secret from the screen and paste them into the right boxes on the Feed Them Social plugin on your website. Save and then go to Dashboard/Feed Them/Settings and click Create a Short-code for Social Network – Twitter Feed. Add in your Twitter name and click Generate Short-code. You can now paste this into a sidebar or post/page.

I like the way the plugin displays the feed on a post – you can select to have the header image plus the follower/like/retweet stats and you can also have videos. I think it works really well. Plus you have the bonus of being able to control Facebook, LinkedIn, Instagram, Vine and Pinterest from the same plugin.

You can find all your apps that you have created on apps.twitter.com by scrolling to the bottom of the screen and clicking on Manage My Apps under Tools.

Now that you have your Twitter API tokens and keys you can set up a number of different plugins. Here are a few useful ones to consider.

For auto tweeting your posts and pages to your Twitter account try **AccessPress Twitter Auto Post** (developer AccessPress Themes).

Once you have activated the plugin go to Dashboard/AccessPress and fill in the key details from the app you have created. Click Auto Publish and then select what you want included in the tweet; for example, the headline and the post excerpt (you will have to make sure your post excerpts stick to 140 characters or at least make sense in 140 characters). Paste the following in the box Post Message Format: #post_title, #post_excerpt, #post_link

Don't forget the post link; otherwise, there will be no connection to your website from your tweet. Then check the boxes that you want to include in the Auto Publish and do the same for the categories. You might not want every single post to be auto tweeted – you might want to only tweet out news, for example. (You can get the option to select individual posts that are not to be tweeted when you create a new post/page. If you can't see this option check the box on the Screen Options drop-down at the top of the screen under the Admin bar on your WordPress site). Hit Publish and you should get an auto tweet.

WordPress sharing plugin **AddToAny** (developer AddToAny) is great for adding social share buttons all over your site. It offers buttons to more than 100 sharing and social media sites. Try it for Facebook, Twitter, Pinterest, Google, WhatsApp, LinkedIn,

Figure 5.21 Manage your tweets with Hootsuite.

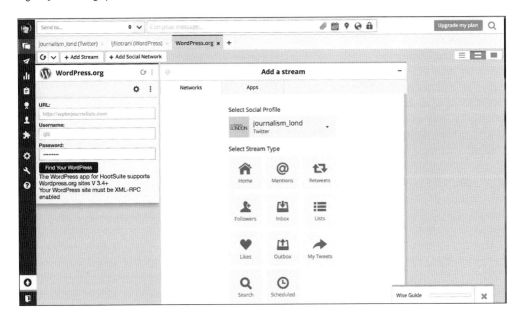

Instagram ... Simply activate the plugin and go to Dashboard/Settings/Addshare and select whether you want a standard bar (my preference) or a floating one (this can cause problems – it essentially means your share buttons won't be fixed to the page/post but will appear wherever you are on the page). Then select which buttons you want to offer your visitors. I would keep it to five or six – don't use them all (Email is always a useful one). Then decide if you want the share buttons at the top of your posts or at the bottom – I always like the top (by the way, you may not need this plugin at all if the theme you are using already offers social share buttons). Then click Save Changes – you should now see social share buttons on your posts.

> Check the top social media accounts on https://socialblade.com

Managing your social media content

Nelio Content – developer Nelio Software

This is a great plugin for managing scheduling – it has an editorial calendar and you can drag and drop posts scheduled for one day into another day. It's really easy. You can also connect all your social media accounts and see exactly what is being published and when.

Go to Dashboard/Nelio Content/Settings/Content. Click on the Analytics Basic box and click Refresh Analytics – this should bring all your current posts on to the calendar – then click Connect your Google Analytics Account (see page 160 for help with setting up your Analytics account). Connect your social media accounts under Social Profiles – Twitter, Facebook Page, Instagram, Pinterest, LinkedIn. You should now see all your posts on Dashboard/Nelio Content/Calendar.

Hootsuite – developer Hootsuite

Hootsuite can be a little confusing to begin with but as you use it it will become second nature. It is incredibly useful for managing your tweets and your posts – you can front-load your tweets and then space them out to publish through the day. For example, you could create 10 tweets and schedule them to go out at 30-minute intervals throughout the day.

Before you do anything though, you need to connect your social media accounts. Once you have signed up for an account, click on your name to go to your account overview. This is on the left-hand side of the screen at the top of the toolbar – this is where you'll be able to add, remove and manage your social networks (Figure 5.21).

You can manage all of your social networks in Hootsuite. Click the Add a Social Network button to get started.

Select the social network you want to add and click the Connect button. A pop up will prompt you to give Hootsuite permission to manage your account. Start with your Twitter account.

Then link up your WordPress site. The account offered by default to connect is the free WordPress.com platform – if you have a self-hosted site (.org) you will need to add an extra app.

Add your website URL, your username and your password. If you get an error message saying:

> Error: Could not find your blog.
> The WordPress app for Hootsuite supports Wordpress.org sites V 3.4+.
> Your WordPress site must be XML-RPC enabled.

... ignore this as your WordPress is XML-RPC enabled by default. There are some other things you should check – here's the advice from Hootsuite:

- Special characters in a password have been found to cause log-in errors. Hootsuite suggests changing your password to one with only letters and numbers.

- Use the URL of your blog's landing page; for example, http://blog.hootsuite.com. Try it with and without 'http://'
- Plugins such as **Bad Behaviour, Block Bad Queries, Better WP Security** and **Login Lock** have been found to cause issues signing in or connecting to the app. Try disabling all your plugins and trying to connect. If this works then add plugins back in one by one to see which one is causing an issue.
- Some users encounter issues with a stream displaying 'No More' for Published Pages and Published Posts. Blogs with **W3 Total Cache** installed, or blogs with a large number of posts, may be causing the app stream to load blank.
- If you still can't get it to connect, contact Hootsuite. Submit a support ticket at https://help.hootsuite.com/hc/en-us/requests/new

Once you have connected all your social media accounts you can add them to your streams – click on Add Stream and select what you want to monitor.

Next, click on the paper airplane icon (Publisher) on the sidebar on the left – this is where you can schedule your tweets/posts. You need to select the social media account where you want it to appear and then you can either choose to post it immediately or schedule it for later. You can build up a bank of tweets here.

You can also add a couple of RSS feeds (see page 118 for help with feeds) in here, which means you will have automatic tweets – this is a great resource. To add a feed, click in Publisher/Content Sources/RSS Feeds and paste in a feed (Figure 5.22).

Remember: once you have connected your WordPress site you will create automatic posts based on your feeds.

The last thing I want to highlight is Hootlet. Find it under Tools on Hootsuite, and drag it up into your Bookmarks toolbar (this is similar to Press This – see page 123 for help with setting up Press This). Whenever you find something you want to tweet you can just click the Hootlet and a box will immediately appear with the headline, an excerpt and a link to the page you were looking at. You can decide to publish it immediately or schedule it.

As I have said, Hootsuite takes some getting used to. Have a look on YouTube for 'How to Use Hootsuite: A Tutorial for Beginners', made by Hootsuite – once you have the hang of it, you'll be hooked.

LinkedIn

Why use LinkedIn? Well, it's the best place to build up a professional network – it's a step up from Twitter in this regard – and you should really think about it as a careers platform. Somewhere to find a mentor, somewhere to seek advice, somewhere to find an internship ... I also use it to ask questions, find sources for interviews and publicise relevant events. It is not for personal chit-chat, and the news must be pertinent to your work/career. It is for professionals.

> We have half a billion members in 200 countries connecting, and engaging with one another in professional conversations and finding opportunities through these connections on LinkedIn. This community represents 10+ million active jobs, access to 9+ million companies – with more than 100,000 articles published every week.
>
> Aatif Awan, vice-president, growth and international products at LinkedIn[30]

Use it to research jobs and to find a contact for a company that you would like to work for.

The first thing you need to do is to create your profile. For inspiration I would have a look at someone else's to see how they have filled in their profile, and use that as a guide. You can look at mine if you like: ljfilotrani. Once you have filled in your profile (make sure your photo is professional-looking – remember, this is about you raising your profile for your career), start searching for people to make

Figure 5.22 Adding an RSS feed to your Twitter account is a great way of ensuring fresh tweets every day.

contact. Once you have found someone you want to connect with, send them a request to connect. When you have a connection they will have '1st' next to their name – this tells you that you are a direct connection and you can email them directly. If there is '2nd' next to their name, this means that they are connected to someone you are connected with. If this is the case, you can ask your connection to introduce you. If they have '3rd' next to their name, this means they are connected to a connection of one of your connections ... If there is no number you aren't connected in any way.

Use LinkedIn as a research tool to build a database of connections. You never know when they'll come in handy.

Connecting your website is easy – just use one of the plugins already mentioned here and your posts will automatically appear in your News on LinkedIn. Be careful though: if you are going to connect, think carefully about what content you want to go on your LinkedIn account. Not everything is going to be suitable.

If you want a plugin specifically for Linke-dIn, try **WP LinkedIn Auto Publish** (developer Claude Vedovini).

Activate the plugin and go to Dashboard/WPlinkedin AutoPublish

The first thing you need to to is authorize the app. To do this you need a client ID from LinkedIn:

- Go to www.linkedin.com/developers/apps and create an application (make sure you are already logged in to your LinkedIn account).
- Click the Create Application button. Fill out all of the general information in the first page of the form.
- In the Authentication tab give your app all permissions and under OAuth 2.0 add the Redirect URL which you will see on the WordPress plugin page.
- In the Settings tab make sure your app's Application Status is set to Live.
- Enter your LinkedIn Client ID and Secret in the boxes on your WordPress plugin page and click Save All Settings.
- Once the page reloads press the Get Authorization Code & Access Token button and then the Save All Settings button.

Instagram

Launched in 2010 and acquired by Facebook in 2012, as of April 2017 there were 700 million Instagram users.[31]

After Instagram itself, Selena Gomez has the most followers with 117 million. Cristiano Ronaldo has 97 million and *National Geographic* has 75 million.

Obviously one of the main reasons for using Instagram is to show fantastic images, but the platform can also be used to link your content online. You can use it to expand on your longer-form written pieces by documenting the story as it is written, for example, teasing your audience with bits of information or serial posts, encouraging them to find the story online to find out more.

When it first launched, the platform didn't provide any way of hyperlinking, so unless you had a feed directly on your website you couldn't connect your images with your site. But now you can.

> Not every news story is necessarily suitable to be presented on Instagram Stories. They must be able to be told quickly and have a strong visual element in order to retain audience engagement. If there isn't a clear visual narrative, it probably isn't worth the effort.
>
> Mark Frankel, social media editor, BBC News[32]

Creating an account is easy – you can either create it from the app or on your desktop.

To create an Instagram account from the app:

- Download the Instagram app for iOS from the App Store, for Android from the Google Play Store or for Windows Phone from the Windows Phone Store.
- Once the app is installed, click the Instagram icon to open it.

- Click Sign Up, then enter your email address (use the same email address that you have created for all the accounts associated with your website) and click Next. You can also tap Log In With Facebook to sign up with your Facebook account (but remember to use the Facebook account you have created for your website, not your personal one).
- If you register with an email address, create a username (make sure you create a username that makes sense for your website – you are trying to create a brand) and password, fill out your profile info (for your website) and then tap Done. If you register with Facebook, you'll be prompted to log into your Facebook account if you're currently logged out.

To create an Instagram account from a computer:

- Go to instagram.com.
- Enter your email address, create a username and password or click Log In With Facebook to sign up with your Facebook account.
- If you register with an email address, click Sign Up. If you register with Facebook, you'll be prompted to log into your Facebook account if you're currently logged out.

You can paste an Instagram photo or a video straight into a post. To do this go to http://instagram.com/[your username] and then click the post to expand it. Click the three dots in the bottom-right corner and select Embed. Copy the embed code that appears and paste it into your post (make sure you are on the Text tab).

All the national newspapers have Instagram accounts but here are a few accounts that I like:

- The *New York Times* – @NYTimes

To get an RSS feed of an Instagram account visit http://fetchrss.com/instagram. Put an Instagram URL in the input field and click Get RSS.

- *New York Magazine* – @nymag. Check out its series of audiograms alongside its 'Cosby: The Women' issue, featuring photos and short audio interviews of some of the women for an example of how to link longer-form pieces on your website with serial posts on Instagram.
- *First News* – @First_news. The only weekly newspaper for young people, with over two million readers. *First News* is the award-winning, family-owned, weekly newspaper for people aged 7–14.
- *Positive News* UK – @positivenewsuk. "Good journalism about good things" and "the world's first positive newspaper". Visit www.positive.news/join
- *MTV News* – @mtvnews. MTV News posts short reporter-led packages that collect the best video from an event.
- @jr. An enigmatic artist whose identity is shrouded in mystery.
- Teenage urban explorer *Humza Deas* – @humzadeas. Humza is a leading member of the 'outlaw Instagrammer' movement – the group of New York photographers who scale buildings and climb bridges, taking pics as they go. The term was coined by Adrian Chen in his article for the *New York Times*, 'Meet the outlaw Instagrammers of New York City'.
- *Yoko Ono* – @yokoonoofficial. A travelogue.
- Photojournalist *Ben Lowy* – @benlowy
- @hawkeyehuey. He is now 8 but he started taking pics when he was 5. Interesting to see his viewpoint.
- Photoblogger *Brandon Stanton* – @Humansofny
- Backstage at *Saturday Night Live* – @Nbcsnl
- @Dogsofinstagram
- *National Geographic* – @Natgeo. Gorgeous.
- *Metro* – @metro.co.uk. *Metro* uses Instagram in its articles really effectively – and lists! And the site runs on WordPress – for example, 'Check out 22 of the world's most popular marathons'.[33]

Video on Instagram is growing. In the first half of 2016, the amount of time people spent watching video on Instagram was up 150%. See @nytvideo: the *New York Times'* video account uses primarily short cuts, outtakes and mood-setting visuals from longer pieces it publishes on its own site.

There are lots of plugins available to display your Instagram account – I like **Instagram Feed** (developer Smash Balloon). It is really easy to set up and you can display lots of different Instagram accounts in the same feed, with lots of options to customize how it looks.

Activate the plugin, go to the Dashboard/Instagram Feed and click on the large blue button to get your Instagram Access Token and User ID. Copy these and then go back to your Dashboard/Instagram Feed and paste them into the relevant Access Token and User ID fields. Click on Customize Page to change how your feed appears. Once you are happy, click on the Display Your Feed to get the shortcode '[instagram-feed]' and paste it into any page, post or widget (text) where you want the feed to appear.

Getting your website posts onto Instagram, however, isn't so easy. There are a few plugins that will do it for you but they are not free. Try **NextScripts: Social Networks Auto-Poster** (developer NextScripts). This is a great plugin for auto posting with numerous options for lots of social media accounts, and some for free – for posting to Instagram you need the Pro version.

Pinterest

Pinterest might not be the first platform you think of when you think about news but it can be a useful tool in building your brand and engaging an audience, and with 175 million active monthly users it is not a platform to ignore (stats correct as of April 2017).[34]

Primarily used by people to source products, it has a massive amount of food and travel content. You could easily jump into these sections to create some conversations for your website. Have a look at how the *Guardian* does it at https://uk.pinterest.com/theguardian

But there is also a space for more serious journalism – check out the *New York Times* at www.pinterest.com/nytimes, and in particular have a look at photojournalist David Guttenfelder's board on North Korea.[35]

There's a great board called Journalism Tools at https://uk.pinterest.com/journalismtools

Ben Silbermann, Evan Sharp and Paul Sciarra co-founded Pinterest back in 2010.

In an article for the *Atlantic* in 2014, Evan Sharp described the platform as

a place where people can go to get ideas for any project or interest in their life. And as you encounter great ideas and discover new things that you didn't even know were out there, you can pin them and make them part of your life through our system of boards.[36]

Creating an account is easy – either sign up with your email account or your Facebook account. Once you have signed in you will be given the option to choose five topics to follow (Figure 5.23).

Then get the browser button (very similar to the Hootlet from Hootsuite – see page 92).

Now you can start pinning things. I would have a look around first and then create a board for your pins. To do this, click on the icon at the top right of the Saved screen – from here you can create new boards and see any pins you have created.

Embedding your Pinterest board on to your WordPress site is easy. You can create a widget on https:///developers.pinterest.com – go to Tools/Widgets and then just paste in your Pinterest URL, select how you want it to look and copy the code (for example, <a data-pin-do="embedBoard" data-pin-board-width="400" data-pin-scale-height="240" data-pin-scale-width="80" href="https://www.pinterest.com/pinterest/official-news/"></a>). Go to your WordPress Dashboard/Widgets and paste the code in a Text widget or straight onto a post or page. Make sure you are in the Text tab.

Remember: you can add Pinterest to Hootsuite (see page 91 for help).

There are lots of plugins on WordPress for pinning your posts on to your Pinterest boards – try **AccessPress Pinterest** (developer AccessPress Themes).

Activate the plugin then go to Dashboard/Accesspress Pinterest and activate it. With this plugin you can pin any image on your site, pin board widgets, profile widgets and the latest pins.

Figure 5.23 There's a great board called Journalism Tools on Pinterest.

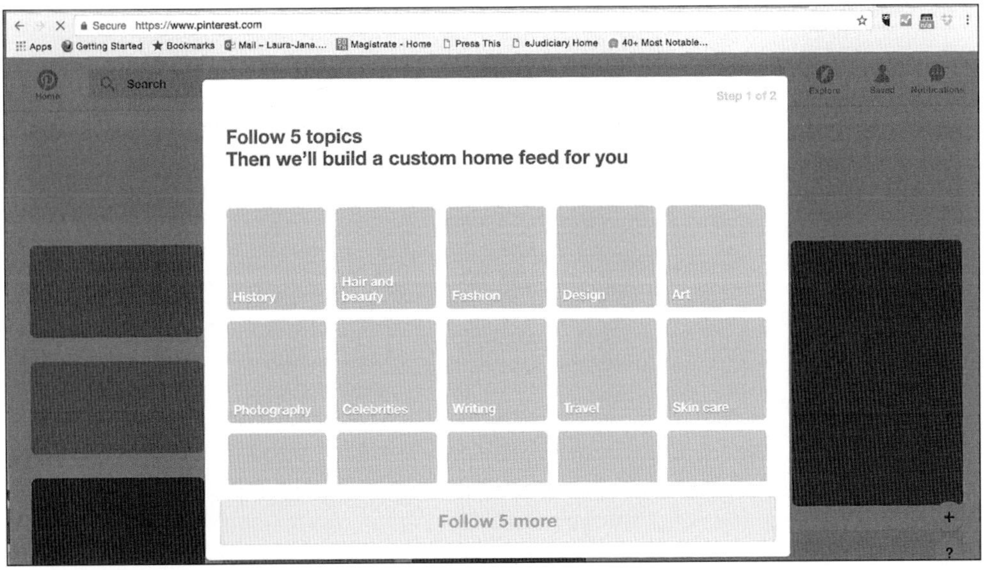

REFERENCES

1   Walsh, S. (2017). Why Quizzes Are Content Marketing's Secret Weapon. [online] Buzz-Sumo. Available at: http://buzzsumo.com/blog/quizzes-content-marketings-secret-weapon [Accessed 12 Nov. 2017].

2   Niemanreports.org. (2017). The Future of Comments. [online] Available at: http://niemanreports.org/articles/the-future-of-comments/ [Accessed 12 Nov. 2017].

3   Price, Alex. (2017). Founder of 93digital – interviewed by LJ Filotrani.

4   WordPress.org. (2017). WP Full Auto Tags Manager. [online] Available at: https://en-gb.wordpress.org/plugins/wp-full-auto-tags-manager/ [Accessed 12 Nov. 2017].

5   Kemp, J. (2017). ManageWP Worker. [online] WordPress.org. Available at: https://en-gb.wordpress.org/plugins/worker [Accessed 12 Nov. 2017].

6   DoubleClick by Google. (2017). Mobile Speed Impacts Publisher Revenue – DoubleClick. [online] Available at: www.doubleclickbygoogle.com/articles/mobile-speed-matters [Accessed 12 Nov. 2017].

7   DeMers, J. (2017). The SEO Industry Is Worth $65 Billion; Will It Ever Stop Growing?. [online] Marketing Land. Available at: https://marketingland.com/seo-industry-worth-65-billion-will-ever-stop-growing-176378 [Accessed 12 Nov. 2017].

8   Fishkin, R. (2017). SEO: The Beginner's Guide to Search Engine Optimization from Moz. [online] Moz. Available at: https://moz.com/beginners-guide-to-seo [Accessed 12 Nov. 2017].

9   Tan, A. (2017). More than Half of Google Searches Now Come from Mobile. [online] Mashable. Available at: http://mashable.com/2015/10/12/google-mobile-searches/#LLG9.FepXuqG [Accessed 12 Nov. 2017].

10 Internetlivestats.com. (2017). Total Number of Websites – Internet Live Stats. [online] Available at: www.internetlivestats.com/total-number-of-websites [Accessed 12 Nov. 2017].

11 Van Deursen, A. and van Dijk, J. (2009). Using the Internet: Skill-Related Problems in Users' Online Behavior. *Interacting with Computers*, 21(5–6), pp.393-402.

12 Schwartz, B. and Schwartz, B. (2017). FAQ: All About the Google Mobile-first Index. [online] Search Engine Land. Available at: https://searchengineland.com/faq-google-mobile-first-index-262751 [Accessed 12 Nov. 2017].

13 WordStream and Cunha, M. (2017). 8 Super-Fascinating Digital Marketing Stats Revealed at SMX East. [online] Wordstream.com. Available at: www.wordstream.com/blog/ws/2015/10/06/smx-east [Accessed 12 Nov. 2017].

14 Sucuri Security. (2017). Sucuri Security. [online] Available at: https://sucuri.net/website-security/website-hacked-report [Accessed 12 Nov. 2017].

15 Eenfeldt, J. (2017). Limit Login Attempts. [online] WordPress.org. Available at: https://en-gb.wordpress.org/plugins/limit-login-attempts [Accessed 12 Nov. 2017].

16 WPPlugins – WordPress Security Plugins. (2017). Hide My WordPress – Security Plugin. [online] WordPress.org. Available at: https://en-gb.wordpress.org/plugins/hide-my-wp [Accessed 12 Nov. 2017].

17 as247. (2017). WordPress 2-Step Verification. [online] WordPress.org. Available at: https://en-gb.wordpress.org/plugins/wordpress-2-step-verification [Accessed 12 Nov. 2017].

18 Digital News Report. (2017). Overview and Key Findings of the 2016 Report. [online] Available at: www.digitalnewsreport.org/survey/2016/overview-key-findings-2016 [Accessed 12 Nov. 2017].

19 YouTube.com. (2017). Press – YouTube. [online] Available at: www.youtube.com/yt/about/press [Accessed 12 Nov. 2017].

20 Kissmetrics. (2017). How Loading Time Affects Your Bottom Line. [online] Available at: https://blog.kissmetrics.com/loading-time [Accessed 13 Nov. 2017].

21 Office for National Statistics. (2017). Internet Access – Households and Individuals. [online] Available at: www.ons.gov.uk/peoplepopulationandcommunity/householdcharacteristics/homeinternetandsocialmediausage/bulletins/internetaccesshouseholdsandindividuals/2017 [Accessed 13 Nov. 2017].

22 Takanakui. (2017). WP Mobile Menu. [online] WordPress.org. Available at: https://srd.wordpress.org/plugins/mobile-menu [Accessed 13 Nov. 2017].

23 Search.google.com. (2017). Mobile-friendly Test. [online] Available at: https://search.

google.com/test/mobile-friendly [Accessed 13 Nov. 2017].

24 Malinarich, N. (2017). BBC Academy – Journalism – Writing for Mobile: Bite-size Basics. [online] bbc.co.uk. Available at: www.bbc.co.uk/academy/journalism/article/art20141202144618106 [Accessed 13 Nov. 2017].

25 Investor.fb.com. (2017). Facebook Reports Third Quarter 2017 Results. [online] Available at: https://investor.fb.com/investor-news/press-release-details/2017/Facebook-Reports-Third-Quarter-2017-Results/default.aspx [Accessed 13 Nov. 2017].

26 Recode. (2017). Mary Meeker's 2016 Internet Trends Report: All the Slides, Plus Analysis. [online] Available at: www.recode.net/2016/6/1/11826256/mary-meeker-2016-internet-trends-report [Accessed 13 Nov. 2017].

27 Nextend. (2017). Nextend Facebook Connect. [online] WordPress.org. Available at: https://en-gb.wordpress.org/plugins/nextend-facebook-connect [Accessed 13 Nov. 2017].

28 Internetlivestats.com. (2017). Twitter Usage Statistics – Internet Live Stats. [online] Available at: www.internetlivestats.com/twitter-statistics [Accessed 13 Nov. 2017].

29 Blog.twitter.com. (2017). Twitter Turns Six. [online] Available at: https://blog.twitter.com/official/en_us/a/2012/twitter-turns-six.html [Accessed 13 Nov. 2017].

30 Awan, A. (2017). The Power of LinkedIn's 500 Million Member Community. [online] Blog.linkedin.com. Available at: https://blog.linkedin.com/2017/april/24/the-power-of-linkedins-500-million-community [Accessed 13 Nov. 2017].

31 Instagram. (2017). 700 Million. [online] Available at: https://instagram-press.com/blog/2017/04/26/700-million [Accessed 13 Nov. 2017].

32 Scott, C. (2017). How BBC News Is Experimenting with Instagram Stories to Engage Younger Audiences. [online] Journalism.co.uk. Available at: www.journalism.co.uk/news/bbc-news-experiments-with-instagram-stories-to-engage-younger-audiences-/s2/a697503 [Accessed 13 Nov. 2017].

33 Metro.co.uk. (2017). 22 of the World's Most Popular Marathons. [online] Available at: http://metro.co.uk/2017/04/23/22-of-the-worlds-most-popular-marathons-how-much-they-cost-and-the-freebies-you-can-get-for-taking-part-6591013 [Accessed 13 Nov. 2017].

34 Pinterest for Business. (2017). 175 Million People Discovering New Possibilities on Pinterest. [online] Available at: https://business.pinterest.com/en/blog/175-million-people-discovering-new-possibilities-on-pinterest [Accessed 13 Nov. 2017].

35 Guttenfelder, D. (2017). Inside North Korea. [online] Pinterest. Available at: https://uk.pinterest.com/nytimes/inside-north-korea [Accessed 13 Nov. 2017].

36 Madrigal, A. (2017). Think Pinterest Is Stupid? This Interview Might Change Your Mind. [online] *The Atlantic*. Available at: www.theatlantic.com/technology/archive/2014/07/what-is-pinterest-a-database-of-intentions/375365 [Accessed 13 Nov. 2017].

CHAPTER 6

Troubleshooting

Launching and running a website is exciting but also scary – particularly when things go wrong. The process can be very stressful, especially at 2am when you're trying to troubleshoot a problem. This is why it is very important to have a clean backup of your site saved, and have a good, reliable, helpful host who offers 24-hour, 365-days-a-week telephone help. As you spend more and more time on your site you'll get to know the most common errors that we all face, and how to fix them. In the meantime, use this guide as your first port of call. But remember: if you haven't backed up your site and you get hacked, there will be no one to blame but you!

COMMON ERRORS

- **Your site is slow**. This is usually a server issue, so first check with your host to see if there are any issues. Next, check to see whether one or more of your plugins is the cause: deactivate all your plugins and check to see whether this has made any difference. If it has, reactivate each plugin one by one to identify which one is causing the issue. This quite often happens when there is an update of either WordPress or an individual plugin; sometimes there are compatibility issues. Have a look at the section on performance (page 73) for tips on improving the site speed generally.

- **You are locked out of the WordPress dashboard.** Have you forgotten your password? Can't access the email account in order to reset it? Don't panic. Here's how to reset your login information:

  1. Log in to your host cPanel.
  2. Find the MySQL database for your website.
  3. Log in to the PHP admin area (this usually involves a different username and password from the ones that you used to log in to your cPanel).
  4. Once you're in your database (make sure you have selected the right server) click on the database name and find Users (Figure 6.1).
  5. Click on Users. Find your username and click Edit.
  6. You should see a number of boxes. Look for user_ pass – it will have random numbers and characters.
  7. Delete this random password and enter your new one.
  8. There should be a drop-down box next to the password or underneath it labelled Functions. Click the drop-down and select MD5 (this will encrypt your password and your password might not work without doing this).
  9. Click Save and try logging in to Dashboard/wp-admin.

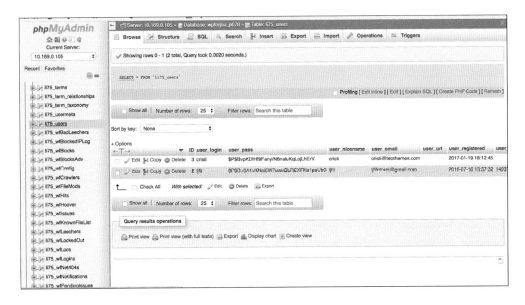

Figure 6.1 Log in to your PHP database area via your host to update your password if you have been locked out of your dashboard.

- **'Error establishing a database connection'.** If you see this message this means that the username or the password in the wp-config.php file is incorrect. This will happen if you have just changed the password to get into your database (please keep a note of all these passwords). To fix this error, find the wp-config.php file using your FTP (see page 38 on setting up an FTP account). Open the file in TextEdit and check to see that there are no errors in either the database name/user or password. Be very careful – spaces, wrong characters and, of course, mistakes will block you from accessing your site. Don't delete the single quotation marks. If you do and you need to put them back, copy one from somewhere

else in the file and use that. I always have a problem with my single apostrophes on my Mac because they are slanted and the code doesn't like them – they must be the straight ones.

- **The database must be repaired.** If you get an error message saying your database needs repairing, find your wp-config file using your FTP and add the following line:

define   ('WP_ALLOW_RE-PAIR', true);

Be careful with the commas and apostrophes. Save this file and then put the following in a browser: www.your domain.com/wp-admin/maint/repair.php

Hit Return. This will activate the process. When it has completed, go back into your wp-config file and delete the line of code. Save the file. That should fix the issue.

> To change Microsoft Word from slanted/curly quotation marks to straight quotation marks, click on Tools – Autocorrect/Autoformat as You Type, and then uncheck the box that instructs the text to change from straight to curly (Figure 6.2).

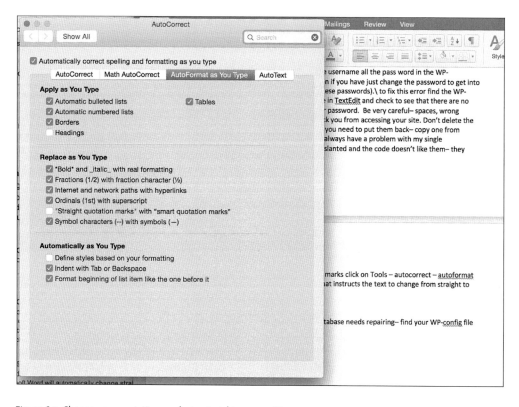

Figure 6.2 Change your quotation marks to straight on your Mac.

- '500 internal server error'. This is such a common error message and not really very helpful because it is just a generic notification which doesn't give you any specifics about what is wrong with your site. Essentially it means there is an issue with your server – but more than that will require some investigation on your part. Start with trying to reload the page you were trying to access, just in case it is something temporary. If this doesn't work, try clearing your browser cache. Next, delete your browser cookies. If you're still getting the 500 message, close everything down and retry. If the issue still exists, go and have a cup of tea. Sometimes the problem is outside of your control and someone else, i.e. your host, will be fixing the problem. If the issue still hasn't resolved itself within a couple of hours, it may well be a permissions error or PHP timeout. For this I would contact your host to help you identify

exactly what the problem is. You'll need more specific help.

- '404 error'. If you see this error when you are trying to access a post or a page that you are sure has been published and is publicly available, one of the first things to try is refreshing the permalinks. Go to Dashboard/Settings/Permalinks and scroll to the bottom of the options and hit Save Changes. This has fixed the issue for me many times. If this doesn't fix it, you might need to manually do this. Find your .htaccess file using your FTP and change the file permissions to 666. This makes the file writable. Save this file and go back to your dashboard and do the permalinks save again. This should sort the problem out. If it does, go back to your FTP and change the file permissions of the .htaccess file back to 660. If you're still getting an error message, contact your host.

- **'403 forbidden access'.** This error message is usually caused by a security plugin not being configured properly, or you could have a corrupt .htaccess file. The first thing to do is to deactivate all your plugins and then reactivate them one by one to isolate the problem. If it isn't one of your plugins, try deleting your .htaccess file. Find it using your FTP server, delete it and then log back into your site. Go to Dashboard/Settings/Permalinks and hit Save. By resaving your permalinks you will force a new .htaccess file to be generated – this should fix the issue.

- **You can't get into your dashboard at all.** Your IP address may have been blacklisted – sometimes this happens when you are trying to update something or change a password and the process gets interrupted. WordPress then blacklists your IP. First, find out what your IP address is by putting http://ip.me.uk in the browser. This will give you your IP address. Once you have this, contact your host and tell them you think your IP might have been blacklisted – they will be able to whitelist you and put you back on track. It's an easy fix.

- **White screen of death.** This will give all new website owners palpitations: your website appears to be gone – with not even an error message, just a completely white screen. Don't panic! This is quite often caused by exhausting the memory limit set by your server. This can be quite easily fixed by increasing the memory limit. By default this is set to 64MB – try increasing this to 256MB. To do this: find your wp-config.php file using your FTP account and add following code just before '/* That's all, stop editing! Happy blogging.*/':

define ('WP_MEMORY_LIMIT', '265M');

> If you can't see a file that you're looking for in Filezilla, click on Server/ Force Showing Hidden Files.

Save this file. That should have fixed the issue if it was a memory limit problem. If not, it could be a rogue plugin, so deactivate and reactivate all plugins to check. Or it could be a damaged theme, so try switching to a WordPress default theme and see if the problem still exists. If it is still there, try installing a fresh copy of the latest version of WordPress via your FTP account. If that doesn't work, you need more help than I can give you here, so contact your host.

- **'Memory exhausted error'.** See *White screen of death* above.

- **'Parse error, syntax error, unexpected'.** This error message should give you exactly where there is a problem – it is a coding issue and means there is some mistake in the code. Quite often it is a missing comma, or the wrong quotation mark (curly instead of straight). The error message will state the location of the problem code and the actual line number where this problem is. What you need to do is locate this file and find the line number. If it is a piece of code that you have just added, then replace it with the original code (that you will have saved prior to making any changes). See if this fixes the error. If it does you need to find out what is wrong with the replacement code. If you can't figure it out, ask your host.

- **'Connection timed out'.** This could be to do with your plugins – deactivate them all then reactivate them one by one to isolate the issue. Or it could be an issue with your theme. Switch to a default WP theme. If this fixes the issue then it is something to do with the theme you are using. Or it could be a memory limit issue – see *White screen of death* above.

- **'Briefly unavailable for scheduled maintenance'.** You can get this message sometimes when you are updating a theme, plugin or WordPress version. It's really just a notification rather than an error message. WordPress creates a . maintenance file during any updates and if the message saying your site is unavailable doesn't go away by itself you will need to find this .maintenance file using your FTP and delete it.

- **Images not uploading/broken links.** Usually if you get an error message when you are trying to upload an image onto the media library, it is because you are trying to upload the wrong file type. WordPress accepts JPEGs and PNGs – it will not accept TIFFs. So the first thing to do is to check the file type. If you have the correct type and are still having difficulties it could be a file permissions issue. Find the upload folder on your FTP (usually in wp-content) and check that the permission is 744 (try 755 if that doesn't work). Check the box Apply to Directories Only, hit OK, then open the file permissions again and check the box Apply to Files Only and put 644 in the numeric value box. Click OK. This should fix the issue. If it doesn't, contact your host.

- **Sidebar below content.** If the summaries in your sidebar appear below your content instead of where they should be, it could be that there is an error in your HTML code or your CSS code, or there is a plugin issue or something incompatible with your theme. First, try deactivating all the plugins and reactivating them one by one to see if this is the issue. If you're still experiencing problems the most likely cause is that there is a <div> tag in your HTML code that hasn't been closed or there is an extra <div> or </div> that isn't needed. To find out which pages/posts are affected, click through your site, making a note of where the sidebar is out of place. Once you have identified the pages or posts, try editing the content first – click on Edit Post/Page and in the Text tab highlight all the text and hit Close Tags on the toolbar. This will add any missing </div> tags. Then check to see you have no extra tags – if you do, delete them. If this doesn't fix the

issue then you will need to check the page/post code. Go to Dashboard/Appearances/Editor and find the single post/page (page.php). Open the file – remembering to make a copy of the code before changing anything – and check through to see if you can find any errors with the <div> tags. If you are still experiencing problems, contact your host.

- **'Are you sure you want to do this?'** This usually appears when you're trying to upload a new theme or plugin. Sometimes it is a problem with the code. First, try deleting the theme or plugin you were trying to upload, and try uploading and activating it again. Sometimes this works on the second try – if it doesn't then the easiest thing to do is to try and find an alternative if it is a plugin that you were trying to upload, or contact the developer if it is a theme issue. If it is neither a plugin or theme issue, it is most likely something to do with the unique keys in the wp-config.php file. You can try opening up your .config file and deleting all the define lines in the Authentication Unique Keys and Salts section. If this doesn't work, contact your host.

- **Not sending emails.** This is a very common problem with contact forms (and newsletters) and one that can drive you mad. My solution is to not use contact forms at all – I just have contact buttons allowing a visitor to email me directly rather than using forms. If, however, you want to use a contact form and you're having an issue sending or receiving emails from the site, this is usually something to do with the configuration of your PHP mail function. Trying to figure out exactly what the issue is can be time-consuming and require some knowledge of email servers – I suggest that you talk to your host before doing anything, to see if it can isolate what the issue is for you. Then you can try and fix it. You can also try adding an SMTP plugin, which will reconfigure the WordPress mail function – this has worked for me in the past. Try **WP Mail SMTP** (developer Callum Macdonald) (Figures 6.3 and 6.4).

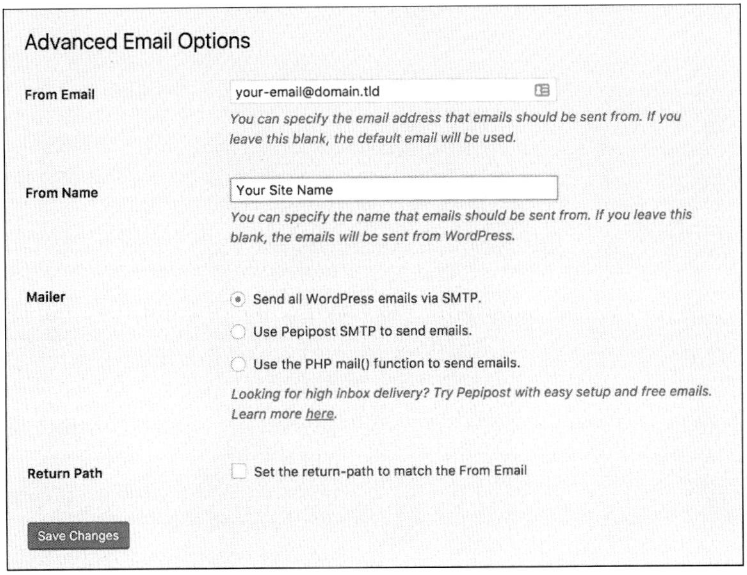

Advanced Email Options

From Email	your-email@domain.tld
	You can specify the email address that emails should be sent from. If you leave this blank, the default email will be used.
From Name	Your Site Name
	You can specify the name that emails should be sent from. If you leave this blank, the emails will be sent from WordPress.
Mailer	⦿ Send all WordPress emails via SMTP.
	◯ Use Pepipost SMTP to send emails.
	◯ Use the PHP mail() function to send emails.
	Looking for high inbox delivery? Try Pepipost with easy setup and free emails. Learn more here.
Return Path	☐ Set the return-path to match the From Email

Save Changes

Figure 6.3 The plugin WPMail SMTP can solve sending and receiving issues with email on your site.

Figure 6.4 Use these settings.

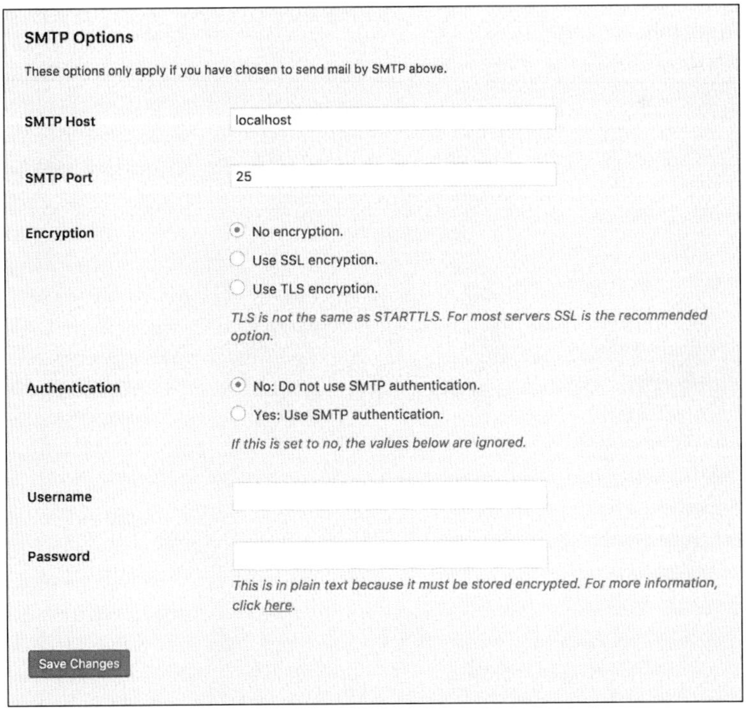

SMTP Options

These options only apply if you have chosen to send mail by SMTP above.

SMTP Host	localhost
SMTP Port	25
Encryption	⦿ No encryption.
	◯ Use SSL encryption.
	◯ Use TLS encryption.
	TLS is not the same as STARTTLS. For most servers SSL is the recommended option.
Authentication	⦿ No: Do not use SMTP authentication.
	◯ Yes: Use SMTP authentication.
	If this is set to no, the values below are ignored.
Username	
Password	
	This is in plain text because it must be stored encrypted. For more information, click here.

Save Changes

CHAPTER 7

Creating content

PAGE LAYOUT

When you first start working on websites (particularly if you have moved from print) it can be a bit frustrating when you realise how limited you are without a good working knowledge of HTML. With a standard Word-Press install and particularly on the free .com sites, what you can do in terms of page layouts is not very creative. The good news is that things have moved on considerably from when I first started building sites, and if you are on a self-hosted site there are now a whole heap of plugins which allow you the freedom to create such things as columns, pull quotes, charts and animations without having to know much HTML. While you still don't have the same freedom as you do working on a print layout, you do have much more control over how your site looks now. One of the most popular plugins and one that is included in many commercial themes is Visual Composer.

All premium Word-Press plugins can be purchased at theme-forest.net (see page 30 for help with installing a plugin that isn't in the WordPress plugin directory).

Visual Composer – developer WP Bakery[1]

When I first discovered Visual Composer (VC) a few years ago, I was very excited. It is an incredible plugin that gives you full control over your layout, with no coding knowledge needed at all. I would go as far as to say it revolutionised my website builds – a game-changer.

For a beginner, VC is fantastic. There are, however, both pros and cons with this plugin. I will address the cons at the end but for now let's start with how to use it.

The first thing to know about VC is that it is a premium plugin, i.e. it is not free. Quite a few commercial themes come with the plugin so you don't need to purchase it separately. However, one thing to be aware of is when the theme you have bought requires an update, the updated version of the theme provided for you will not include an updated version for the VC plugin (usually). This will mean you will (more than likely) have to pay for a new version of the VC plugin so that it works properly.

VC claims to work with any theme. The plugin basically adds functionality to Edit Post/Page, allowing you to drag and drop elements onto the page. For example, you could create a page with two columns of text, a pull quote, a pie chart, an RSS feed, a sidebar ... You have complete flexibility with how your content is laid out. You can save your pages/posts as templates so when you create a new piece of content, you can select the

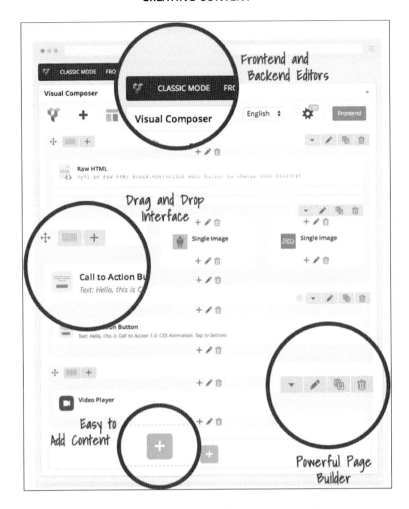

Figure 7.1 Visual Composer allows you great control over the layout of your posts/pages.

saved template. And if you activate your download of VC with the licence, you can access a library of ready-made templates.

You can also control how elements of the page appear: you can add/change borders; change colours, fonts, padding and backgrounds; add parallax images, a video background or image filters … In short, it will pretty much allow you to customize even the most basic of themes, utilising all the most up-to-date elements available on WordPress (Figure 7.1).

Once you have activated the plugin go to General Settings for VC on the dashboard and select Role Manager (Figure 7.2).

By default, VC is available on pages only, so change the Post types to Custom and then select Posts as well. This will give you control over all your content (this will change for the admin only – if you want editors to have the same access to VC scroll down and change the settings for User to Role Editor too). If you have bought the plugin, activate it by clicking on Product License. This will give you access to full support and any updates (you need the licence code – see page 33 for how to find a licence code).

There are other settings you can play around with but leave these until you are more familiar with the plugin. For now, go and edit

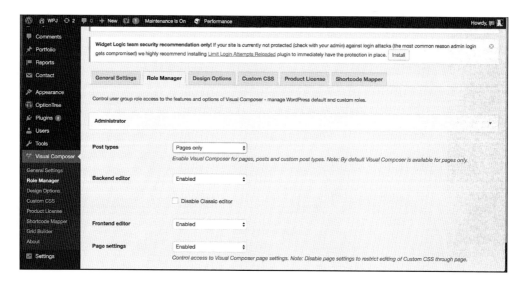

Figure 7.2 Once you have activated VC, adjust the settings starting with allowing the plugin to work on all content.

Figure 7.3 On Edit Post/Page you are given the option to use VC by clicking Backend Editor.

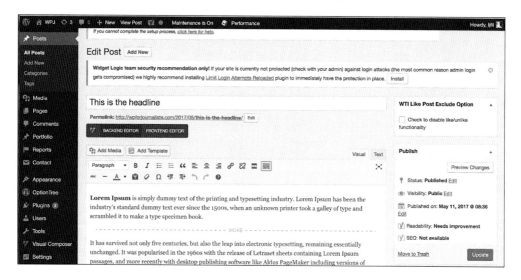

an existing post or page and you will see a new bar of buttons has appeared (Figure 7.3).

Click Backend Editor and you will see your content is now in boxes. The way to think about VC is that all content is put into containers – these are the grey boxed areas. You can add elements (blocks) into these containers by clicking on the plus sign. This pulls up all the available elements. Select a text block to start

with and click Save. You will see the text block is now in a grey container running the full width of the area. Next, divide the container into two columns. Click on the box with the lines and select the ½ + ½ option (Figure 7.4).

You will now see that you have two separate containers – one with the text block you have just created and another empty one where you can add another element. Try

Figure 7.4 Create columns in a text box by clicking on the icons of lines.

adding a custom heading block in the empty container. (You can change the font, size, colour – this is quite a good element to use for pull quotes.) Click Save, publish or update the post and go and have a look on the front end to see what your layout looks like.

As you can probably already see, VC offers you a huge range of options, elements and flexibility. I am not going to go through every single element or every single function that it offers – it is up to you to explore and find out for yourself what works and doesn't work on your website. What you need to know is that you can edit both the container that any element sits in and the individual elements.

For example, you could change the settings for the columns that you have just created by clicking on the pencil in the grey container. Have a play around (every time you make a change, check it out on the front end). To edit the element – in this example, the text block – click on the pencil in the green box (which comes up if you hover over the text block). You can change the text in the same way you usually amend/add text in WordPress, and you also have some design options.

You are offered options to edit for every element and every container, giving you full control over your layout. You can also move containers and elements around by dragging and dropping the boxes – click on the Move icon (be careful: you can sometimes drop containers into containers, and then they will behave differently).

Some of the functionality that is particularly useful is being able to add one of your sidebars into your post – and if you have a customizable sidebar plugin (see page 72) you can essentially create a widgetised area specific to this particular piece of content. Another element I have found useful on a news site is being able to add any number of RSS feeds, and the post grid is useful too – use this to pull in content from around your site by category.

So, a fantastic plugin to have. There are, however, some things to consider when using VC. One is that although the developers claim that the plugin is compatible with

Padding adds space between your blocks.

all themes and most other plugins, I have experienced issues many times with specific themes and other plugins, forcing me to disable VC altogether. I have also found that sometimes, depending on the combination of theme and plugins, the site is very sluggish. And last, and the reason that I no longer use VC, is that although a site can look amazing on a desktop, it can quite often look a mess on mobile. This, coupled with the fact that quite a lot of the elements offered in the plugin come already built in to some commercial themes, so you don't need them (and if they aren't there, individual plugins are available for every single thing you could possibly dream of doing on WordPress), plus there are lots of elements never needed … all of these points mean it is no longer a go-to for me.

Once you know what you are doing on WordPress you don't need a plugin such as VC – but for a beginner it is fantastic (and fun).

Gutenberg – developer Gutenberg Team

Something that could render VC obsolete in the future is the development of the plugin Gutenberg. Named after Johannes Gutenberg, the first European to use the printing press (in 1493), the plugin is designed to allow people to publish content using blocks, much along the lines of VC. It is thought this will allow people greater control over how their pages and posts look without requiring HTML knowledge.

Here's what the developers say about the plugin:

> The goal of this new editor is to make adding rich content to WordPress simple and enjoyable. This whole post is composed of *pieces of content* – somewhat similar to Lego bricks – that you can move around and interact with. Move your cursor around and you'll notice the different blocks light up with outlines and arrows. Press the arrows to reposition blocks quickly, without fearing about losing things in the process of copying and pasting.[2]

At the time of writing the plugin is still in beta, meaning it is still being tested but it should have been released by the time you are reading this (Figure 7.5). At the moment the jury is still out on whether it is going to be included as core or whether it will remain as an optional plugin. Judging from the reviews so far, my guess is the latter, but we shall see.

Figure 7.5 Gutenburg is another plugin which will give you control over the layout of your pages/posts.

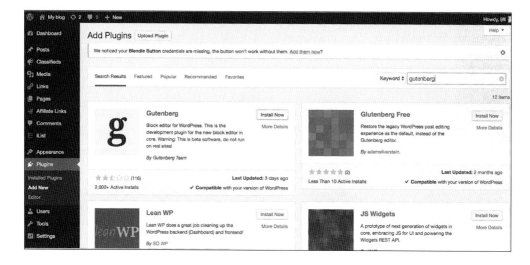

Once you have activated the plugin, the first thing to note is that you now create posts under Gutenberg and not under Posts, although when you need to edit a post you find your post in the usual place, under Posts/Edit, and then you have to select Gutenberg (Figures 7.6 and 7.7).

To create content, you simply click on each box and type it straight in; it's a more streamlined (some may say basic) version of VC. You are shown options for each box on the right-hand sidebar (make sure you have clicked Block rather than Document) and you can add more boxes (elements) by clicking on the circle with the cross in it at the top of the screen (Figure 7.8).

Some of the features are much better than the original WordPress way of editing a post; for example, making the text bigger and adding colour is a lot easier (Figure 7.9).

Figure 7.6 Create posts under the Gutenburg tab.

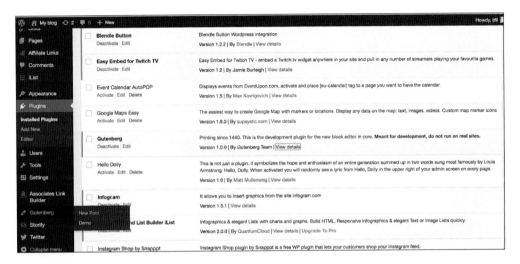

Figure 7.7 Edit existing posts by locating them in All Posts and then selecting Gutenburg.

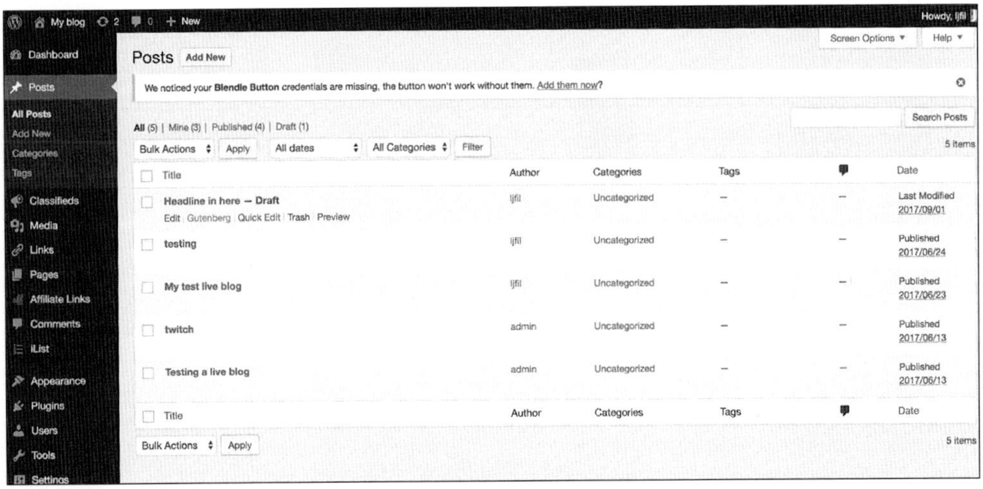

Figure 7.8 Add elements by clicking on the circle with the cross in the top right of the screen.

Figure 7.9 Changing font size and colour is very easy with Gutenburg.

You don't have to fiddle around with any HTML and you can immediately see any changes you make.

All in all, I think it is quite an intuitive plugin and I like what it offers so far, though I can definitely see that people are going to be

The button to flick between Visual and Text view so that you can see the HTML is hidden in the top left of the edit screen (Figure 7.10).

in two minds about it as it feels like it is aimed just at beginners – fantastic for WordPress.com but not so relevant for WordPress.org. If you know what you are doing in WordPress, it offers little extra and actually feels a bit like a regression.

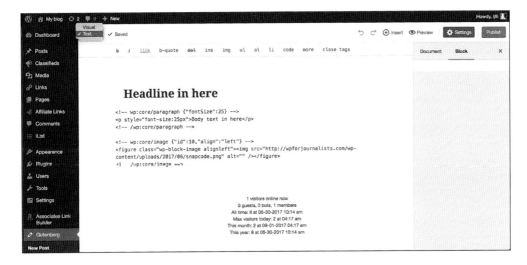

Figure 7.10 Flick between visual and text on a post by clicking on the button in the top left corner on your dashboard.

HTML AND CSS

First things first: HTML stands for Hypertext Markup Language and is the language a browser understands. This language allows you to put anything you like on a web page – images, text, videos, etc. – and it is also a way of allowing websites to connect with each other through links (hyperlinks). It works by using shortcodes in a text file. On a page/post in Edit, click on the Text tab to see the HTML (Figure 7.11).

CSS, on the other hand, stands for cascading style sheets. As already mentioned in Chapter 1, the concept of CSS was proposed in 1994 by a member of the World Wide Consortium (W3C), Håkon Wium Lie. The proposal was in response to the problems developers and designers were beginning to face due to the

Figure 7.11 On any post or page you can see the HTML by clicking on the text tab.

phenomenal growth of websites. Essentially the creation of CSS allowed for site-wide changes of how the content was presented (colours, font type, font size, styling around images …). They could be controlled by one page – a .css file.

So, CSS is a way of controlling how your whole site looks and feels, and HTML allows you to add whatever content you like to an individual page. You can make changes to your whole site by editing the .css file, which you can find on your dashboard under Appearance/Editor, and on an individual page/post you can adjust how the content that appears in the text box looks by editing the HTML under the Text view in Edit Post.

Most of the time you will not need to change the .css file as you will have bought a particular theme because you like the style. However, you may well find that some of the elements need a bit of tweaking here and there so it's a good idea to familiarise yourself with the file (Figure 7.12).

> **For practice with HTML, go to the website w3schools.com – it is a fantastic resource and will give you everything you need.**

You can see, for example, in the CSS in the figure that the heading sizes are defined as:

/*heading*/

h1, h2, h3, h4, h5, h6, .h1, .h2, .h3, .h4, .h5, .h6 {color:rgba(28,28,28,1.0); font-weight:bold; margin:0; line-height:1.2}

h1, .h1 {font-size:40px; letter-spacing:1px; padding-top:5px; padding-bottom:7px;}

h2, .h2 {font-size:32px; padding-top:2px; padding-bottom:3px;}

h3, .h3 {font-size:26px; padding-top:4px; padding-bottom:5px;}

h4, .h4 {font-size:20px; padding-top:6px; padding-bottom:6px;}

h5, .h5 {font-size:16px; padding-top:1px; padding-bottom:2px;}

h6, .h6 {font-size:14px; padding-top:2px; padding-bottom:2px;}

You can change the sizes here so that when you are on an individual page/post and you select the size h4 the text will automatically appear in a

Figure 7.12 You can edit your theme's CSS file from the dashboard under Appearance.

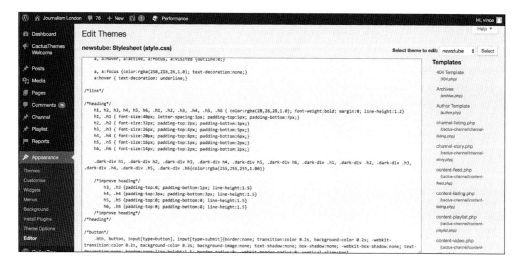

font size of 30px, instead of 20px as it is in this example. You can adjust any of the elements you like in the curly brackets and this will enforce a change site-wide. Just be careful: before you start fiddling, copy the whole style. css sheet and keep it safe. Then, if you muck up somewhere, you can paste the original file back over your errors. Also, it's a good idea just to make one change at a time so that you can track what works and what doesn't.

As I have said, you most probably won't be adjusting your style sheet. What you will be adjusting much more often is the HTML on your individual pages/posts, and for this it is a good idea to have a basic grasp of some of the most commonly used HTML.

So let's have a look at an individual post and what HTML is used for the content in the text box.

First, open up an existing page/post which has some content in the text box.

In terms of formatting your text, most of what you need will already be available for you on the toolbar in Edit Post but it is a good idea to know some basic HTML in case you hit problems.

> **To view the HTML in Edit Post/Page select the Text view.**

Here's some HTML from one of our posts on journalism.london:

<h4>The Best Picture award at the Academy Awards is the most prestigious prize that an aspiring filmmaker could work towards. But, with so many films having won this Oscar, are there any trends that you should follow to ensure you get a look in?</h4>

<a href='http://journalism.london/wp-content/uploads/2017/06/visme-eg-1.eps'><img class='alignleft wp-image-39,614 size-large' src='http://journalism.london/wp-content/uploads/2017/06/visme-eg-1-382x1024.eps' alt='win an Oscar 2017' width='382' height='1024'/></a>

The first thing to look at is genre, and incredibly, almost half of the best picture winners have been Drama's. This includes

films such as '<a href="http://www.imdb.com/title/tt2562232/">Birdman</a>' from only a couple of years ago to '<a href="http://www.imdb.com/title/tt0020629/?ref_=nv_sr_1">All Quiet on the Western Front</a>' winning in 1929. And whilst we're on the topic of 'Western', this is a category you'd be well advised to avoid, with only one Oscar winner coming in 1992 with '<a href="http://www.imdb.com/title/tt0105695/?ref_=nv_sr_1">Unforgiven</a>'.

We'll now take a look at duration. The length of your film may seem unimportant, but it's more relevant than you may imagine. No films of under an hour and a half have managed to make it all the way to Best Picture. Definitely something to keep in mind if your feature is coming in at a mean hour and twenty five minutes. The shortest on the list is '<a href="http://www.imdb.com/title/tt0048356/?ref_=nv_sr_4">Marty</a>' coming in at exactly ninety minutes whereas the longest is the 1939 epic '<a href="http://www.imdb.com/title/tt0031381/?ref_=nv_sr_1">Gone with the Wind</a>'.

One of the first things you should know is that all the commands/instructions start in an angle bracket <> and close with a forward slash </>. These instructions are called tags. You can see in the example code above that every command starts with a tag. See if you can identify all the different commands.

If you wanted to make the word 'help' appear in bold you would use the tag (give the instruction) <strong> or <b> – both work.

Try typing the following in your Text tab on a post:

I want the word <strong>help</strong> to appear in bold.

Click on the Visual tab to see if that has worked.

Here are a few of the most-used HTML tags. Have a go with each one on a post – remember to close them with </>

- **
** This tells the browser to go to the next line – so it is a bit like hitting Return in Word.
- **<p>** This tells the browser that it is a new paragraph, and it puts an empty line between your paragraphs. Open the tag at the beginning of where you want a new paragraph and close the tag at the end of the paragraph with </p>
- **<hr>** This adds a horizontal line across the page.
- **<h1>** This is a title tag – the h1 tag is usually only used on the headline on your post/page – it is the biggest text on the page.
- **<h2><h3><h4>** etc. These are title tags too. Each denotes a smaller text size than the next and should be used to help with page hierarchy. The exact size of these will be dictated by your theme style.css file (as already explained). You can easily change the size, font and colour for these title tags.
- **<a href='url'>** This is called the 'a tag' and is an important one. It is the instruction for a hyperlink. You close it by adding </a>

'Page hierarchy' means organising your content so the eye goes to the most important information first – you can do this by using different font sizes, colours, images and layouts.

Try typing the following sentence:

I want to link directly to the fantastic website journalism.london

And now hyperlink the words 'journalism.london' to the actual URL, which is http://journalism.london, by adding the a tag:

I want to link directly to the fantastic website <a href='http://journalism.london'>journalism.london</a>

Notice the link words – the words you want people to click on – are outside of the tags. Save and publish the post and check the link works.

- **<img>** This tells the browser to show an image (you will need to add your image to the media library unless you are using an image on another site).

Try uploading an image to your media library and copying the URL for the image. It should end in either .jpg or .png depending on the file type you uploaded. Then try adding it to your post using the following tag:

<img src='http://yourdomain.com/wp-content/uploads/2017/02/imageyouuploaded.jpg'>
    </img>

Switch to the Visual tab to see whether it has appeared. If it hasn't, check the code carefully – are you missing a quotation mark?

You can also add in the alt text and the width and height of an image – images without this information can affect the speed of a page load, so it is always worth checking to see if your images have the correct information. You can add any missing information directly in the HTML. For example:

<img src='http://yourdomain.com/wp-content/uploads/2017/02/imageyouuploaded.jpg' alt = 'my image example' width '300' height '600'>
    </img>

Remember: images are measured in pixels. Notice that the information the tags refer to is always within single quotation marks.

- **<body style='background-color:blue'>** This will change the background colour – if you want the whole post to be on a blue background, open the tags at the beginning before any other text and then close the tag with </body> after the last word.

- <h1 style='color:blue;'> this would change the h1 text to blue.

Colours in HTML can be specified by name (for example, 'blue'), by an RGB value (such as '0,0,255') or by a HEX value (for example, #0000ff) – I tend to prefer using HEX values. Use an HTML colour picker to find your codes – w3schools.com has a good one.

If you wanted to change a font colour for a few words in a sentence try using <span style= ' '>

Type the following sentence:

My dog Ella loves the green trees in the woods

Now make the words 'green trees' green by adding the following:

My dog Ella loves the <span style='color: #00FF00;'>green trees</span> in the woods

Have a look on the Visual tab to see if you have made it change colour.

The HTML instructions are written using American English – therefore 'colour' is 'color', 'centre' is 'center' and 'grey' is 'gray'. Pay attention, because if the spelling is wrong the HTML won't work.

The only other thing I want to mention here is the structure of the pages/posts is also controlled by HTML – to see the structure of the pages you need to go to Appearance/Editor/Yourtheme on your dashboard. You will see on any of the page/post.php templates that there are tags. One of the most important that you should familiarise yourself with is the <head> tag.

Quite a lot of information about your page that doesn't appear on the front end is included in this tag. This could be the title of the page, <title> – which is important as this is what the search engines will display on a search results page. The <head> tag is also where you are instructed to place some code for Google Analytics in order for your site to be verified, so it is a good idea to familiarise yourself with where this tag is. It can be on a number of pages (Figure 7.13).

Depending on your theme, it might be in a header.php file, as it is in my example, but it can also be on the frontpage.php or homepage.php or main.php – you will have to spend a bit

Figure 7.13 The head tag is where you place your Google Analytics code.

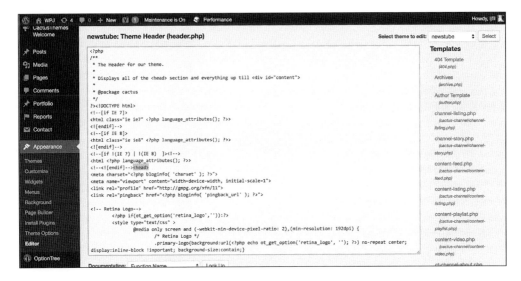

of time trying to locate it because you will eventually need to know where it is.

There is of course much more to learn if you want to be a master of HTML, but what I have outlined here is enough for you to be quite competent in troubleshooting any issues and being able to make changes to the formatting of your posts and pages. Almost everything you need will be done automatically for you by clicking on a button or by adding a plugin but it is good to know some of the basics yourself.

RSS

RSS stands for Really Simple Syndication (sometimes it might be referred to as 'Rich Site Summary'). An RSS is a live feed from another website of its content, and I am a big fan of RSS – particularly when you are starting out. It is a really easy way of keeping your site fresh with up-to-date content (there is nothing more off-putting than finding a news site and realising that the last piece of content was posted weeks ago). Having an RSS feed from a website such as the BBC will mean you are always going to have current news headlines visible on your site. Each time there is new content on the area of the BBC website that you have a feed for, the headline and snippet of the article will appear in your feed, and hence on your website. There are various options for how often a feed will check for new content, which we will look at with a plugin towards the end of this section.

RSS is not just for your homepage though. You can also use RSS feeds on different areas of your website that are pertinent to a particular category. For example, you could have a sports feed, a fashion feed,

> **There are plugins which will paste any code into the <head> tag for you without you having to find the page in the editor. Try Head and Footer Scripts Inserter (developer Arthur Gareginyan).**

> **To add some white space try adding ' ' on a separate line or between words – it will add real space to your text.**

a food feed, a London feed … Using RSS is a wise way of populating your site with useful, current content for your visitors. You can even get feeds that have quotes of the day, poetry, quizzes … (Try searching for RSS feeds on www.wingee.com.)

There are two things you need to know:

1. How to find an RSS feed of the content you want.
2. How to add the feed to your site.

Let's start with how to find an RSS feed.

It used to be very easy – all sites used to display the RSS icon. You could just click on it and this would show the feed for the page.

Most sites have stopped doing this. Now each site has its own way of housing its RSS feeds. I am going to go through a few of the ones I have used, and ones that cover the variety of ways to find an RSS.

Guardian News and Media (GNM)

The *Guardian* is fairly simple – just add /rss to the end of any URL. For example, if you wanted a feed of UK news, from the homepage click on the category 'UK'. This will bring up the URL www.theguardian.com/uk-news. To get the feed for this page, simply add /rss – so the feed would be www.theguardian.com/uk-news/rss. This system allows you to search for anything and then add /rss, so you can really tailor the exact content you want. You can even create a feed for a particular journalist – I searched for my name and added /rss for the feed: www.theguardian.com/profile/laurajanefilotrani/rss (though it's been a while since I worked there so there won't be any new content!).

The New York Times

The feeds are not as intuitive as GNM's but they are collated for you in one place, which is very helpful. Unlike GNM's, you can't just search for content and create your own RSS; you have to use the feeds already created for you. Having said that, the feeds offered are quite extensive, so you will more than likely find one that suits what you are after. To find its feeds go to www.nytimes.com/services/xml/rss/index.HTML

Then click on the section you want a feed from. For example, the feed for Arts is: rss.nytimes.com/services/xml/rss/nyt/Arts.xml

You will notice that rss is at the front and the file type is XML – this is what you should look for.

Sky News

You can find links to a number of feeds at news.sky.com/info/rss. For example, the feed for UK news is: feeds.skynews.com/feeds/rss/home.xml

BBC News

The BBC helpfully still has the RSS icon on most of its category pages, so you can just click on the area you are interested in – for example, news in London – and find the icon

> **XML is a file used to share formats and data on the web. It stands for Extensible Markup Language and is is similar to HTML.**

(usually on the right sidebar). Click on the icon and that will give you the feed.

The feed for news in London is: feeds.bbci.co.uk/news/england/london/rss.xml

You can search for more feeds on Google – try searching for 'sports rss' and see what you can find.

How do you get the feed onto your website?

Go to Dashboard/Appearances/Widgets and find the RSS widget. Drag and drop it into the sidebar where you want the feed to appear. If you have custom sidebars you can create a specific one for a specific area of your website and tailor your feeds (Figure 7.14) – for example, your website could be about football news with categories for every football club in the Premiership. You could create a custom sidebar for each club and then find a feed for news about that club. For example, a sidebar for West Ham United could have a feed from Talk Sport: talksport.com/rss/football/west-ham-united/feed.

Figure 7.14 The RSS widget allows you to add feeds to your sidebar.

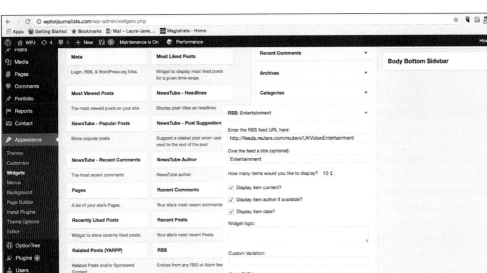

Paste in the URL of the feed, give the feed a title and select the number of headlines you want to pull in. Check the boxes for displaying the content (this will give you a snippet of the article as well as the headline), the date and the author (you may have more options depending on the theme you are using). Click Save and go and have a look to see how it appears on the front end.

Dealing with your own site feed

You can create feeds for your own site so that visitors can get your content onto their sites. The first thing to do is to check in Dashboard/ Settings/Readings that you have checked the box Summary for the option For Each Article in a Feed Show ... This will ensure your feed pushes a summary of your content. Then I would add a plugin which allows them to pull in your featured images as a thumbnail to go alongside the headlines – this makes the feed much more interesting. There's a lovely plugin that does this for you called **CyberSyn** (developer CyberSyn). This plugin is a very useful tool because not only does it add featured images to your feed, it also pulls in syndicated content, creating posts on your site. I'll pick up on this in the next section.

Feeds on a WordPress site are very easy – you just add /feed at the end of the URL. So, to make things super-easy on your site, create a page with links to all the different feeds for your category pages – for example, http://wpforjournalists.com/ category/cars/feed – then put the RSS icon on the homepage which clicks through to this page. You can also put an RSS icon on each of the category pages with a link to that category feed.

Or add a plugin to do it for you – try **Category Specific RSS Feed Subscription** (developer Tips and Tricks HQ, Ruhul Amin).[3]

Some more useful RSS plugins which will pull in images, video and audio as well as text are:

- **WP RSS Aggregator** – developer Rebel-Code, and
- **RSS feed** – developer POWr.io.

RSS feeds are still certainly a highly effective way of feeding data, and allowing people to aggregate feeds into one place. Lots of people think RSS is dying somewhat, but services like Feedly (https://feedly.com/) continue to grow and help to keep RSS alive. Alex Price, 93digital[4]

SYNDICATED CONTENT AND CURATED CONTENT

Strictly speaking, RSS feeds are 'syndicated content' – the term just refers to third-party content with back links that you are able to use on your own site, and vice versa. There are plenty of plugins available which offer this service and there are hundreds of premium plugins that charge you to push your content through syndication to third-party sites. Content marketing companies are built around syndicated content.

Content curation is slightly different: you are still using third-party content but you are generally manually searching for similar content around keywords and pulling it onto a page for your audience. We'll be covering this in more detail in the next section.

The reason for using both syndication and curation is that by sourcing other content from external sites and creating links on your own site to this content, you are increasing your chances of being found in an organic search and thereby increasing your site ranking. It's also a way of improving the quality of your website – populating it with interesting content that you don't have to create yourself. Done correctly, both syndication and curation can be an excellent way of getting a rich source of news on your site regularly.

As I have said, there are plenty of plugins to choose from – I am going to concentrate on a few that give you a range of options. I am going to start with syndication and then move on to look at content curation.

The four plugins I have selected are **CyberSyn**, which I have already mentioned, **FeedWordPress**, **Press This** and the *Guardian* News Feed. All are fantastic tools for getting original content onto your site which you can tweet out without having to create yourself. The difference between these plugins and simple RSS feeds is that they create posts for each piece of content – some of which you can publish in their entirety. One thing to be aware of, though, is that part of the deal (particularly with the *Guardian*) is that you republish the articles exactly as they are – bringing in all the links, including any ads. This is a small price to pay though.

CyberSyn – developer CyberSynSEO.com

Full disclosure – this plugin can be hit and miss and it will require you to spend some time finding feeds that will allow reposting articles in full instead of just summaries. However, once you find them you will have access to regular, media-rich original content and it's a good plugin to illustrate how a syndicated content plugin can work (Figure 7.15).

Figure 7.15 Cybersyn allows you to pull full posts from other websites to populate your own site.

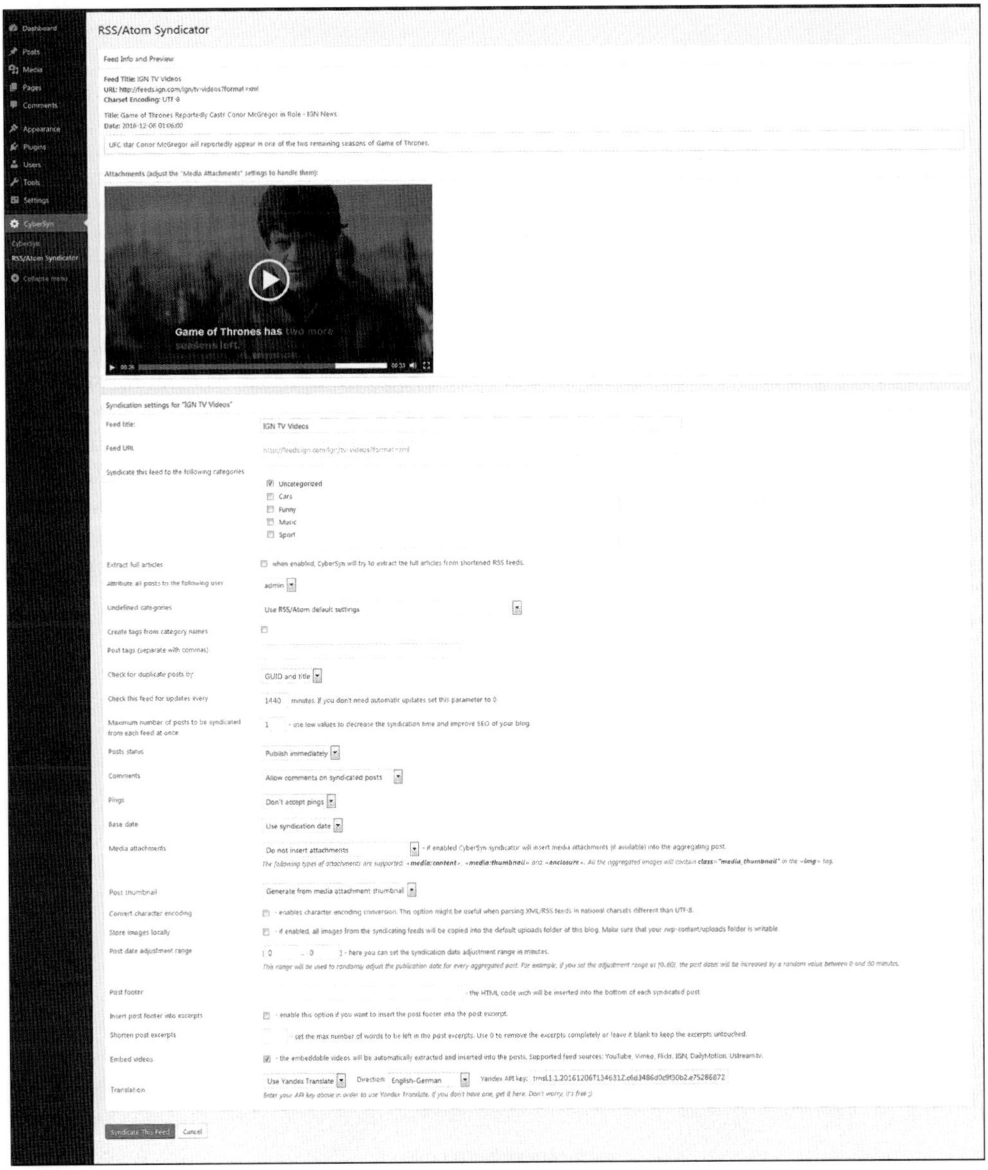

Activate the plugin – you can leave all the general settings – and click on CyberSyn/RSS/Atom Syndication. This is where you add the feeds you want to pull content from. Try adding IGN TV videos (this is a good example to learn from) in the New Feed URL box and click Syndicate Feed: http://feeds.ign.com/ign/tv-videos?format=xml

You will then have some options to choose from. Decide what category you would like the posts to be assigned to (you might want to create a new category) and check the box that says Extract Full Articles – this will pull the whole article rather than just an excerpt. Scroll down and find Media Attachments. Select Insert Attachments at the top of the posts, then find Post Thumbnail – select Generate From the First Post Image, and check the box that says Embed Videos (Figure 7.16).

You can leave all the other options the same. Click Update Settings.

The feed should now appear in your list. Check the box next to the feed and click Pull Selected Feeds Now – if there is any content you should get a box saying one post was added. If you have a box with this message, click on All Posts and see if a new post has been created with the content (Figure 7.17).

Figure 7.16 Don't forget to select Insert Attachments if you want any images or video content to be included.

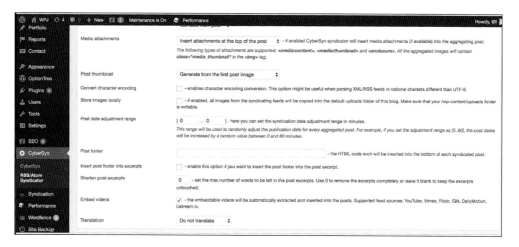

Figure 7.17 Posts will be automatically generated by a feed.

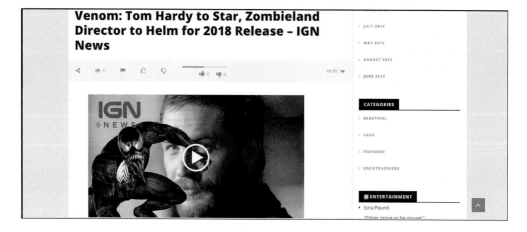

You should see the post with the embedded video plus the feature image. You can now tweet this out to your followers.

FeedWordPress – developer Charles Johnson

This plugin follows the same process as Cyber-Syn but does not embed multimedia content – it creates posts with headlines and snippets only. However, you can embed the video content yourself if you are given the option to share the video. Try the following:

- Activate the plugin and on Dashboard/ Syndication/Syndicated Sites add your feeds. Add Reutersvideo: Breaking Views – http://feeds.reuters.com/reuters/ USVideoBreakingviews
- Click Syndication/Posts and Links and set the permalinks to 'The local copy on this website' (you might want to change this on different feeds which don't have embeddable content to share – see Figure 7.18).
- Hit Save, then pull in some content. Click on Syndicated Sites and check the box next to the feed, then click Update Checked.

You should see a new post created. You can find it in All Posts. Edit the post that has just been created. You will see that only the headline, standfirst and a link to the video have been uploaded. However, Reuters provides you with an embed code for all its videos so you can find the video yourself and embed it.

To do this, copy the headline of the post, open another window and search for the video with the headline. Once you have found the video, copy the embed code which you will find if you click <> underneath the player on the Reuters site. Copy this code and go back to your post – making sure you are on the Text tab – and paste the embed code. Hit Publish/ Update. You should have the actual video embedded in your post – click on View Post to check.

You can now tweet this out to your followers.

Press This

This is a great tool that allows you to grab bits of content from other sites and create posts with this content. It requires you to manually do this – it is not an automatic feature such as FeedWordPress but it works pretty well and in my opinion not enough people use it. It comes with a standard WordPress install so there is nothing to actually activate. Find it on Dashboard/Tools/ Available Tools (Figure 7.19).

Figure 7.18 Settings for FeedWordPress can be customised for individual posts.

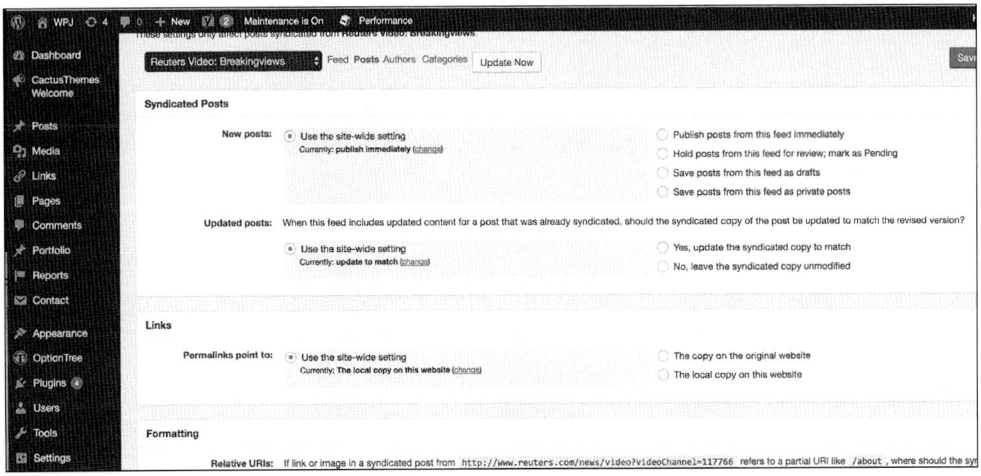

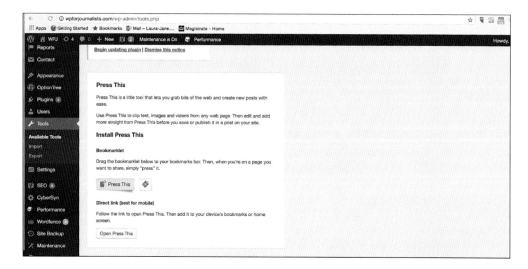

Figure 7.19 Find Press This under Tools.

To use it, drag the bookmarklet into your Bookmarks bar on your browser (you may need to make your Bookmarks bar visible first) and when you find some content, an article or a video on another site that you want to create a post for on your own site, click on the Press This icon on the Bookmarks bar. This will create a post with the snippet of content on your site.

Tip: a word of warning: if you have Word-Fence activated you will get a message asking you to override the block – this is fine to do, just check the box that says 'I am certain this is a false positive'.

You can edit and add your own text, but do make sure you keep the hyperlink back to the original content. You won't be allowed to publish the whole article – it just brings a snippet, with an image, if available, and links back to the original.

The Guardian News Feed – developer Daniel Levitt

This is my favourite plugin – it is absolutely brilliant. With this plugin you can publish nearly any article you like from the *Guardian* and the *Observer* in full! It is marvellous. Once you have activated the plugin you will find the articles on the dashboard under Posts/Guardian News Feed.

To use the plugin you need to register for an API Key first. This used to be completely free for all, but now a charge has been introduced for commercial sites. However, if you are a student you can register for a free developer key, which will give you access to all the articles.

To register for a free key, go to https://bonobo.capi.gutools.co.uk/register/developer. Fill in the required information (the product URL is your website) – don't worry about a company URL – and if you are a student put in your university as the company name. In Reason for Key put something about being a student. Check the box that you accept the T&Cs and click Register. Find the email and copy the key, then go back to your website and on Dashboard/Settings/Guardian News Feed paste the key into your API Key box and click Update Options. You should get a message saying you have a valid key.

Have a look under Dashboard/Posts/Guardian News Feed and you should see all the content you can choose from. Some of the content on the *Guardian* and *Observer* is not allowed to be published, but the vast majority is. The search facility is not brilliant in my experience, so I often do a search on guardian.co.uk first and when I find content that I want to use, I copy the headline and then come back to my site and paste that headline in the search box on the feed.

To publish a post is very simple – once you have found something you want on your website, just click Save to Drafts – this will create a post with the whole article. Find this in All Posts and click Edit. Add a standfirst in place of the italicised text 'Please note: . . .' I always go and copy the standfirst from the *Guardian* and use that. Then leave everything else exactly the same. Give the post a category and a featured image. Hit Publish.

A note on the featured image: there is a grey area over whether you can or can't use the image that is on the article on the *Guardian*. There are no actual guidelines forbidding you to do this but there are no guidelines saying you can, either. I would advise, as always, to find your own *Creative Commons License* images if you can just to be on the safe side. More on images in the next section.

One last word on this plugin: it hasn't been updated since 2015. It still works but who knows for how much longer. Get it while you can.

(There is now a button at the bottom of all content on the *Guardian* which is a request to reuse the content. So even if the plugin disappears, you should be able to still share its content – though it is quite a laborious task to fill in a form for each article you want to syndicate.)

CURATION

Running a news and features website is not just about producing original content – it should also be about providing a central point for your audience for all the great content online surrounding your topic area. You as a website owner should be across all trending discussions, all breaking news and every mention of something relevant for your audience. The term to describe this is 'curation'. When it is done effectively it can elevate your website to a position of authority on a topic. To do it successfully needs a certain level of automation as there is far too much content online for you to keep across, but it also requires you to choose the content to share.

There are lots of tools you can use on your WordPress site – here are the ones that I have used very effectively.

Storify

When Storify was launched in 2010 by Belgians Burt Herman and Xavier Damman, everyone went mad for it, covering live events and creating stories on their websites with it. The tool essentially allows you to create posts using tweets, posts, videos and images from a number of different social media streams – including Twitter, Facebook, YouTube, Instagram and Google. Once you have signed up you are able to search by keywords across all of these accounts and then pull in any relevant content to make up a new post. It can be very effective and many newspaper sites have used Storify to cover live events.

There is a caveat: in 2013 the startup was bought by another startup, Livefyre, which was in turn bought by Adobe in 2016. Unsurprisingly (as Adobe offers its own publishing platforms) the WordPress plugin is no longer being updated (which is a shame as you used to able to create a post automatically with it) and the launch of Storify 2 sees the service go from a free to a costly paid-for service aimed at big companies.

However, at the time of writing, you are still able to create stories and embed them into your site for free.

Here's how, once you have signed up to Storify via storify.com (Figure 7.20).

Connect your Twitter, Facebook or Instagram. (Storify searches these services via their Search APIs, which is why any searches must come from an authorized account. You only need to do this once at the beginning when you start using it – and you can use any account you like. It's just really a verification step.)

Then you can start searching for content to pull in to create a story – for example, 'festivals 2017'. You can pull in tweets, videos and images and you can write your own comments, creating a story around the

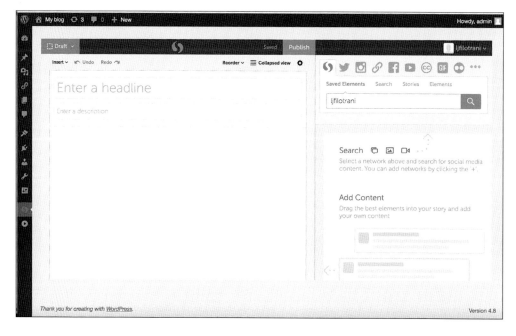

Figure 7.20 You can pull in content from a number of social media platforms on Storify.

content you have sourced. When you are happy with your piece, publish it – this will automatically publish the story under your account on Storify (everyone can see it, so make sure you are ready to publish). Once it is published, click on My Stories and you should see it on your Storify dashboard. If you click on View Story you can grab the embed code for your story (Figure 7.21).

Figure 7.21 Embed your Storify content directly on a new post on your website.

Copy the code, go back to your WordPress site and create a new post, pasting in the embed code on the Text tab. Make sure you give your story a proper headline, standfirst and a featured image. That's it – then you can share it.

Paper.li

I found Paper.li very useful to grow my number of Twitter followers. It is an automatic service set up around keywords which creates a daily newspaper, pulling in tweets from your time-line that mention your keywords. You can set it to send out notifications to Twitter accounts that make it onto the newspaper.
The thing that you need to be careful of is that because it is automatic, some of the content it pulls in is not always relevant to you – this is particularly true if your keywords/topics are general rather than specific.

Sign in with your Twitter account then click on Manually Select Content Sources in the top-right corner (Figure 7.22).

Add a keyword (the topic of your newspaper – the more specific the better), click Your Twitter Feeds and Connect Your Facebook Account.

Then select a paper layout – click Create My Paper. You can then change the settings for your paper by clicking on the Admin wheel in the top-right corner. From here you can change the title of your newspaper, add a subtitle and change the sources from where the content is pulled in (Figure 7.23).

Click on Social Media Agent and connect auto sharing on your Twitter account. Now your paper will be tweeted every time it is published.

To connect this newspaper really well with your website (other than through your Facebook and Twitter feed) you have to upgrade to the Pro version – which at the time of writing was $9 a month. If you upgrade you can embed the whole paper into a page on your website – it will then essentially run on your site. It will also give you an RSS feed of your site, and the Pro version allows auto posting to your Facebook and LinkedIn accounts.

Just a word of warning – because this is a piece of content created automatically via keywords you do need to remember to check what is being posted and delete anything that isn't relevant. Think very carefully before connecting

Figure 7.22 Try to be quite specific with keywords on Paper.li otherwise you will end up with a lot of random content.

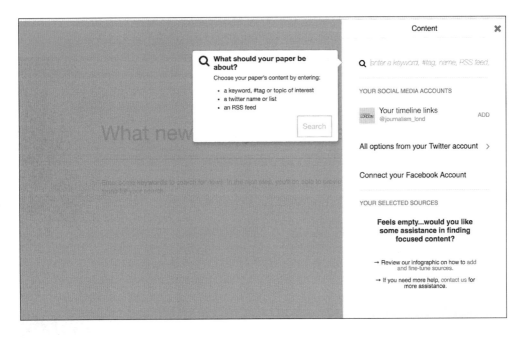

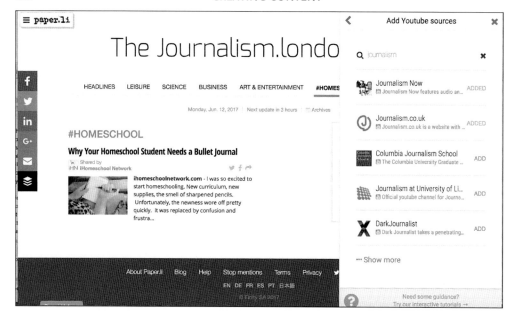

Figure 7.23 You can choose to pull content from a variety of social media sources.

it to LinkedIn. My advice is to leave LinkedIn unconnected.

Scoop.it

Scoop.it essentially works in the same way as Paper.li but it isn't automatic; it is a manual service. It is automatic in that you set up keyword searches, which is the automatic bit, but it is manual because it requires you to select from the search which content you want to appear on your page (a bit like the newspaper created by Paper.li). What makes it different from Paper.li (and why I used to absolutely love Scoop.it) is that from an app on your phone you can source articles/videos/content that you want on your site, hit Scoop and a post is automatically created on your website with the headline, an excerpt, an image, video and whatever content is available around your keywords. This is then automatically tweeted out. This used to be completely free and I found it absolutely wonderful at increasing audience engagement and encouraging traffic to a site. I would scoop a few articles in the morning on the bus, at lunchtime, whenever I had a few minutes, constantly feeding my websites with new content (and tweets).

The service is still fantastic, but it is expensive now and aimed at companies with marketing budgets (at the time of writing, to connect your website costs $67 a month – and you have to pay for the year). You can still use it to curate content but the integration between your Scoops and your website is now too expensive for students, so you really are just connecting via tweets, and to be honest if you are not going to pay for the connection to WordPress it's not really worth it anymore – such a shame.

Feedly.com

Another great service that curates content from a range of sources' feeds. To connect to your WordPress site you need to sign up for the Pro version, which is $5 a month – you can then paste your feeds directly onto your site.

IMAGES

Images can make or break a website so you need to spend some time thinking about how you want to handle them. Some things to consider are: where are you getting your pictures from; what is your house style in terms of sizes, captions, portrait or landscape, etc.; and what plugins do you need.

Where to get your pictures from

Be very careful with using pictures from other people's sites without their permission. It is very easy for companies to track down images of theirs that are being used without the appropriate licence. If you are in breach of copyright, you could face a hefty fine if you are found out, so be warned. This is particularly true if you're using images from a big agency such as Getty.

So how do you get good quality images?

1. Take your own

The best and easiest method is to take your own. This is more challenging, of course, if you are covering breaking news – getting hold of pictures at the scene can be difficult – so

> When captioning images, you should try and sum up what the picture is about – perhaps you could take a quote from the article, name anyone that needs naming, or name the location or venue if appropriate, and then credit the image if you have taken it from another source.

you'll have to think laterally about how you can represent the stories visually. Think about generic pics and suggestive images.

2. Use Creative Commons License images

Any image which has a Creative Commons License is available for you to use – sometimes with some conditions. To find Creative Commons images go to Google and click on Images. Click on Advanced Search Settings and check the box Usage Rights – select Free to Use or Share (Figure 7.24).

Now, when you search for an image the results will only pull up images that you can use. If you find one that you want to use, click on Save Image and then open it so that you can resize it and upload it into your media library. Remember to give your image a proper filename, not a number. Make a note of where

Figure 7.24   Search for images that are free to use or share even commercially.

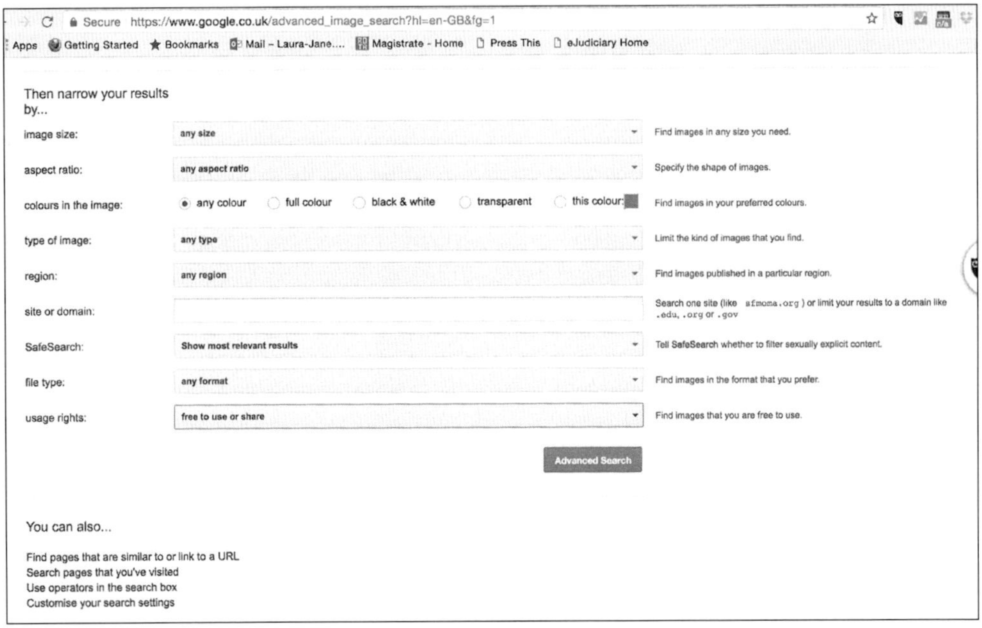

the image came from so that you can credit the source properly (and Google is not the source!).

How you write your captions will be up to you to decide – whatever you decide, though, make sure you follow this style consistently throughout your site. This then becomes your house style. Something else to consider is where your caption appears. It should be outside of the image box, underneath it or by the side, and not in the box – this is to increase SEO and will allow you to hyperlink any information you like. Therefore don't add the caption in the media library – add it directly on a post underneath the image. Hyperlinking the photographer, the agency or the site you got the image from is always helpful.

3. Buy an image

There are plenty of sites offering you the chance to buy an image. For stock images I often use 123rf.com – you can also buy video and audio content here as well. The platform works on credits – you need to buy some credits, and go for on-demand rather than signing up for a plan. Twenty credits will be enough to get going – at the time of writing this was £18. On average, for the images you will need a maximum of three credits for each one – you only need web use (72 dpi) and unless you're using it for a wide slider you should go for a size around 800 pixels.

Istockphoto.com is another very good site (and is actually run by Getty), but the images are considerably more expensive.

To find more sites that offer you the chance to buy images, do a search for 'royalty-free images' (this is not the same as 'copyright-free' – 'royalty-free' means you can buy the rights to use them, not that they are free from copyright). In the past I have used pixabay.com and pexels.com – both have excellent stock pictures to go with feature articles.

What is your house style?

You should decide on how you want your posts to look and standardise them throughout your site. Will your posts have one image or two? Will you use any landscape images or will you only use portrait? Where is your caption going to go: underneath or on top, or on the side? Or at the bottom of the post?

Write a list of the image sizes and make sure you resize and crop any image to the right size before you upload it to the media library. Keeping everything to a house style will give your website professionalism and will help its credibility – and if all your images are correctly named, with alt tags, you'll also please Google. (For more help with the media library, see page 58.)

Which plugins do you need?

Hopefully you have selected a theme that is appropriate for your content – so if you have an image-heavy site you will have picked a theme which has built-in plugins and functionality that allows you to fully control this content (for some inspiration regarding good commercial themes for photography, see page 42).

If, however, yours is a text-heavy news site you may well have a theme that could do with some extra plugins. Here are a few useful additions:

Sliders/galleries

It is very unusual now for commercial themes not to have an image slider installed, but if you don't have a slider option with your theme, there are lots of plugins to choose from. Some are easier to use than others. Most sliders/galleries work on same basis as each other, so if you understand how one works you'll be able to figure out most of the others.

NextGEN – developer imagely

This is perhaps the most downloaded plugin for adding image galleries and sliders on WordPress. You can create thumbnail galleries and slideshows, choose how to switch

> **Add an image optimiser to help with sizes and page load times – see page 73 for a good plugin for this.**

between texts (fade, for example, or swipe), upload batches of images and group images into albums, and there are many other features.

To use it, activate the plugin and go to the page or post where you want to add a slider/ gallery. You will see that a NextGEN icon has been added to the toolbar – this is usually a green square. Click on this and you can start to build your gallery/slider (Figure 7.25).

You can control all the settings for these slides shows/galleries on Dashboard/Gallery/Gallery Settings and, in Other Options, you can set the size that all images should be resized to. You can also add a watermark to images if you want to make sure that they aren't used without your permission.

NextGEN also gives you a couple of widgets that you can drop into your sidebars – go to Dashboard/Appearance/Widgets and try dropping a slideshow into your sidebar. You must have created a gallery first. Specify that

> 'Lightbox' – a lightbox is a pop up which houses your images. Instead of displaying a gallery on the page/post, if you have enabled a light box the images will appear in a box on top of the page/post.

the width is to be the same as the width of the sidebar – try 300 pixels and see how that looks.

Soliloquy – developer Soliloquy Team

This is another great plugin for creating sliders – it's very easy to use. Simply activate the plugin and on the dashboard go to Soliloquy/Add New. Give your slide a title – for example, 'Test slider' – and click Select Files From Your Computer. Edit each image and then give them a proper name and alt text (Figure 7.26).

There are options in All Config Slider but I would leave everything as the default in the first instance – come back and adjust these if you need to. The rest of the settings are for the Pro version, which you may consider upgrading to – particularly for an easy way of integrating images from Pinterest and Instagram.

Hit Publish and you will see that a shortcode has been

Figure 7.25 NextGen is probably the most popular plugin for creating sliders and galleries.

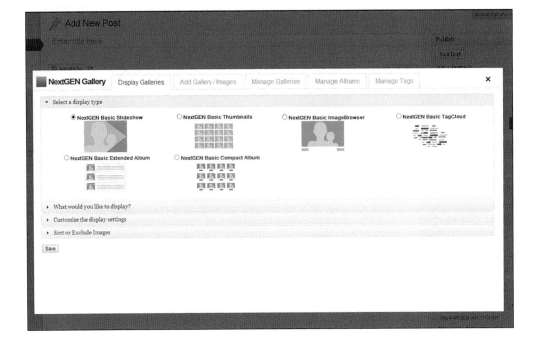

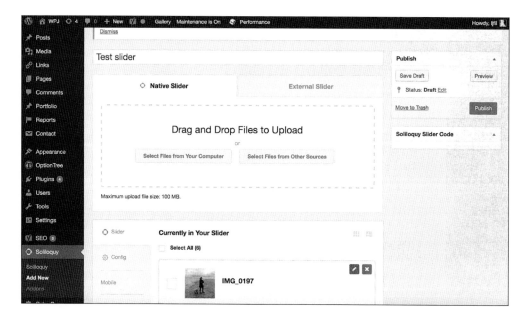

Figure 7.26 Soliloquy is another good plugin for creating sliders.

generated. Copy the shortcode and open up the page or post that you want the slider to appear on. Paste the shortcode in the Text tab – save and publish it and see what it looks like on the front end. You may need to go back and adjust the settings in Config.

You can also add the shortcode in your sidebar – go to Dashboard/Appearance/Widgets and paste a shortcode into the HTML/Text Widget and drag onto the sidebar. You should now have a lovely slideshow in your sidebar.

Parallax

The biggest trend that happened in the past couple of years in terms of images was the introduction of the parallax functionality. It essentially adds a scrolling effect on images – quite often a background image, so that as you scroll down the page the image appears to be revealed slowly. It is very effective and has transformed how images are used. Most commercial themes now have this functionality built in – it's something you can look for when choosing your theme. The *New York Times* was one of the first to adopt this new style back in 2012 with its interactive piece 'Snowfall: The avalanche at Tunnel Creek' by

John Branch. This was a complete game-changer in the way content was handled by newspapers online.[5]

You will see that instead of a static image it has used videos of the mountains – incredibly effective. Read about how it was created and some of the reaction to the piece on Storify: https://storify.com/williams_paige/inside-snow-fall-1

For more amazing *New York Times* interactives go to www.nytimes.com/interactive/2016/12/28/us/year-in-interactive-graphics.HTML

If you want to achieve this effect and do not have the option in the theme you are using, try the plugin **Smart Slider 3** (developer Nextend).

Activate the plugin (make sure you have deactivated all other slider plugins – you only need one). Go to Dashboard/Smart Slider (Figure 7.27).

To create a slider, on the Smart Slider dashboard have a look at the template library and have a go at placing a forward slider on the page. First, import the template that you want (you'll have to register an email address first). This should now appear in the Smart Slider dashboard – click on Edit and you will see that

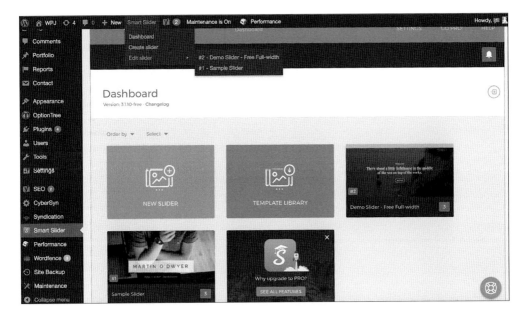

Figure 7.27 For a plugin to create parallax images try Smart Slider 3.

three slides have already been created. Before you make any changes copy the shortcode [smartslider3 slider=2] and paste this into the page/post where you want the slider to appear. Make sure you're in the Text tab. Hit Publish and see what it looks like.
Then go back and edit the slider.

My advice is to try editing the slides that have already been created before creating your own, because then you will see how the slides are made up. Change the background pic by clicking on the Background button and selecting a new image. Make sure it is wide enough, otherwise it will be pixelated (Figure 7.28).

Figure 7.28 Try editing the example slides first before creating your own – this will help you understand all the functionality.

Then have a play around with all the other options. Adding text is easy – just click the text boxes you want to change. Have some fun! You can hit Preview to see what your slider looks like before publishing it on a post.

When you're happy with it, copy the short-code and paste it into a post. It's all fairly self-explanatory.

Now, to add the parallax function you need to go Pro – at £25 for a single domain it's well worth the money. One word of warning: make sure you buy the WordPress version and watch the help video at smartslider3.com/parallax-slider

Don't be freaked out by how many options there are – like everything with WordPress, you just have to follow the instructions. My advice is to make sure you're fully comfortable with the free version before installing the Pro version – that way you will understand the standard func-tionality and the extra parallax won't throw you. Have some fun – it's a fantastic plugin.

Interactive images

Being able to make images interactive is parti-cularly useful when you want to embed a map. Putting hotspots (markers) on certain locations and allowing your visitors to access extra con-tent such as videos, audio snippets, posts and links to external sites can make your images incredibly rich.

Thinglink is the go-to tool for this. It isn't a plugin – it's a third-party site where you create your image and then use the embed code to transfer it to your website. Go to thinglink. com – once you're registered you can upload an image that you want to make interactive and then simply click where you want to add a tag for more content.

You'll then be given the option to add a hyperlink and some text. It used to be that you could drop video and audio content in for free as well, but now this is a premium function (and quite expensive – at the time of writing it is $125 a month if you want to use video), so just stick to text. Give your image a title and once you're happy save it and then click Share. This will bring up the embed code. Copy the code and then paste this into the Text tab on the post on your site where you want the interactive image to appear. It works really well.

The *New York Times* used Thinglink for its coverage of the Boston Marathon.[6]

There are a number of plugins that you can activate on your site which will do the same thing as Thinglink, although not quite seamlessly, such as **Draw Attention** (developer Tyler Digital and Purple Pen Productions). This plugin is pretty good and the premium version is not so expensive. You can add video and audio and you have more customizable tools.

1. Activate the plugin and go to Dashboard/ Draw Attention/Edit Image.
2. Put the title in your image.
3. Add the image.
4. Click Update and then scroll down to Hot-spot Area.
5. Click on the image where you would like a hotspot (Figure 7.29).
6. Add the title of your hotspot.
7. Select the action Show More Info.
8. In the Description box add some text or embed a video and hyperlink.
9. Add an image.
10. Click Update and copy the shortcode [drawattention]
11. Paste this shortcode in the post/page where you want the interactive image to appear, and hit Publish.

The only issue with the free version is that you can only create one image per web-site. If you want more than one interactive image you need to get the Pro version, which at the time of writing was a one-off payment of $75. This is considerably less than Thinglink and will give you unlimited images and lots more control over the look and feel of your images. It's well worth the money if you have maps or venues, or if you are reviewing make-up or fashion – being able to add where to buy a piece of clothing, for example, is a really good tool.

Figure 7.29 Draw Attention is a great plugin for making images interactive.

For inspiration on making images interactive, check out the *Washington Post* article 'The math of mass shootings'.[7]

VIDEO

According to stats on YouTube, in 2017 the platform had more than a billion users watching hundreds of millions of hours every day . . . staggering.

According to tech giant Cisco, video will account for 82% of all internet traffic by 2021.[8]

Video content is vital on a website – it is the way you will get new visitors and keep the ones you have – as the figures above from Cisco demonstrate. But video content is not just about story packages or vlogs – video content can be used to add atmosphere, give context and illustrate aspects of a written article. They can be just a few seconds long – just enough to give a flavour of an event. The thing that you need to know about video content on your website is that you do not host a video directly in your media library. You do not host the video at all on your site. What you do is upload your video to a third-party platform such as YouTube or Vimeo and then you embed its player with your video onto a post.

The reason for this is because video files are comparatively large and require lots of memory and space in order for them to load and play properly. You do not have the capacity to do this in the same way as a platform such as YouTube. Another reason for using a third party such as YouTube is that by using such a big platform with such a huge reach, you are increasing your chances that your content will be seen.

The process for embedding content is the same for whichever player you use. I'll use YouTube in this section as the example – but whenever you are looking for video content to use on your site, look for the embed code, which is usually under a Share button. This is the code you need. Use the following example with YouTube to learn about embedding video content.

To upload your own video, you must first have a YouTube account – and in order to have a YouTube account you must have a Google account. So, first things first: create a Google account – you should have one anyway because you will need it for lots of plugins, not least for Google Analytics, which we will be discussing in the next chapter. Once you've got an active Google account, use it to sign into YouTube.

To upload a video, click on the Upload icon, which is in the right-hand corner of the screen. Select the video file you want to upload (the longer the video the longer it will take to upload – and it's best to do this when you're connected to the internet via an ethernet cable; trying to upload a video while on Wi-Fi can take hours).

Add a proper headline and a proper description, thinking about keywords, and add tags. Make it Public, and once it has finished uploading hit Publish. Once your video is live, find the embed code by clicking on Share and Embed – you can change the dimensions of the player by clicking on Show More and selecting a different size from the drop-down. I actually prefer to replace the frame width with '100%' instead of the pixels – this will then fill your page/post, whatever the size, to 100% of the width (Figure 7.30). For example, instead of:

<frame width '853' height ='480' . . .

it would be

<frame width '100%' height='480' . . .

Copy this code and then go back to your website and paste it into the Text tab of the post or page where you want the video to appear.

Sometimes, depending on your theme you may have the option to select a video format page and will be asked for the URL rather than the embed code – in this case it is usually the URL in the browser with the word 'watch' in it. For example:

YouTube.com/watch?V=Jt2LVIDhZUC

Approximately 20% of the people who start watching a video on YouTube leave it after the first 10 seconds, so make sure your beginning is brilliant![9]

If you're having difficulties with the video not showing up, double-check what URL you have added.

Also check the embed code. Or it could be that your video is set to Private rather than Public on YouTube (Figure 7.31).

You can change this by clicking on Video Manager or Creator Studio on YouTube and then Edit Videos. The box next to the title should say Public and not Private or Unlisted.

Figure 7.30 You can adjust the size of the player by changing the width and height values.

Figure 7.31 Make sure your video is set to public on YouTube otherwise it won't play on your website.

You can also embed a playlist instead of a single video – first, create your own playlist and add videos to it or copy someone else's playlist if it is public (for example, www.YouTube.com/playlist?list=LLkOcbg-bAxzqSjboenjHmRJA). Click on Share and then Embed – follow the same process as above.

Most of the major news organisations have YouTube channels, including the *Guardian*, the BBC, Sky, Channel 4, Vice and the *Sun*. Just do a search for news channels and you'll find lots to choose from.

You can also stream live programmes on your website using YouTube. This is something the journalism students do from our newsroom at London South Bank University. More on this in the next section on live streaming.

There are plenty of places other than YouTube to look for video content for your site – most of which are enabled to allow you to embed their videos straight into a post. Here are a few popular places to look:

Vimeo – Vimeo.com

Embedding a video from Vimeo is even easier than on YouTube as you can just paste the URL of the video you are watching straight onto a post. For example, try adding this video of No Back Dan – https://vimeo.com/218543813 – onto a post. Easy, right?

Flickr – Flickr.com

To embed a video from Flickr, find the video you want and then click on the share arrow at the bottom of the screen. Copy and paste the URL that pops up straight onto a post – you don't even need to be on the Text tab. For example, copy and paste https://flic.kr/p/5ZkyeQ

Something to note: all Flickr images/videos are Creative Commons License by default, so unless otherwise stated you can use any content you like. If you do use someone's image, though, please give them credit and hyperlink back to their Flickr account. It's only polite! And it may well pick you up one more visitor.

Instagram – Instagram.com

Instagram is not only great for images, it is also a great platform for short videos. For inspiration, have a look at 'Video Meals' by Australian Slim Geransar, a winner at the 2017 Shorty Awards run by the Real Time Academy of Short Form

Arts & Sciences. (The Awards are comprised of leaders in technology, journalism, business and culture – the awards aim to recognise excellence in content production on social media.)[10]

According to research in 2016 by Later-gramme (a scheduling tool for Instagram posts that was started at a hackathon in 2014; now called Later.com), the best times to post on Instagram for engagement are generally lunchtime (11am to 1pm) and in the evening (7pm to 9pm), and weekdays are best, with Wednesdays and Thursdays driving the most engagement and Sundays driving the least:[11]

- Sunday: 5am,
- Monday: 7pm and 10pm,
- Tuesday: 3am and 10pm,
- Wednesday: 5pm,
- Thursday: 7am and 11pm,
- Friday: 1am and 8pm, and
- Saturday: midnight and 2am.

TedTalks – Ted.com

I love TED talks – and now you can embed them straight onto your site. Go to any Talk page (for example, www.ted.com/talks/giorgia_lupi_how_we_can_find_ourselves_in_data), and hit the <> embed button.

If you are planning to run a site with video as the main content, you should look for a theme that is designed for this purpose. Try **OneVideo** (developer Upcode).

Snapchat – Snapchat.com

> Ephemeral should be the default. The landscape has changed.
>
> Snap CEO Evan Spiegel[12]

Originally launched in 2011, Snapchat has become one of the most popular social messaging and photo/video-sharing apps worldwide. The company reported an average of 158 million people using Snapchat daily, with more than over 2.5 billion snaps created every day at the beginning of 2017.[13]

The thing that makes Snapchat different from any other social media platform is that the content disappears after a set time – you as the user get to decide how long you want the content to survive: between 1 and 10 seconds. This is why CEO Evan Spiegel talks about ephemerality when he talks about the platform. It's actually quite a beautiful concept when you stop to consider it. The fact that the content you share, the thoughts that you project, are deleted after a short time is a counter to the relentless tracking that we all experience with other social media platforms – here's Spiegel explaining what Snapchat addresses at a keynote speech back in 2014 at LA Hacks at Pauley Pavilion:

> Every time we express ourselves, we do so with the understanding that things we say might become permanently and publicly known. We are encouraged to express ourselves in ways that are accepted by the largest possible audience. We lose our individuality in favor of popular acceptance.[14]

Well, Snapchat is the counter to this: it is about experiencing the moment and then moving on. There is something quite freeing in this approach – the medium allows for experimentation; it allows for mistakes; it allows for you to change your mind, your mood, your feelings; you are not recorded, traced, tracked … It is a refreshing change. As Spiegel says, it isn't about putting yourself on display; it's about living in the moment. It is no wonder that it is so popular.

But how do you make it work for your WordPress site? There is no way of integrating Snapchat with your website – instead it is essentially a way of establishing your brand and connecting directly to your readers. You can use the platform to put out exclusive content, and you can put codes on your snaps and get your followers to use this code to download something on your site, or encourage them to comment on an article or join a discussion in one of your forums. You can also show teasers of your content on Snapchat – with the full articles, videos, audio available on your site …

Some companies have even used it to put out job ads.

Most of the major news organisations have a Snapchat account and most of them now even have Snapchat editors – this is a real role! Snaps work really well for showing behind the scenes in a newsroom or a radio studio, showing how organisations work and of course showing live events (which is why I have put Snapchat in this book between video and live streaming rather than in the section on social media).

The *Sun* launched its Snapchat channel in July 2016, and appointed Sophie Tighe as its editor. She says:

Since the Sun went live with Snapchat in July 2016 our readers say they use it all day, every day – they say they can't imagine a day without Snapchat.

One of the things I found most interesting when moving onto the platform is that although Snapchat is an image-based service, it's about the text you put on top of the image rather than just the image, whereas by comparison Instagram is about beautiful images. Snapchat is messaging with pics.

It's a conversation rather than an end point. Understanding this made me rethink how people are using Snapchat.

We look at data analytics every day to see what's working and what isn't – for example, anything to do with UK celebs. Stories covering stuff going on in 'Love Island', for example, they are our bread-and-butter stories. Round-ups of what's happened in these shows do so well for us. Also tips and advice work really well – how to stay cool in the summer, for example. These feature pieces are popular. We keep them light-hearted, fun and visually eye-catching.

You can't link out from Snapchat. We have a whole Snapchat content management system which automatically archives everything but this archive is not public-facing. Readers can't access it. Snapchat is the entity in itself.

So many celebrities use Snapchat now [that] I think for a lot of younger journalists it's overtaken Twitter as a potential source for stories.[15]

Getting started is really easy. Download the Snapchat app and create a new account (be careful with your username as you can't change it once you have entered it – remember: this is a professional account so it should reflect your website). Enter all the rest of the information and then find some friends (you have to allow access to your contacts), then tap Share Username – this will make your profile visible to everyone.

Taking a snap is really simple – Snapchat opens straight into your camera, so just take a pic or record a video (you can switch the view to take a selfie of course, and you can add lenses from this view). Then you can draw on the image or video by using the Doodle tool, and you should add a caption – remember: you are telling a story. You can add a sticker and you can also add filters (if you swipe right or left on the Preview screen you can choose different filters). Then you can choose where to send it and how long you want it hanging around – by default this is three seconds but you can set it to have no time limit if you like.

Use the Discover button to find accounts – try following these for a start:

- @thenytimes
- @huffpost
- @entertainment_weekly
- @cosmopolitan
- @thesunuk

Make sure you let your visitors on your website know that you have a Snapchat account for them to follow. If you don't have one of the social share plugins already mentioned in this book – see page 91 – then add a plugin such as **Snapchat Snapcode Widget** (developer Pipdig).

Activate the plugin and then go to https://accounts.snapchat.com/accounts/snapcodes to get your snapcode (a PNG image). Go back to Dashboard/Appearance/Widgets and drag the

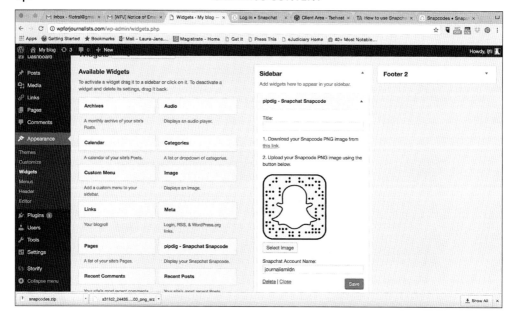

Figure 7.32 Create your Snapchat code and put it in your sidebar for a direct link to your Snaps.

Pipdig Snapchat widget into your sidebar.
Upload the PNG here (Figure 7.32).
You can also join in with our people's snaps, to
contribute to the Our Story section. This is great
if you are at an event. Once you have created a
snap and you click to send it, choose the option
to send it to Our Story ... if there is a story that
you can add your content to, of course.

> I promise you every view counts. You may
> look at a video and only see 246 views and
> write it off. But one of those 200 viewers
> might be a producer at CNN, or might be
> the CFO of a big company that you're
> trying to reach. And in 10 years that con-
> tent creator could become a massive celeb-
> rity and all of the sudden your interview
> has a million views.
> Gary Vaynerchuk, entrepreneur and CEO
> and co-founder of VaynerMedia[16]

LIVE STREAMING

Live streaming follows on from videos – it
simply means being able to broadcast live to

your audience – and there are a number of
ways of doing it. You can use Facebook Live,
you can use Twitter's Periscope, you can use
YouTube, you can use Snapchat. Choosing
which platform to use will to some extent
depend on why and what you are streaming
and what you want to do with the content
afterwards. It also depends on your preference.

Why go live in the first place? Well, you
might want to cover an event, you might want
to pick up on breaking news, you might want to
set up a Q&A with you and your followers or
you and an expert, you may want to interview
someone, you may want to broadcast a performance, or you may want to take us behind the
scenes – we often do this for our JLDN Live
shows on journalism.london.

Going live can be fun and if you get it
right can really engage your audience.

Facebook

The easiest way to do this is by using your
smart phone. First, though, you should create
a Facebook page for your website – this is so
that you can keep your professional account

separate from your personal. This is all covered in the chapter on social media – see page 85.

Once you have created your page, going live is very easy. On your phone (log in to your Facebook app – if you haven't got one you will need to download one), simply go to your page and click Publish, then select Live Video and when you are ready click Go Live. When you are live make sure you respond to any of your fans if they comment. When you are finished, make sure Public is selected and post the video. It will then appear on your page timeline. If you have connected your website with your Facebook page (see page 85 for advice on setting this up) your live broadcast (now a video) will be on your website too.

Facebook also offers the service of being able to embed a player showing the live broadcast straight onto a page of your website, but this is a premium service (around $250 a month). Major media publishers such as ITV News have used the platform really successfully. For inspiration, read this case study on how ITV used Facebook Live to cover the EU referendum in 2016 – it will give you some good ideas about how you can use streaming:

1. Using Facebook Live ITV broadcast a Referendum Result Live programme, giving users the opportunity to comment on events as the night unfolded.
2. ITV News Political Editor Robert Peston broadcast live from a mobile phone as he travelled across London, going to events organised by Remain and Leave campaigners to get instant reactions as results came in.
3. And back at ITV Headquarters, producers set up a Facebook Live booth, where a range of guests answered

questions submitted live by the audience. Entrepreneur Theo Paphitis discussed Brexit and business, and former Labour Party leader Lord Kinnock engaged on what the political implications of a Leave vote would be.[17]

YouTube

We use YouTube for our live streaming. It allows you to embed the live stream straight onto a post on your website – a service which, unlike that of Facebook Live, is free (currently). There are a few extra steps you need to follow – including downloading an encoder – but once you have set it up, it works really well.

Here's how to do it:

Follow this link for some tips from Facebook on successfully streaming on its site: https://live.fb.com/tips

- Sign in to your YouTube account and go to the Creator Studio tools – click on Live Streaming. From here you need to verify your channel first by adding your phone number (you'll get an access code), then you need to download some encoding software. You can find a list of the recommend software to use at: https://support.google.com/YouTube/answer/2907883?hl=en We use **WirecastPlay** (developer Telestream) – simply fill in the details and get your download link. Once you have downloaded it, open the application (click the free version for now) and on the toolbar click Output/Settings (Figure 7.33).

- Add your YouTube username and click Authenticate. The application should automatically add your account. Click OK (leave the encoder settings as they are for now – if you have problems then you should come back and check the settings).

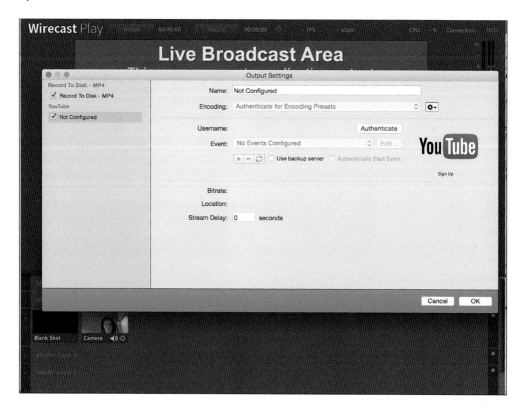

Figure 7.33 You need to download an encoder to stream live to your website via YouTube.

You are now ready to stream. As soon as you click Stream on the WirecastPlay application, whatever your desktop camera is picking up will be streamed live to your YouTube channel. We have cameras hooked up to ours, so you don't need to use the built-in camera – but this is for you to investigate; I am just covering the basics here.

Once you have connected WirecastPlay with your YouTube account, you need to add a player onto your website so that your audience can watch your live streams on your site. Create a new page for your live stream on your website. Then back on YouTube, on the Stream Live page, find the Share box (it's towards the bottom of the page). Click Watch Page and then you can copy the embed code from here. Now you can use this to embed a player straight onto your website which will allow your users to watch

your stream live from your website (see page 135 for help with embedding a YouTube player).

There is also the option to stream live from your mobile but you need 1,000 YouTube subscribers before you can do this.

Periscope

When Periscope first launched in 2015 it was an incredibly exciting app – it allowed you to watch what was going on live in all corners of the world in a way that had never been possible previously. I remember watching people simply driving in their cars in Tel Aviv in the dead of the night, and being thrilled at being connected so immediately with strangers. Not only that, but being able to message them, and for them to be able to address my questions by speaking to me, was so addictive.

Now the app has really been overtaken by Facebook Live and to some extent Snapchat, but there is still a place for it – particularly for raw, personal content. It has a visceral quality that is missing in more polished platforms such as Facebook Live. I am not sure of its future though – it's really difficult to get hold of any up-to-date stats – so it's difficult to assess what is going on. The last stats Twitter released about Periscope were on the first anniversary of the app in March 2016: "As of today, over 200 million broadcasts have been created on Periscope and over 110 years of live video are watched every day on iOS and Android."[18]

However, there have been some developments which point to its survival – namely the opening up of Periscope Producer, which allows all users to hook up external sources such as encoders for professional cameras (much in the same way as YouTube) and the launch of 360-degree videos (although at the time of writing everyone on Twitter and Periscope can watch live 360-degree videos but only select partners can go live in 360 degrees via Periscope).

The app was created by developers Kayvon Beykpour and Joe Bernstein. Beykpour was travelling in Istanbul when protests in Taksim Square broke out. He came up with the idea of Periscope because he was frustrated that he could get text updates on Twitter letting him know was happening, but couldn't *see* what was happening. Twitter bought the app in 2015 and that's when it launched properly.

In May 2017 @TravellerKaskus, part of @Kaskus – one of Indonesia's largest online communities – used the app to broadcast regular content during Ramadan: from tips on what to do during Iftar and unique Iftar food from different cities in Indonesia to the preparations for the homecoming season.

How to get started with Periscope:

- Download the Periscope app and log in with your Twitter account.
- Create a Periscope account and log in.
- Enable your camera, your microphone and your location.
- Open your broadcast preview.
- Tap the Broadcast tab at the bottom centre of the screen (or the camera icon at the bottom right of the screen if you are on Android).
- Give your broadcast a title (think 'Headline – keywords' – you are trying to get viewers so say it like it is).
- Choose who you want to share it with by clicking on the icons by the Go Live button.
- When you are ready, hit Go Live.
- When you are finished, swipe the screen down and tap Stop Broadcast.

Since December 2016 you can broadcast straight from Twitter – simply hit the Live button when you are composing a tweet and that will open up the broadcast screen.

When you are watching someone else's content, click on the heart symbol – hearts are a way for you to show you are supporting the broadcast.

It's a good idea to change your settings so that you save your broadcasts as videos – this way you can use the content by uploading it to

> Keep your phone steady and don't move around too much. Give your audience time to see what you are seeing, and remember to talk! You are broadcasting – so unless you are filming someone else speaking, make sure you are talking to your audience. Explain what is going on, why you are filming, what you think, how you feel … and pay attention to the comments from your Twitter followers. Make sure you mention anyone who comments – answer their questions and thank them for watching. This is your chance to engage.

YouTube and embedding it into a post.

To change your settings, click on your profile and click Settings. Scroll down and find Camera Roll and enable Auto for Save to Camera Roll and Save in High Definition (if you are on Android this would be Save to Gallery rather than Save to Camera Roll).

Connecting your Periscope account with your WordPress site

While there is no free integration which allows for live streaming onto your website from Periscope, you can alert your visitors that you are live with a button:

- Download the plugin Twitter (developer Twitter).
- Activate the plugin. Fill in your Twitter name and then go to Dashboard/Appearance/Widgets – here you will find a Periscope On Air button which you can drag into your sidebar. This will show your visitors when you are live on Periscope and allow them to click straight through to the stream. The button will change colour when you go live on Periscope.

Tip: if you are serious about live broadcasting I would suggest you invest in Wirecast Studio 7.5, which now offers you the chance to stream Periscope live to your website (and Facebook Live and Twitch.tv – and a few others). At the time of writing it was $495 for the licence.

US Open sponsor Chase used Periscope in 2016 to give tennis player Andy Roddick's fans the ultimate viewing experience – they could hear Andy's real-time commentary and were able to ask him questions as they watched matches with him at court-side. The live streams generated nearly 9.1 million impressions and drove nearly 2.5 million video views. There were 185,000 unique viewers on a single Periscope broadcast and 385 hours of Periscope video watched.[19]

Twitch.tv

Twitch is a live streaming platform for gamers. Launched in 2011 (and now owned by Amazon) it is phenomenally popular – according to stats on its site close to 10 million visitors gather to watch in 2017 and talk about video games with more than 2 million streamers every day.

It's easy to sign up with Twitch (you can sign in with your Facebook account), but in order to stream you will need to download an encoder. XSplit Broadcaster is the package to use for streaming – it's fantastic, gives you loads of exciting features and is also really affordable (around $5 a month for a premium licence). Unfortunately it is only available on PCs – if you are on a Mac you will need to use something like Wirecast Studio 7.5, as mentioned above (I have covered how to set up Wirecast for streaming to YouTube; see page 142 for help with this). OBS is an alternative – the Open Broacaster Software is free and works on Macs or PCs, so it's a good one to try out before investing in Wirecast or signing up with XSplit.

Once you have connected your encoder (on OBS you need to change the broadcast settings to Mode: Live Stream; Streaming Service: Twitch; Server: Closest Geographical), you need to get the Play Path/Stream Key from your Twitch dashboard. You can find this under Stream Key: click the Show Key button. Copy this and go back to OBS and paste the key in. There are other options but this should get you up and running – if not, there are lots of places online with help. Once you are connected with whichever package you are using, and are ready to start streaming, you should connect your Twitch content with your website.

The easiest way to do this is simply copy the embed code in the same way you would if you were embedding a YouTube video (see page 135 for help with this). You can also embed the Chat box, which is quite fun. Try adding this into a text widget on your sidebar.

If you want to add some channels, try the plugin **Easy Embed for Twitch TV** (developer Jamie Burleigh). This adds a 'rail' of the streams you are watching.

Activate the plugin then go to Dashboard/Settings/Easy Embed for Twitch TV and customize the feed. Make sure you select Published at the bottom of the screen; otherwise, it won't show up. Then you can paste the shortcode [getTwitch-Rail] anywhere you like on your site – try creating a post and pasting the shortcode in the Text tab. Remember: you can do this on a text widget too so that you can put this rail in your sidebar.

AUDIO

- 4.7 million adults in the UK listen to podcasts according to RAJAR, the body responsible for providing the audience measurement service for the UK's radio industry[20] (in the US, according to podcast researcher Edison,[21] the audience is 57 million!).
- The largest podcast age demographic in the UK is 25- to 34-year-olds.
- Podcasts reach their highest audience between 8.15 and 8.30am.
- Listen-again or catch-up radio is mainly used in the evening – it peaks between 11 and 11.15pm.

Audio is a fantastic medium – it is intimate, immediate and accessible, so it is not surprising that the trend for producing podcasts is growing in popularity. One of the factors behind this is that it seems that once a listener gets hooked on a podcast they become loyal followers. Something to consider when you are thinking about producing content for your website!

Like video, the first thing you need to know is that you do not host audio directly in your media library. (Unless you want to just add a snippet in a written piece – have a look at the *New York Times* interactive 'Two gunshots on a summer night' for a good example of this.)[22]

You do not host the audio on your site at all. What you do is upload your audio to a third-party platform such as SoundCloud or Audioboom and then embed its player with your audio onto your post.

Like video, the reasons for this are the size of the files and also because you want to have your content on a larger platform so that it can reach a greater audience than your own website is likely to have.

The process for embedding content is the same as for video (in fact for anything you want to embed): always look for the embed code, which is usually under a Share button. This is the code you need. I am going to talk you through the process using SoundCloud but use this example to learn about embedding content in general (Figure 7.34).

Figure 7.34 Audio content should be uploaded to a third party host such as Soundcloud.

To upload your own audio you must first have a SoundCloud account. The easiest way to set this up is to sign in with your Google account. You do have the option to sign in with your Facebook account but be careful with this – ask yourself, 'Is my Facebook account personal? And if so, am I OK for the content to be linked to the professional journalism website that I am trying to build?' If the answer is no, either create a new Facebook account or use your Google account.

Once you are signed in, click on Upload, which is in the top-right corner of the screen. Select the audio file you want to upload (the best file type is an MP3, as it is compressed and so will take less time to upload).

Add a proper headline and a proper description, thinking about keywords, and add tags. Select the appropriate genre, add a featured image and make sure the track is public. Once it has finished uploading, save it – this will automatically publish it and will open another page giving you some share options and the URL of the track. Click on Go to Your Track.

It's from here that you should click on Share to get the embed code for your post. I prefer to use the middle option, which will give you a long thin player (Figure 7.35).
Copy this code and then go back to your website and paste it into the Text tab of the post or page where you want the audio to appear.

Sometimes, depending on your theme you may have the option to select an audio format page and will be asked for the URL rather than the embed code – find this in the browser or click on Share.

If you're having difficulties with the audio not showing up, double-check what URL you have added and the embed code. Or it could be that your audio is set to Private rather than Public on SoundCloud.

Like YouTube, you can also embed a playlist instead of a single track. First, create your own playlist and add audio to it or copy someone else's playlist if it is public. Click on Share and then Embed – follow the same process as above.

Figure 7.35 Check on share to get the embed code for your podcast.

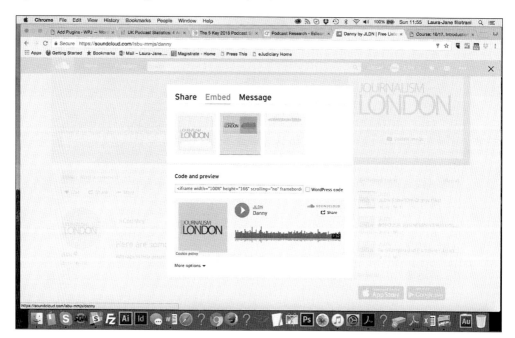

```
<iframe width='100%' height='450' scrol-
ling='no' frameborder='no' src='https://w.
soundcloud.com/player/?url=https%3A//
api.soundcloud.com/playlists/
102596628&color=ff5500&auto_play=fal-
se&hide_related=false&show_comment-
s=true&show_user=true&show_reposts=-
false'></iframe>
```

If you look at the code above you can see you have some options that you can manually change if you like: you can change the colour – it is set to hex code: ff5500 but you can go and find another colour using an HTML colour wheel (see page 117 for more help with this); you can turn autoplay on – changing 'false' to 'true' will play the content as soon as someone opens the page; you can hide related content from showing up by changing hide_related from 'false' to 'true' ... Have a play around.

Once you are happy with your content, why not submit it to iTunes as well? If you have it on iTunes as well as SoundCloud you are increasing your possible

audience. You can embed either the iTunes player or the SoundCloud player on your website as you please. I would stick with just one though – don't have two different players on your site. You will need an RSS feed of your content, and you can get this from your SoundCloud account:

1. Go to your profile and click Edit.
2. Fill in the Bio – this will be used by iTunes as the description for the content.
3. Click on Settings – you find this in the drop-down underneath the three dots in the top left-hand corner of the screen (Figure 7.36).
4. Click on Content and you should have your RSS feed (check the box underneath so that by default all your podcasts will be included in the RSS feed). If you want only selected content to appear, uncheck this box – you will have to manually check the box in the settings of the track that you want to add to the feed.

Once you have your RSS feed you can add it to iTunes – check out the instructions at https://itunespartner.apple.com/en/podcasts/overview

> **Remember: HTML is written in American English so be careful with the spelling – 'colour', for example, is 'color'. If you spell HTML using UK English it won't work.**

Figure 7.36 Find the RSS feed of your content under settings on your Soundcloud account.

Most of the major news organisations have iTunes accounts. Search for news channels and you'll find lots to choose from.

There are plenty of other places to look for audio content for your site – here are a few of the ones I use:

This American Life

'This American Life' is a weekly public radio show broadcast on more than 500 stations to about 2.2 million listeners.

There are tons of great shows to listen to, but try the spin-off show which brought in huge audiences in 2014: https://serialpod cast.org/season-one It's an investigative piece (a true story) on who killed Hae Min Lee, a teenager in Baltimore, in 1999. Her ex-boy-friend Adnan Syed is arrested for the murder, but did he do it? This podcast follows the case. It is gripping and brilliantly produced.

Rookie Podcast – developer Gutenberg Team The 'Rookie Podcast' is hosted by Tavi Gevin-son – an American writer and magazine editor who is best known for her fashion blog Style Rookie, which she started when she was just 12. This podcast is the spin-off from the blog. She interviews people she admires and has teenagers ask semi-qualified grown-ups for advice.

Radiolab

'Radiolab' is described as "a show about curios-ity, where sound illuminates ideas, and the boundaries blur between science, philosophy, and human experience."

The Guardian *GroundTruth*

'GroundTruth' is "a podcast about global reporting on the front lines of the planet's most urgent issues – from terrorism to global warm-ing to income inequality".

Reliable Sources with Brian Stelter

'Reliable Sources' examines how journalists do their jobs and how the media affect the stories they cover in this weekly CNN program.

Anna Faris Is Unqualified

Actress Anna Faris hosts this advice/call-in show – expect relationship advice mixed in with interviews and some quizzes. Quirky and friendly.

If you want to add a snippet of audio content directly into a written article – in the same way as the *New York Times* interactive I mentioned earlier in this section, 'Two gun-shots' – simply add the track in your media library. Make sure it is an MP3 and very short! The longer it is the bigger the file and the more your site will struggle to load properly. Or try **Soundcite** from Knight Lab. This online tool allows you add inline audio to your story.

In an age where consumers have many entertainment choices, local radio main-tains its strength and popularity in the marketplace among national and local advertisers.
Mark Fratrik, senior vice-president and chief economist at BIA/Kelsey, 2017 Investing in Radio report[23]

LIVE BLOGGING

Live blogging is a great way to engage an audience and really good fun – if a little stress-ful! My students love it when we do a live blog. The best way, really, is to have two of you – one to listen and comment and the other to trans-late the comments into a post – but you can do it by yourself if you are prepared.

The key to a live blog is research. Before you start you must do your homework thoroughly – make a list of all the names of people who will be involved, along with their job titles and any other information that might come up or be useful to clarify for your audience. Research the topic – make a list of any points, stats/details, names of locations, names of venues … anything which you will need to cover (think about doing a live blog of the Eurovision Song Contest, for example – how stressful would this be without a list of all the countries/contestants in advance?).

Once the event starts you should try and offer commentary as well as facts – aim to get your thoughts down, backed up by details and observa-tion. This is what will keep people engaged. With something complex like the Budget, you should be translating how what is being delivered by the

Chancellor will affect your audience. Never forget who you are talking to – this should guide you in deciding what information to include and how to include it.

There are quite a few plugins that you can use but the one I like is the official one from WordPress, **Liveblog** (developer Wordpress.com VIP, Automattic).

To see it in practice have a look at politico.eu at www.politico.eu/article/european-council-live-blog-2

The thing that makes this plugin better than many others is that you can post updates right from the front end of your site, so there is no need to use your dashboard – plus you can drag and drop photos right into the Liveblog area. Unlike other plugins, you don't need to create an account with a Liveblog platform – this plugin essentially turns any post into a live blog (even existing ones; for example, if you had written a post about an upcoming event, when the event actually starts you can simply add your live blog to the end of the post by enabling the function – no need to create a new post).

To use it is very simple: activate the plugin and then create a new post/page (or use an existing post). Scroll down to the bottom and you will see a button asking you to enable the live blog function – enable it and then click on Visit the Live Blog. This will take you to the front end, where you can type straight into the box and pull in images from your desktop – no need to upload them to the media library (Figure 7.37).
Don't forget to add hyperlinks.

This is a good plugin for live blogging from your phone too, as you don't have to be connected to any other site. Simply log into your website (not via the WordPress app – just on a browser) and then click onto your live blog post. Click View Post and you will be able to type straight into your post.

The other tool I have used successfully is 24liveblog.com – there used to be a plugin but now you just have to copy and paste the embed code straight onto a post on your site. It's free to use most of the starter features, and it is fun.

For some inspiration of how to run an interesting and engaging live blog, have a look at:

Figure 7.37 Liveblog turns any post into a live blog and you can post straight from the front end.

- The UK General Election 2017 on the *Guardian* site: www.theguardian.com/politics/live/2017/jun/08/general-election-results-2017-uk-live-labour-tories-corbyn-may-election-results-live-news-line
- The 2017 Oscars from *Empire* magazine: www.empireonline.com/movies/features/oscars-2017-live-blog
- Premier League football fixtures 2017/18 from the *Mirror*: www.mirror.co.uk/sport/football/news/premier-league-fixtures-201718-live-10615276
- The 2017 Google I/O annual developer event from Mashable: http://mashable.com/2017/05/17/google-io-2017-live-blog/#ArIVN3RANgqx

INFOGRAPHICS

Infographics are a way of using data to tell a story visually. They can be incredibly satisfying to work on and can be a really useful way of making something complex or simple or to drive home a staggering fact. The trick to infographics is simplicity. You should be able to tell what the story is without too much figuring out. The images you choose, the colours, the fonts, the stats – they should all work without too much explanation. A good place for examples is www.informationisbeautiful.net

If you think you will be including quite a few infographics on your site, it is worth considering choosing a WordPress theme that has data visualisation features built into it. Try **Infographer – Multi-Purpose Infographic Theme** (developer QODE).

Or look for a theme that has graphics as a prominent feature.

If you want to create an infographic as a piece of content to upload onto your website, there are a number of ways of doing this. You can find a template you like on a site such as 123rf.com – buy it and then drop your own data/content onto it. The only problem with this is that you buy a JPEG, which means each element won't be editable – it is one flat image.

There are other sites that offer templates – some for free; what you should look for is a template that is an Illustrator file (.ai) or an EPS (.eps). Both of these file types will mean that you are bringing in all the individual elements that make up the image, so that you can edit each element (instead of a JPEG, which brings all the elements flattened and joined together as one – meaning you have to modify the actual image rather than being able to edit an element).

An alternative is to build an infographic online and then export it. There are quite a few tools online that you can use – most will allow you to create an infographic for free, but before you start working on one, check whether you are able to export it or can get an embed code for it; otherwise, you won't be able to create a post with it on your site. Most of the tools charge you for exporting.

One of the tools I have used in the past is Infogram.com (formerly known as infogr.am).

Infogram is free if you just want to embed (it is a premium service if you need to export your infographic as a JPEG or PDF). You can sign in with your Gmail account and it has a WordPress plugin which makes adding the infographics to a post super-easy. Its charts and infographics are fully responsive by default, which means they automatically adapt and are optimised to mobile devices of any screen size, and it offers a wide range of templates for you to use.

Before you download and activate the plugin, sign up online at https://infogram.com and get your API Key – you will need this to connect your Infogram account with your WordPress site. You'll find your API credentials in your account settings (click on your name at the top-right corner of the screen) in Infogram.

Once you have your API information go to your WordPress site, download and activate the plugin (developer Torbjon) and go to Dashboard/Settings/Infogram and paste in your API Key and API Secret. Now, when you create a new post or page on WordPress you will see on the toolbar that you have the option to embed an infographic that you have created on Info-gram. One word of warning though: I have found this plugin quite sticky – if for some reason the infographic that you have created isn't showing in full, just paste in the embed code from Infogram instead; choose the Responsive embed code.

On Infogram creating your infographic is fairly simple. You can choose to add maps, graphics and counters – add an element from the left-hand sidebar and then save your own data over the top by adjusting the data on the right-hand sidebar (click on the element and then click Edit Data). You can upload a data set straight onto the site – your data should be an .xls file or a .csv file – or you can add it manually. Then adjust the size of the graphic and the colours. When you are happy with your infographic click Share. This will now be in your library and will be available on your WordPress site to paste into a post. Or copy the embed code, as explained above.

Other tools to try include **Piktogram** and **Visme**. Here's first-year journalism student Pascal Kempson of London South Bank University on using Visme (see his infographic on genres that win the most Oscars at http://journalism.london/2017/06/win-oscars-best-picture):

I chose Visme largely due to the ease of use. The online software provides you with tools to create a plethora of designs relatively simply, whilst still permitting flexibility. It's also free, which never hurts.
The software is very simple even if you've never used anything of the type before. It's mainly drag-and-drop with a set of standard formatting tools. An obvious tip is to regularly save your work as you go – a more specific tip would be to consider purchasing the Pro version. Visme provides hundreds of free stock images/cartoons, but you have a much wider selection with the paid-for option.
The main difficulty of putting my infographic together was matching the right images with the right categories. Despite the vast selection available, trying to find exactly what I wanted became a slight issue with Visme. If you're looking for something

very specific I would recommend using Adobe Illustrator.
Using and understanding data seems like a daunting task but a key factor is to take an angle you're interested in. Once the data is understood, it helps to be inquisitive. I took what I could see from the data and began to ask further questions about it – the answers of which weren't immediately clear.
With my infographic I wanted to turn quite boring data of Oscar Best Picture winners into an accessible story that would be fun to look at. I gave it a 'step by step guide' style similar to something you'd see online for advice. It allowed me to show what the key features of the 'best' films were, in a way that's exciting to read and perhaps inspiring for filmmakers.[24]

There are also a number of plugins that you can add on WordPress so that you don't have to create your graphics on a third-party site.

Try **Infographic Maker iList** (developer QuantumCloud). This plugin allows you to create charts, graphs and text lists – all responsive.

Activate the plugin then go to Dashboard/iList/New iList.

Try creating a simple doughnut as an example:

- Add a new iList: put in a headline – 'Boys and girls', for example; select Graphic Lists; click on Choose Template and select the first image – this is [image-template-one] (you'll see that there are more choices for the Pro version of the plugin, which you may want to buy once you have explored the free version).
- Click on Create iList Chart; select Doughnut as the chart type; give the chart a title – 'Boys and Girls'; give the dataset the same name and then under Label put 'boys', value '50', colour 'blue'; on the next row put 'girls', value '50', colour 'pink '. Then click Generate Chart (to add more data simply add a row). Publish the post.
- Go to Dashboard/iList/Manage iList Items and you will see the chart that you have just

created with a shortcode. Now, you can either copy this shortcode and create a new post – in the Text tab paste this shortcode. Save and publish and you should see your chart with half in pink and half in blue. (Try to grab some stats and have a go at creating more complex charts.)

- Or you can simply create a new post. You will see a new iList icon on the toolbar of Edit Post (Figure 7.41).
- Click on this icon and you will be able to select the chart from a drop-down (I have had some problems with this way of doing it, so I stick to copying the embed code and pasting it in myself).

What you need now is some data! To get you started, here are a few places to find some stats:

- **Office for National Statistics.** The UK's largest independent producer of official stats and the recognised national statistical institute of the UK.
- **UK Data Service.** The UK Data Service is funded by the Economic and Social Research Council with contributions from the University of Essex, the University of Manchester and Jisc. Its Open

Data collections are available for anyone to use.

- **Data.gov.uk.** Here you can "find data published by government departments and agencies, public bodies and local authorities. You can use this data to learn more about how government works, carry out research or build applications and services."
- **UK Government statistical data sets.**
- **UK Police Data.** This is the site for open data about crime and policing in England, Wales and Northern Ireland.
- **The NHS.**
- **The World Health Organization.**

Other WordPress plugins to try:

- **Blazing Charts** – developer Massoud Shakeri,
- **TablePress** – developer Tobias Bäthge, and
- **WordPress Charts and Graphs** – developer Themeisle.

Maps

Maps can be a great way of adding interactive content onto your site. Of course, you can use maps to show people where things are and to

Figure 7.41 Once you have activated the plugin iList you will see a new icon to create graphics on your posts and pages.

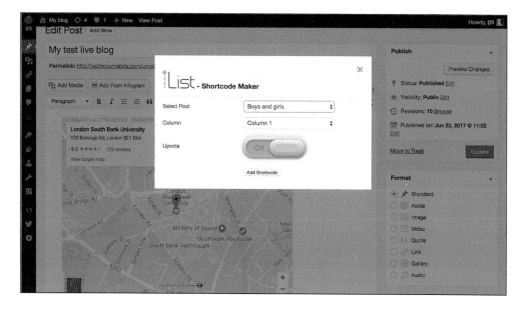

add more information about a venue or an event, but they can also be used to tell a story. You can add information about people, neighborhoods, murders ... Need some inspiration? Here are some examples of story maps:

- 'Election 2017: What do the mapped out visits of Scotland's leaders tell us?' See www.bbc.co.uk/news/uk-scotland-scotland-politics-40162504
- 'The future of "fake news"? A misleading map of "refugee crime" in Germany distorts reality': https://www.thebureauinvestigates.com/stories/2017-02-27/the-future-of-fake-news
- 'Geography, class, and fate: Passengers on the *Titanic*' – a map of travellers' hometowns that its developers say "reveals the immigrant status of most third-class passengers, who also suffered the highest fatality rate": http://storymaps.esri.com/stories/titanic

The *Titanic* story map was created with software by **Esri.com** – a premium service. For a free alternative you can visit Knight Lab (Northwestern University Knight Lab). Knight Lab offers a great online tool, **StoryMap**, which allows you to pull in content from a variety of sources, such as Twitter, Flickr, YouTube, Vimeo, Vine, Dailymotion, Google Maps and Wikipedia, and you can embed it straight into a post.

Here are a few examples of what you can create with StoryMap:

- 'Lewis Hamilton beats Sebastian Vettel to Chinese Grand Prix pole' – the *Evening Standard*: www.standard.co.uk/sport/other-sports/lewis-hamilton-beats-sebastian-vettel-to-chines-grand-prix-pole-a3510531.html
- 'Crime spree in Norwich March 2017' – the *Eastern Daily Press*: www.edp24.co.uk/news/crime/see-the-moment-man-suspected-of-norwich-crime-spree-is-arrested-1-4954490
- 'Aberdeen's biggest works of art' – the *Evening Express*: www.eveningexpress.co.uk/fp/news/local/map-to-find-nuart-aberdeens-biggest-works-of-art

- 'Game of Thrones: Arya's Journey' – Knight Lab: https://storymap.knightlab.com/examples/aryas-journey

It is not just the StoryMap tool that is useful on the Knight Lab site – there are a couple of others you should explore. **Timeline** is one, and the other is **Juxtapose**, with which you can put two images side by side to illustrate a change.

Here's a good example of Timeline in action:

- 'Rory Best stokes the flames by insisting Ireland have more to play for than just denying England the Grand Slam' – the *Independent*: www.independent.co.uk/sport/rugby/rugby-union/international/six-nations-ireland-vs-england-grand-slam-rory-best-a7636366.html

And an example of Juxtapose:
- 'Then and now: California comes back to life after years-long drought' – the *New York Post*: http://nypost.com/2017/04/12/then-and-now-california-comes-back-to-life-after-years-long-drought

Northwestern University Knight Lab describes itself as "a community of designers, developers, students and educators working on experiments designed to push journalism into new spaces". The projects they work on are all open-source, which means you can use them and contribute to their development. Check out their project page for what they are working on at the moment: https://knightlab.northwestern.edu/projects/#toolbox

Back to maps – if you don't want to use any of the tools already mentioned, there are many WordPress plugins you can activate on your site for embedding maps onto a post. Before we look at some options, it is worth pointing out that if you just want a simple map, Google Maps offers an embed code which you can customize and paste onto a post without the need for any plugin.

It is very easy to do: go to Google Maps, search for the area you want a map of and then click Share. Copy the embed code, go back to your WordPress site and paste the code in the Text tab of a post/page (Figure 7.42).

You can change the size of the map in the embed code on your post – simply put in the required width and height. For example, here is the code for a map of London South Bank University:

```
<iframe src='https://www.google.com/
maps/embed?pb=!1m18!1m12!1m3!
1d2483.8170890313827!2d-
0.10427488445472513!
3d51.498223979633686!2m3!1f0!2f0!3f0!
3m2!1i1024!2i768!4f13.1!3m3!1m2!
1s0x487604a03afbd695%3A0xffafoe
f7e5c357e4!2sLondon+South+Bank+Uni
versity!5e0!3m2!1sen!2suk!
4v1498315064750' width='600'
height='450' frameborder='0' style='bor-
der:0' allowfullscreen></iframe>
```

To change the size, change the width and height. Remember: these are pixels. You can also put in '100%' instead of a value – this will make the map 100% of the width of your post. You can also add a frameborder and a border – try adding the value '1' to both and see what this does to the design of the map.

More fun is to embed the street view – simply drop the man icon onto Google Maps to make the map the Street View version, click Share and copy the embed code.

If you want to create a story map such as the ones above – or even just a map which has information about points of interest – you need to be able to add markers. If you want to add markers to a map (and drop in extra content – even videos and audio snippets at certain points) then you are going to need a plugin (unless you have chosen a WordPress theme that has this functionality built in – I have listed a few themes with good maps at the end of this section).

There are lots of plugins to choose from and they all work on pretty much the same basis. I have used **WP Google Maps** (developer

Figure 7.42 It's very easy to embed a Google map on your website – just look for the embed code.

WP Google Maps) in the past. It is the one I have found to be most compatible with the other plugins I am using – particularly caching plugins – and it has lots of great functionality, including the option to create as many maps as you like, a number of themes to choose from and support for Street View, and you can animate your markers. To access all this functionality you need to pay for the Pro version, which at the time of writing was only $39 – worth it if you are going to be using maps a lot.

To use WP Google Maps, activate the plugin and go to Dashboard/Maps.

The first thing you need to do is grab the API Key (if you have worked your way through this book you should be well versed in this process!). Click on Create an API Key – you will be taken to a page where you should select Create a Project. Opt out of email updates but select Yes, you agree with the T&Cs. Click Agree and Continue. Your API Key will now be generated. Be patient; it can take a minute or so. Once it is created you will automatically be taken to the API Manager – Credentials. Here you should click Create (don't worry about key restrictions). You should then get your key – simply copy this, go back to your website and paste it into the box asking for the API Key.

If you are using the free version you will only be able to create one map. click Create Map and then you can drop markers on it by typing in the location. You can put on as many markers as you like (remember to move the zoom level so the map shows just the area you want; otherwise, you will get a whole world map). Once you are happy with your markers (you will see all the things you can add if you have the Pro version – including images and videos) click Save and the shortcode will be generated. Copy this and paste it into the Text tab of a post.

You can change how your map looks by changing the theme. There's a fun plugin called **Snazzy Maps** (developer Atmist) which will do this for you and gives you loads of different styles to choose from. It doesn't add maps but does add different styles to your existing maps. It's really easy to use. Once it is activated go to Dashboard/Appearance/Snazzy Maps. Simply select the styles you like under Explore and save the ones you like – these will appear under Styles. You can then enable the one you like, and this will be applied to all maps (you can have only one style across the whole site).

If for some reason you can't get WP Google Maps to work, there are lots of alternatives. Try:

Google Maps Easy – developer supsystic.com

First, get yourself an API Key at https://developers.google.com/maps/documentation/javascript/get-api-key

This is probably the best plugin because of the free bits it offers – you can create a map with lots of markers and drop videos/images/text and hyperlinks onto a marker, which is excellent. The reason I didn't use this as my main example is because I have found it a little buggy and I also think it is a little confusing. But if you can get it to work it may well be the best option. There are of course lots of premium functions that come with a licence.

Leaflet Maps Marker – developer MapsMarker

This has lots of functionality for free but you can create a map with only one marker. You can add video to that marker, and a description and a hyperlink, but you can only have one marker for free. To add more markers on the same map you need to create a new layer, and adding more than one marker to a layer requires the Pro version. This is quite an interesting plugin actually, because it also offers you the chance to add markers to AR maps via **Wikitude's Augmented Reality** browser. Check it out. This is going to be more of a feature going forward, for sure.

You can also use maps to show how many people are actually on your site at a time – this is quite fun to see (but not if you have absolutely no traffic – then it can be a bit depressing!). Try **Visitor Map** (developer Blixt Gordon).

Now, if you are really serious about having maps as part of your storytelling, I would pick a theme that offers this functionality as part of the code (just make sure you check out how the blog posts are displayed too: you don't just want a directory site, you need something that displays text, video and audio well). Try **Javo Spot** (developer Javo Themes) or **WPVoyager** (developer Purethemes).

REFERENCES

1   CodeCanyon. (2017). WPBakery Page Builder for WordPress (formerly Visual Composer). [online] Available at: https://codecanyon.net/item/visual-composer-page-builder-for-wordpress/242431 [Accessed 14 Nov. 2017].

2   Medium. (2017). Welcome to the Gutenberg Editor – Matthias Pfefferle – Medium. [online] Available at: https://medium.com/@pfefferle/welcome-to-the-gutenberg-editor-e655ae35e8b1 [Accessed 14 Nov. 2017].

3   Tips and Tricks HQ, Ruhul Amin. (2017). Category Specific RSS Feed Subscription. [online] WordPress.org. Available at: https://en-gb.wordpress.org/plugins/category-specific-rss-feed-menu [Accessed 14 Nov. 2017].

4   Price, Adam. (2017). Founder of 93digital – interviewed by LJ Filotrani.

5   *New York Times*. (2017). Snow Fall: The Avalanche at Tunnel Creek. [online] Available at: www.nytimes.com/projects/2012/snow-fall/#/?part=tunnel-creek [Accessed 14 Nov. 2017].

6   *New York Times*. (2017). A Moment From the Boston Marathon, Audio and Stories. [online] Available at: www.nytimes.com/interactive/2013/04/22/sports/boston-moment.HTML?mcubz=0 [Accessed 14 Nov. 2017].

7   *Washington Post*. (2017). More than 50 Years of U.S. Mass Shootings: The Victims, Sites, Killers and Weapons. [online] Available at: www.washingtonpost.com/graphics/national/mass-shootings-in-america [Accessed 14 Nov. 2017].

8   Cisco. (2017). Cisco Visual Networking Index: Forecast and Methodology, 2016–2021. [online] Available at: www.cisco.com/c/en/us/solutions/collateral/service-provider/visual-networking-index-vni/complete-white-paper-c11-481360.HTML [Accessed 14 Nov. 2017].

9   YouTube.com. (2017). Press – YouTube. [online] Available at: www.youtube.com/yt/about/press [Accessed 15 Nov. 2017].

10   Instagram.com. (2017). Simple, Quick, and Healthy (@videomeals). Instagram photos and videos. [online] Available at: www.instagram.com/videomeals [Accessed 15 Nov. 2017].

11   Chacon, B. (2017). The Best Time to Post on Instagram in 2017 – Later Blog. [online] Later Blog. Available at: https://later.com/blog/best-time-to-post-on-instagram [Accessed 15 Nov. 2017].

12   Live.theverge.com. (2016). Dive into Mobile Live. [online] Available at: https://live.theverge.com/dive-into-mobile-live-blog-google-microsoft-snapchat/iframe.html [Accessed 15 Nov. 2017].

13   Snap. (2017). Form S-1 Registrations Statement. [online] Sec.gov. Available at: https://www.sec.gov/Archives/edgar/data/1564408/000119312517029199/d270216ds1.htm [Accessed 15 Nov. 2017].

14   Evan Spiegel. (2014). 2014 LA Hacks Keynote. [online] Snap.com. Available at: www.snap.com/en-US/news/post/2014-la-hacks-keynote [Accessed 15 Nov. 2017].

15   Tighe, S. (2017). Snapchat editor, The Sun UK – interviewed by LJ Filotrani.

16   Vaynerchuk. (2017). Why 1 View is Everything – Gary Vaynerchuk – Medium. [online] Medium. Available at: https://medium.com/@garyvee/why-1-view-is-everything-3fe415cf3678 [Accessed 15 Nov. 2017].

17   Facebook Live. (2017). Global News Publishers Find Success With Facebook Live. [online] Facebook Media. Available at: www.facebook.com/facebookmedia/success-stories/globalnews-live [Accessed 15 Nov. 2017].

18   Periscope. (2016). Year One – Periscope – Medium. [online] Medium. Available at: https://medium.com/periscope/year-one-81c4c625f5bc [Accessed 15 Nov. 2017].

19   Marketing.twitter.com. (2016). Chase Teams with Andy Roddick to Present the US Open through Live Periscope Video. [online]

Available at: https://marketing.twitter.com/
na/en/success-stories/chase-teams-with-
andy-roddick-to-present-the-us-open.HTML
[Accessed 15 Nov. 2017].

20 RAJAR. RAJAR Midas Audio Survey Winter
2016. (2016). [ebook] Available at: www.
rajar.co.uk/docs/news/MIDAS_Win
ter_2016.pdf [Accessed 15 Nov. 2017].

21 Edison. (2017). The Infinite Dial 2017.
[online] Edison Research. Available at: www.
edisonresearch.com/infinite-dial-2017/
[Accessed 15 Nov. 2017].

22 Bogdanich, W. and Silber, G. (2013). Two
Gunshots on a Summer Night. [online]
nytimes.com. Available at: www.nytimes.
com/projects/2013/two-gunshots
[Accessed 15 Nov. 2017].

23 Main, S. (2017). Radio Is Expected to Surpass
Newspapers in Local Ad Revenue by 2021.
[online] Adweek.com. Available at: www.
adweek.com/digital/radio-is-expected-to-sur
pass-newspapers-in-local-ad-revenue-by-
2021 [Accessed 15 Nov. 2017].

24 Kempson, P. (2017). Student – interviewed by
LJ Filotrani.

CHAPTER 8

Understanding users

Understanding the visitors to your website should be key in determining your content strategy – or rather, defining who you are trying to reach should be. Without this and a clear vision for your editorial, your target audience will elude you. Thankfully there are some tools you can use to help, which is what we are going to cover here.

I am going to give you a heads-up before you read on – there is a lot in this section that will be confusing. Don't try and understand it all immediately. Understanding your audience and the metrics used to measure them is an organic process and will only start to make sense over time – and in context. When you start to ask questions about what is working and what isn't working on your site, the stats will become more important to you. So for the moment, just take in what you can and leave the rest for another time.

Remember: the whole purpose of understanding the stats is so that you can adjust your content – making it more relevant, more accessible and more engaging. The bigger your audience the higher up in the rankings you will be.

> When you are trying to find information about a company's audience, try searching for its media pack – this is usually produced by the company's commercial department and will include all the information that someone looking to advertise with it might need to know; for example, its demographic.

MANAGING USERS

Let's start by looking at some of the terminology used when talking about online audiences.

Bounce rate

This can refer to both a single page or the whole website and can be tricky to work out – it basically refers to how many pages a visitor is clicking on, compared with how many visitors arrive on your site. For example, if 100 visitors arrive on your homepage but only 50 go on to other pages, this gives you a site *bounce rate* of 50%.

All you really need to know at this stage is that if your bounce rate is high for the whole site or an individual page, it means that your visitors are leaving without clicking on other bits of content. If this is happening, you need to look at the pages and see what you can do in order to encourage your visitors to click on more pages. Ask yourself: is the content relevant to your audience? Do you have other content that the visitor might be interested in promoted on the page?

One thing to be aware of when looking at your bounce rate: if a visitor comes to your site via a direct link to that page and leaves after just that page, your bounce rate will show as 100%. This would be cause for concern if you didn't take into consideration time spent on the page.

Some reasons people click away from a site:

- A slow page load time,
- Pop ups (these can be very annoying – especially if the pop up appears every time you click on a page),
- Banner ads (especially animated ones),
- Music that plays automatically with no way of turning it off (playing a nice jingle on your homepage might sound like a good idea but it quickly becomes irritating if you can't turn it off and it plays again from the beginning every time you click),
- Videos that auto play with no way of stopping them,
- Unrelated content – keep it relevant,
- Headlines and standfirsts that do not sum up the content – don't make your visitors hunt for the content; make it easy with clear headlines and excerpts,
- Bad site design – i.e. no house style, pictures all different sizes, clashing colours, inconsistent fonts,
- Awful navigation – content is really difficult to find, the menu bar is not helpful, and there are no tag clouds or drop-downs or an About page,
- Images do not load,
- Keywords are attracting the wrong audience, and
- Broken links.

Benchmark bounce rates are different depending on what kind of website it is; for example, for an ecommerce site where a visitor goes to buy something, the benchmark bounce rate in 2017 was around 33%. However, on a news site where content is the driver, the benchmark bounce rate was between 40% and 60%. In general, the advice is that you should be aiming for a rate of below 40%, but I wouldn't get too hung up on this figure.

Time spent on page

This is arguably more important than the bounce rate. It simply measures how long a visitor is spending on a page. This tells you how engaging your content is (although it doesn't tell you if a visitor clicks on a page and then goes away to make a cup of tea before returning to your site and closing it down!).

Exit rate

This is a measurement for individual pages and is calculated from the number of people who click away from your website from a specific page. If you have a page which is showing a high exit rate – i.e. a lot of people are leaving your site from it – ask yourself why.

Uniques

This is the word used to describe visitors who visit your site once within a given period. For example, you might talk about 'daily uniques' – the number of visitors you have in a single day. (Each visitor is counted only once even if they visit your site in the morning, go away and come back again in the afternoon. Each visitor is recorded from their IP address.) Or you might talk about 'monthly uniques' – the number of single visitors over a month (again, a visitor is only counted once in the month no matter how many times they come back to your site – if they are using the same IP address, of course).

Visits

This counts all visitors to your site, no matter how many times that individual comes back. So if your site has only visitor to your site on one day – that day's visits may show as 100 but the uniques will show as only 1.

Page views (also called impressions)

This is how many times a page has been clicked on – you can find out how many pages a visitor looks at on average.

Landing page

This is the first page a person visits when they come to your site.

Traffic

When you talk about visitors to a site you talk about how much traffic the site has.

Traffic sources

This is where your visitors have come from – what has sent them to your site. A visitor could come to your site because they already had the URL, which is called 'direct'; or it could be from a hyperlink from somewhere – this is called 'referral'; or it could be from searching a keyword – this is called 'organic search'; or it could be from an advert, which is called 'PPC' (pay per click). So the four traffic sources you will mostly likely come across are: *direct, referral, organic search* and *PPC*.

GOOGLE ANALYTICS

Armed with all of these terms, let's look at the most popular analytical tool: Google Analytics.

By way of illustration let's look at a couple of examples from 2017:

- The *Guardian* reaches 155 million unique browsers a month globally.
- It has 35.3 million monthly global unique visitors.

- It has a 25.4 million UK monthly cross-platform reach.
- There are 6.9 million average daily unique visitors.
- The site is visited for 26 minutes on average per visitor.

Uniques per month:

- The *Guardian*: 24 million,
- *The Huffington Post*: 6 million, and
- *Vice*: 4 million.

Google launched its web analytical application in 2005 and since then it has pretty much dominated the market for tracking and reporting website traffic. Most website stats that are quoted are sourced from Google Analytics and if you are even just a little serious about working online, you need to know your way round its tools.

Some of the things you can learn from the application include: the demographic of your visitors – who they are, where they live; the behaviour of your visitors – what time of day they visit your site, how long they spend on your site; how your content is viewed – which articles are getting the most views, which pages are keeping your visitors engaged; how is your site being found – by referrals, in organic search . . .

There are a number of plugins that you can install on your website which will translate some of the data for you, from very basic to more complex, but the first thing you need to do is connect your site with the application. To do this you must create a Google Analytics account.

> Today's world is driven by data. Having insight into how your website is performing will allow you make real decisions that have real world impact. You will be able to see how long people are on your site, where they come from, what content they view and much more, allowing you continue evolving your site to be more effective.
> Alex Price, 93digital

> Create a Gmail account just for your website and use this account for all your Google tools and any other platform/application/social media account – keep all your accounts registered to one email.

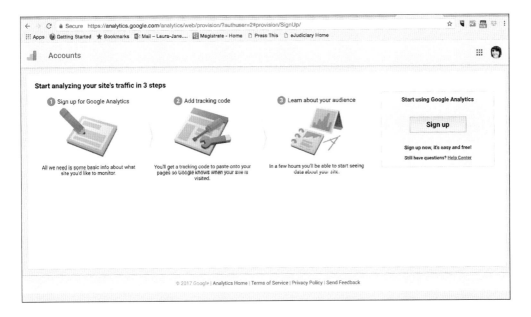

Figure 8.1 Sign up for Google Analytics.

I am going to walk you through a basic set-up and then highlight a few areas that I think you should be monitoring. Google Analytics can be used in an incredibly detailed way – it is a complex application – or you can use it just to get an overview. Don't worry if you don't understand everything. If you can get an Analytics account up and running, and you can connect your website, that will be enough for a start.

Step one

- Set up a Google Analytics account – google.com/analytics will take you to the sign-up page. If you have already set up your Google account you will be asked to sign in and then click Access Google Analytics. Click Sign Up (Figure 8.1).
- Fill in the required information. Put in your name as the account name or, if you like, put in a brand name. Put in your website name and then paste in the URL for the site including 'http://'. Select the industry and then, importantly, choose the time zone – this will

have an impact when you are looking at your visitor behaviour to see what time of day the site is being accessed (Figure 8.2).
- Click the blue box at the bottom, Get Tracking ID.
- You will first be asked to agree to the T&Cs. Click the UK as your country of residence. You will then be taken to your dashboard and you will see the Tracking ID – it starts with 'UA-'.

Step two

- Add a plugin on your WordPress site that will connect your site using the Tracking ID you have just created. Try **Google Analytics Dashboard for WP** (GADWP; developer Alin Marcu).
- Activate the plugin, and in Dashboard/ Google Analytics/General Settings click Authorize Plugin.
- Click Get Access Code. This will take you to the Google log-in page. Select the email you have just used to set up your Google Analytics account.

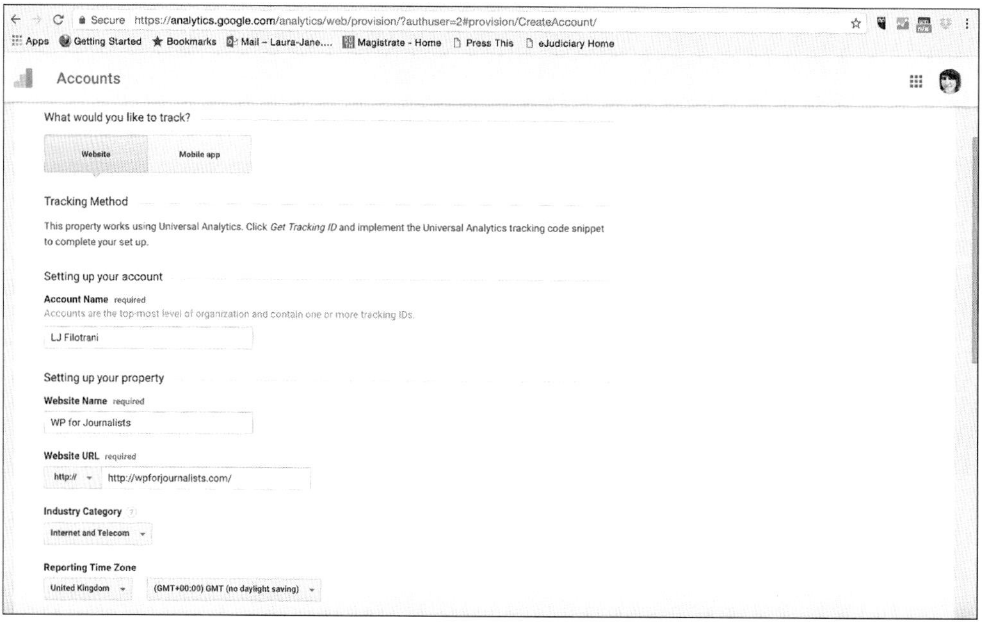

Figure 8.2 Don't forget to set your time zone for accurate stats.

- You will then be asked for permission to connect the plugin GADWP with your Google Analytics account – click Allow (Figure 8.3).
- Copy the code and go back to your website and paste it in the box where it says Access Code. Hit Save Access Code.
- You should now see your website in General Settings.
- Hit Save Changes.
- Now click on your dashboard and you will see a widget has been added (Figure 8.4) with dropdowns allowing you to access different data. You won't have any stats if you have only just set it up, but it won't be long before you start to get some figures. I like to keep an eye on Real-time, especially when I have just tweeted out some content – keeping this view open will show you real-time activity. It can be a bit addictive.

This plugin will give you the top line. To drill down on what's going on your site you really need to be logging into your Google Analytics account. Go to your Google Analytics account

and make sure you are still signed in. To get to your admin area – which gives you control over everything – click the wheel at the bottom left of the screen (Figure 8.5). Click the arrow below it to make the sidebar full and you will see on the left you have the following options: **Customization, Real-time, Audience, Acquisition, Behaviour, Conversions.**

You will have to spend some time exploring. As I said at the beginning of this chapter, Google Analytics is a complex application and you can really get a lot of detailed information about your site from it. At the beginning, of course, there won't be a lot of data, so here are the areas I think you should explore first:

- **Real-time** This gives you all the information about the visitors that are on your site right now: what country they are in, where they have come from (a search, for example), what content they are looking at, etc.
- **Audience** This gives you information over a period of time. You can select a day, a number of days, a week – however long you

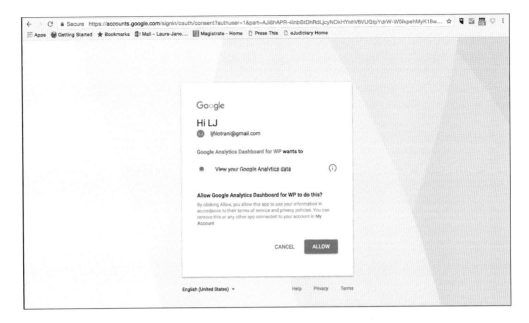

Figure 8.3 Authorize the GADWP plugin.

Figure 8.4 You will have a widget for stats now on your dashboard.

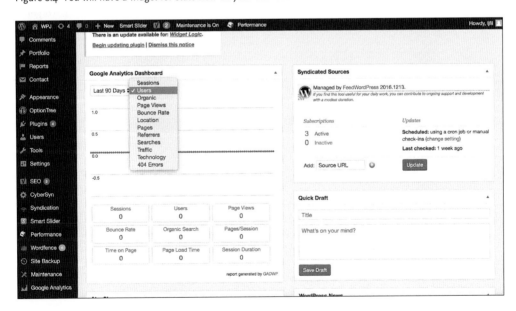

like – and see the breakdown of the audience.

■ **User Explorer** This shows you exactly what content an individual user has been looking at,

how much time they spent looking at it and what time of day they accessed it (Figure 8.6).

■ **Behaviour** This is where you can access information about your content. Click on Site

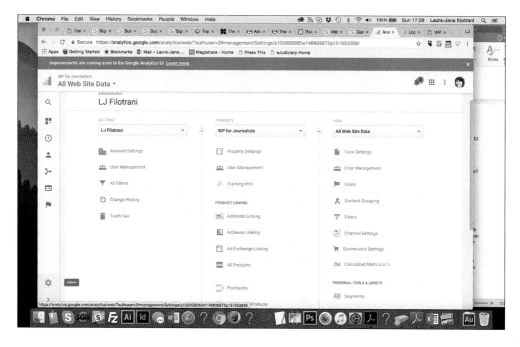

Figure 8.5 On Google Analytics click on the wheel to find your admin area.

Figure 8.6 The User Explorer area will show you exactly what your visitors have been clicking on.

Content for information about all your pages, and then individual articles/videos/podcasts – anything published – on Content Drilldown.

There is so much more on Google Analytics than I have covered here, but I think that is enough for you to be getting on with. Use the information to start building up a picture of how your site is functioning. You should set a time to produce a regular report – weekly or monthly if you are not very active. Export it and keep it so that you can refer back to see any trends.

Use these reports to get together a content strategy of when and what to publish, and set yourself some targets.

Managing users

We covered setting up users on your site at a basic level in Chapter 4. Here we are going to look at some plugins that will help you manage your users as your site grows. The plugins mentioned are going to be particularly useful if you run a multisite with a number of admins and a number of subdomains.

User Switching – developer John Blackbourn

This is a very useful plugin if you have multiple users on your website. It allows you to quickly switch to their account so that you can test what they can see and troubleshoot any problems they have. You do this without having to log out and log back in. Very useful.

Members – developer Justin Tadlock

This is a plugin which allows you to modify and add capabilities to the default roles available for users on WordPress. As already mentioned, by default the roles are:

- **Administrator** This user has access to all options and features.
- **Editor** This user can manage and publish posts.
- **Author** This user can publish their own posts but not anyone else's.

- **Contributor** This user can write posts but cannot publish them – they have to submit their posts for review.
- **Subscriber** This user has basic functionality, such as changing their profile and leaving comments.

The Members plugin allows you to amend the capabilities of these roles and also create bespoke roles for individuals. You can also assign a user multiple roles if you need to. One of the things that is particularly annoying, for example, with the default roles is that only the administrator is allowed to embed content. Having the Members plugin allows you to give this capability to your editors (Figure 8.7).

Some of the functions the plugin allows are:

- **Role Manager** Allows you to edit, create and delete roles as well as capabilities for these roles.
- **Multiple User Roles** Give one, two or even more roles to any user.
- **Explicitly Deny Capabilities** Deny specific capabilities to specific user roles.
- **Clone Roles** Build a new role by cloning an existing role.
- **Content Permissions** Gives you control over which users (by role) have access to post content.

Inactive User Deleter – developer Korol Yuriy aka Shra

This is a good plugin for cleaning up inactive user registrations – you can filter and bulk delete. Very handy.

Restrict User Access – WordPress Membership Plugin – developer Joachim Jensen, Intox Studio

This plugin allows you to create access levels for your users – so you can keep posts and pages restricted; give your users gold, silver and

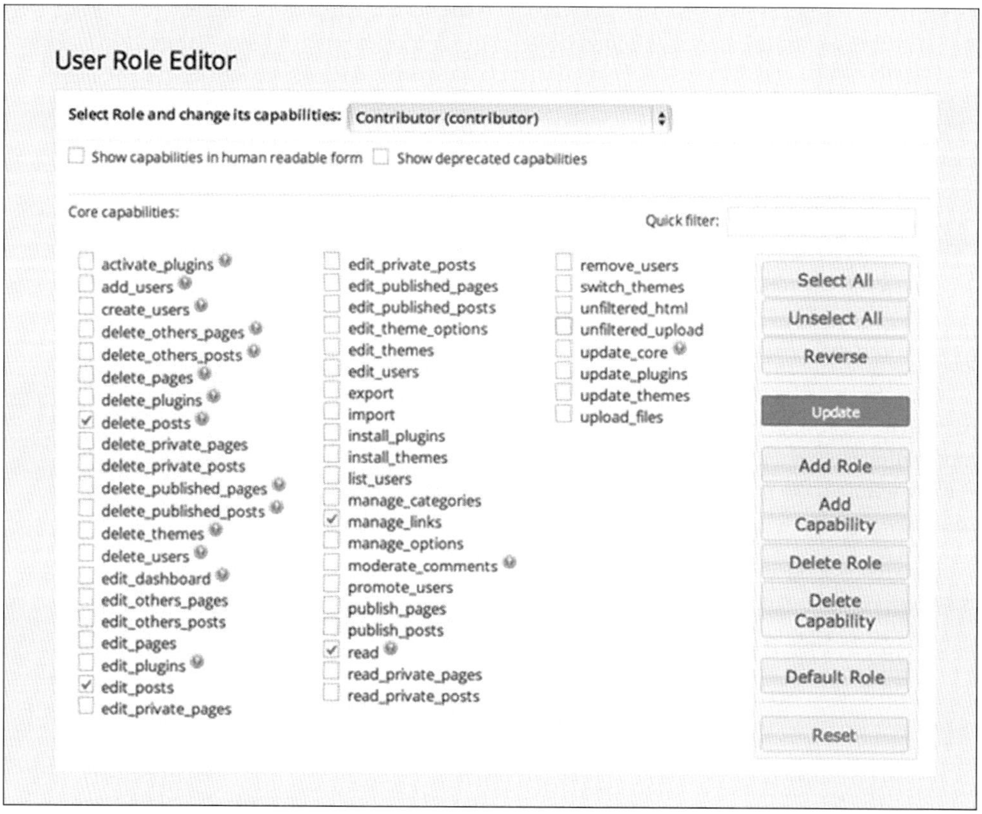

Figure 8.7 Being able to change permissions for a user is very useful. The Members plugin gives you this functionality.

bronze membership; and even introduce a paywall to access certain content. More of this in Chapter 9.

Bulk Password Reset – developer Ruben Woudsma

A great plugin when you have multiple users – change everyone's password with one click.

Dynamic User Directory – developer Sarah Giles

If you have a lot of contributors and you want to list them on the front end so visitors to your site can see who they are and what content they have published and read a bit about them, this is the plugin for you. Highly customizable and very useful.

FORUMS AND Q&AS

Being able to communicate with the visitors to your site is very exciting when you first start out. You can do this at the most basic level by having comments turned on for your posts. But if you really want to get a conversation going you should look at running a forum area on your site. A forum is simply a place where you can group conversations and allow users to respond to each other. Most support areas on websites are forums.

The Student Room at www.thestudent room.co.uk is a good example of a forum.

The thing to remember with running a forum is that it takes time to grow – you need to seed conversations and be active in encouraging people to join in. One of the ways you can do this is by posting a question yourself and then actively finding someone to respond to it. This is when a good healthy contacts list in LinkedIn comes in handy. Message the people who you think might be able to answer your question and post a link asking them to respond. Don't be despondent if 9 out of 10 people don't – it's a numbers game and at the beginning of a new forum it is incredibly slow going. The other thing to do is try and get a team of friends to join and post comments for you – and if you can stretch to it, pay for a few hours of their time a week. You need to dedicate time to growing a forum – think about it like tending an allotment.

The other thing you need to consider – particularly if your forum starts to take off – is moderation. 'Moderation' refers to the checks you are going to put in place so that your forum runs how you want it to.

Two of the questions you will need to ask yourself are:

- **Is your forum going to be pre or post moderation?** By this I mean are you going to review each comment that is posted before it is published, or are you going to allow the comments to be published immediately and then check them (and take them down if they are inappropriate)? There are pros and cons of both systems. I personally prefer post moderation as you want people to be able to see their com-ment as soon as they have written it. If it has to go into a moderation queue before it passes in order to go live, you may well lose the interest of those posters. On the other hand, you run the risk of having inap-propriate comments on your site, so you need to be vigilant. Either way, you need to have decided what your system is going to be and how you are going to manage it.
- **Who is going to moderate?** Is it going to be you? Is it going to be a team of people? The Student Room has been very clever – it runs its moderation teams using student volunteers and then has a paid team who manage them. This works very well for it.

Tip: you will need to think about the guidelines for your users, i.e. rules for posting.

If you do get a forum going it can be a very rich source for story ideas for your site. You can see what conversations are popular and which questions are generating the most responses. You can create content to address any issues raised and then post links to the content in the forum. You can also post links to conversations in your articles – relevant ones, of course.

The other thing you can do with a forum is run live Q&As. This was very successful at the *Guardian*. I introduced live Q&As so that job hunters could ask panels of experts for help with a particular sector. We would invite a number of industry professionals to be online at a given time and then publicise the live Q&A, inviting people to log on. If they wanted to, they could send in questions prior to going live. On the day, we would open the forum and keep the conversation flowing by linking comments, asking for clarifications, posting hyperlinks to more information, researching unanswered questions … Then, after we closed the live chat – they usually lasted for an hour and ran over a lunchtime – we would collate all of the best bits of advice into a post. Have a look at a few examples at www.theguardian.com/careers/live-q-a (the CV clinics were always popular).

So, how do you get a forum on your WordPress site? There are a couple of of ways. You can install a specific community-based theme, which will have forum functionality built in, or you can add a plugin to your existing site.

The system that most commercial themes offering integrated forum areas use is **BuddyPress**. You can get BuddyPress as a plugin too (developer The BuddyPress Community), adding it to your existing theme, but if you are serious about running a community platform, or at least a forum area, you should really look at getting a theme that has this as a central function. This is because all your formatting (the style, the layout) will be designed with this in mind, whereas if you are tagging it on to an existing theme you may find that it looks unprofessional.

One thing to consider though: if you are picking a community-based commercial theme make sure that it also offers a good layout and site architecture for posts – you will need to have both. Quite a few of the community themes are designed to handle forums and not news and features, so just keep that in mind.

Here are a few I would recommend:

Huber – developer Ghostpool

http://huberdemo.wpengine.com

This is a good theme for reviews and has both BuddyPress integrated and bbPress, which is the forum element. It also works with the WordPress Social Login plugin, so your users can log in via Facebook, Twitter, Google+, etc.

Boombox – developer PX-Lab

https://boombox.px-lab.com/

This is a good all-rounder and has the look and feel of a Buzzfeed site. Not so suitable for more serious news sites.

OneVideo – developer Upcode

http://demo.touchsize.com/themes/?
theme=onevideo

This is a good community theme based around video content.

Multinews – developer Momizat

http://themes.momizat.com/themes.php?
theme=multinews

Lots of features – more than you'll ever need, probably.

If you don't have a theme with BuddyPress installed you can add it as a plugin.

I am not going to go through all the instructions for running the plugin here, but I am going to highlight a few pointers. As BuddyPress is an official WordPress plugin it should work with most themes.

For you to run forums you also need to add **bbPress**. This is a separate plugin (developer The bbPress Community) – you can activate this without BuddyPress if you just want to have forums, without the social connections between your users. Simply activate the plugin and then create a new forum at Dashboard/Forums/Newforum.

There are options in Dashboard/Settings/Forums for controlling how the users post in your forums which you can play around with. You have the option to give your users different roles – automatically on this page or by going to Dashboard/Users/Allusers.

You will see that you now have the option to give your users the following roles: Keymaster (this is like the admin), Moderator (permission to review/delete/block comments), Participant (permission to post comments), Spectator (permission to view but not post), and Blocked (self-explanatory!).

You will also see that you have two new areas: Dashboard/Topics – this is where each forum will appear by topic – and Dashboard/Replies – this is where replies from your users will appear. Every time you get a new reply a number will appear alerting you to the fact that there is a new reply or a new topic has been created.

To take your forums to another level you need to install **BuddyPress**. This is probably the most widely used plugin for creating a community platform. Be warned: you will need to spend some time with this because getting your head around how it works can be a little complicated. But there are heaps of sites offering support online – see https://buddypress.org/support

Once you have activated the plugin, click Get Started and check the options you want to activate. I would leave everything as the default to start with. Click Save Settings.

You will see you have new pages created showing your members and activity, and you have two new areas on your dashboard: Dashboard/Activity and Dashboard/Emails.

You need to make sure you have allowed registration on your site – go to Dashboard/Settings/General and then check the box Anyone Can Register.

From here you will have to play around. Wpmudev does a comprehensive BuddyPress guide – find it at https://premium.wpmudev.org/blog/buddypress-guide

Some good examples of forums:

- The *New York Times* – Room for Debate, at www.nytimes.com/roomfordebate

- Digital Spy, https://forums.digitalspy.com
- AnimeUK, https://forums.animeuknews.net
- The Student Room, www.thestudentroom. co.uk

If you don't want a full-blown community platform you can opt for something lighter like a questions-and-answers plugin, such as **CM Answers** (developer CreativeMindsSolutions).

I really like this plugin – I like the layout and the easy functionality. The limitation is that it restricts your forum to a Q&A format, which may not be suitable for all. It is very easy to use: activate the plugin, keeping all the settings the same for now, and create a new question. Go to Dashboard/CM Answers/Questions and Add New Question – this will pull up a standard post, which will be the question. You can put as much detail in the text box as you like, and add pictures, videos, whatever you like. Publish it, and your question will be live. It is super-simple to use. My advice, though, is to upgrade to the Pro version – at the time of writing it is $39 – as you will have many more options to help make it look and feel exactly as you want it

to. It will also integrate with BuddyPress if you have that installed (and it also makes it compatible with a multisite).

The last functionality that I'd like to cover in terms of users is that of polls. Being able to offer polls is a really easy way of interacting with your users and can provide good story leads. There are quite a few plugins to choose from but try **Poll, Survey, Quiz, Slideshow & Form Builder** (developer OpinionStage.com) – it offers you so many options.

Simply activate the plugin, sign up with your email and then select the type of poll you want to create at Dashboard/Poll, Survey, Quiz Form (Figure 8.8).

This will then take you to opinionstage. com, where you will create your poll. When you are happy with it (you can preview it from here), click Save and then Embed. This will bring up a box which will give you the option to copy a WordPress shortcode (Figure 8.9).

You can copy this and place it on any post or page, or you can add the OpinionStage widget (Dashboard/Appearance/Widgets) and drag it in to a sidebar (Figure 8.10).

Figure 8.8 Polls are a great way of interacting with your visitors.

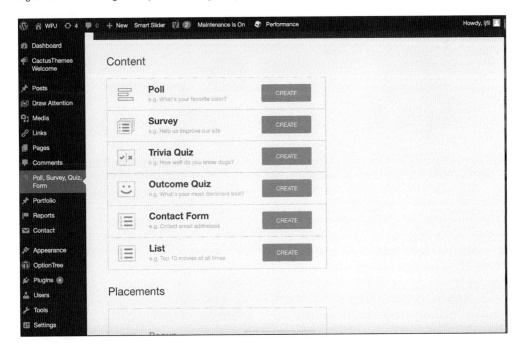

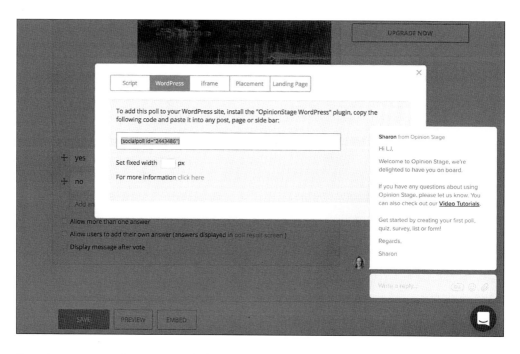

Figure 8.9 Paste your poll onto a post with the embed code.

Figure 8.10 Being able to run a poll in a sidebar next to an article can be really useful.

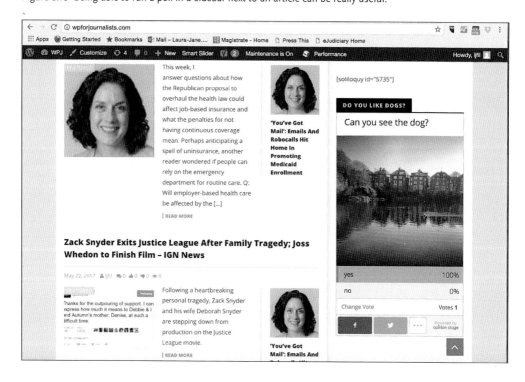

CHAPTER 9

Commercialisation

Full disclosure before we begin this chapter: it is incredibly difficult to make money from content online as a startup! Sorry to start with a negative, but better you know this from the off. Even huge publishers such as the *Guardian* have difficulty making money digitally, so you will need to think laterally if you are going to make yourself sustainable via your website.

Just to give you some idea, despite an audience of 155 million monthly unique visitors (April 2016), the *Guardian* reported losses of £69m with digital revenues down £2m in the financial year of 2015/16 from the preceding year.[1] The newspaper points to Facebook and Google taking mobile advertising from the publisher as partly responsible for this loss.

Some of the publisher's strategies to change the decline in revenue include investment in membership – it has 230,000 members (March 2017) who pay a minimum of £5 a month, 185,000 digital and print subscribers and 190,000 one-off contributors.[2] As part of a strategy for the future called Project 2021, the company has plans to grow this to 1 million members – on top of this, it is seeking to boost revenues further by asking readers for voluntary donations online.

According to a report produced by Deloitte for News Media Association, the UK's trade body for publishers, the vast majority (81%) of news media organisations' revenue continues to come from print readership, with only 12% coming from digital.[3]

However, when looking at social media platforms such as Facebook you can see where the money is going – in Facebook's first-quarter report for 2017, the social media giant reported $8.03 billion in revenue with 1.94 billion users globally.[4]

And, while it is difficult to pin down exactly how much money YouTube makes for Google, estimates are around the $9 billion mark – not surprising when you consider YouTube has more than 1 billion users, almost one-third of all people on the internet, and each day those users watch 1 billion hours of video, generating billions of views.[5]

The top three YouTubers of 2016 were:[6]

1. PewDiePie. Earned: $15 million. Subscribers: 49,756,391.
2. Roman Atwood. Earned: $8 million. Subscribers: 10,152,692.
3. Lily Singh. Earned: $7.5 million Subscribers: 10,296,350.

So, the money is there ... it's just accessing it!

(Something to pay attention to when you are planning your site is the type of content you are producing. While video content has been a very attractive proposition to advertisers over the past few years, according to BIA/Kelsey's 2017 Investing in Radio report, by 2021 radio will surpass newspapers and become the fifth-largest media category among advertisers.[8] Something to keep in mind.)

I am going to tackle this area in four sections: **Ecommerce** – arguably the easiest way to make money as you are selling a product (other than content); **Subscriptions** – a massive growth area for newspapers in particular (as already highlighted by the *Guardian*); **Advertising** – arguably the hardest way to make money online (particularly as so many people have ad blockers now); and lastly something you probably haven't heard of before, **Affiliate marketing**.

ECOMMERCE

You are going to need an ecommerce site if you have a product to sell. You might want to sell tickets, audio clips, T-shirts ... Whatever your product is, you will need a way of displaying it (merchandising), taking money, keeping accounts and building a database of customers, and for that you will need an ecommerce platform. WordPress offers some brilliant themes with ecommerce functionality built in using the platform **WooCommerce** (which was bought by Automattic, WordPress' parent company, in 2015).

WooCommerce comes with lots of payment gateways so you can accept money for your products, including via PayPal (using PayPal accounts and credit card payments), BACS, Amazon Pay and even cash on delivery, and there are lots of extensions for more. You

> **Estimate your potential YouTube earnings with the YouTube Money Calculator from Social Blade (though since 2016 the new rules on YouTube mean you can't start earning money until your channel hits 10,000 lifetime views).[7]**

> **Above all, remember: good-quality content will pull an audience in but a bad user experience will drive an audience away. You won't get a second chance, so make sure you do it right (and test, test and test!).**

can also control your inventory, database of customers, accounts, sales, taxes, shipping costs ... everything really to run a successful online shop. Plus, there are tons of extensions, some free, some premium.

It can get quite complicated – so start small. In fact, before you even begin you should consider how much time and work you are going to need to get it going. Don't underestimate this – it is incredibly time-consuming and, actually, setting the site up is the easy part. Getting your audience, keeping your site up to date and growing your business all require time and planning – this is the hard part. Make sure you know exactly who you are selling to and how to reach these people, and ask yourself why would they buy from you. What are your credentials? Why should someone trust you? Do you know who your competition is and how you are different/similar?

WooCommerce actually powers 28% of the world's online stores.[9] Here are a few sites that are up and running using WooCommerce for a variety of sales:

- **yoto.org** This site is using a modified free WordPress theme, **Tempera** (developer Cryout Creations). This is a not-for-profit site for homeless young people in Tucson, US, and it uses WooCommerce to accept donations.
- **vicfirth.com** This site uses the commercial theme **Dante** (developer Swift Ideas). Vic Firth is a percussive/drumming company. It uses WooCommerce to sell

drumsticks, sound-isolating headgear and more, and also as an education resource library.

- *ripleys.com* This site uses the commercial theme **Presso** (developer Envirra). This book publisher uses WooCommerce for books, tickets, memorabilia and more.

When you are choosing your theme, if your main content is news and features you need to pick an ecommerce theme which handles this content well – you don't want a theme that is good for displaying products but the blog posts look a mess.

Here are a few ecommerce themes which I think are suitable for running a news and features site:

- **unPress Magazine** – developer Favethemes,
- **MikMag** – developer Themedutch, and
- **Multinews** – developer Momizat.

If you don't want a full-blown ecommerce site and you just want to accept some small payments for individual items, you can connect your site to PayPal through some buttons on your posts and pages and in your sidebars (you will need to set up a PayPal account first – and I would recommend that if you are serious about making cash from your site, you create a business account with PayPal and keep this separate from your personal accounts).

Here are a few useful standalone plugins:

Paypal Donations – developer Tips and Tricks HQ

Allows you to add a PayPal donation button with shortcode that you can paste anywhere on your site.

WP Easy Paypal Payment Accept – developer Tips and Tricks HQ

Add a PayPal Buy Now button anywhere on a WordPress post or a page.

Snapppt – developer Snapppt

This is a great plugin that turns your Instagram images into shoppable links. Once you have got your ecommerce site up and running, activate the Snapppt plugin developer. This will integrate your website with your Instagram account, offering a seemless way for your followers on Instagram to buy by clicking on your images – which will bring your followers straight to your products on your website (or to a third-party site). You can also embed shoppable Instagram galleries and carousels onto your website.

Easy Digital Downloads – developer Easy Digital Downloads

If you have got files you want people to be able to download and you want to charge for them, this is a great plugin. You can set it up to charge for any type of media file.

RO Blendle Button – developer Reporters Online (RO)

RO is a platform for freelance journalists who want to sell their articles directly to readers. It's actually a Dutch site but accepts content in English.

The most interesting thing about this venture is the link with **Blendle**. Blendle has been called the Spotify of journalism – created by Alexander Klöpping, it is an online newsstand which allows people to browse through lots of journalism and just pay for the stories they like. So, no more signing up with different paywalls for every newspaper. Users pay with a single click, and only for the articles they read.

If you are a freelance journalist and you are signed up with RO you can request a Blendle button, and then any content that you submit to RO will appear on Blendle. Once connected, you can place the button on any content, giving your users the option to pay for it or not. You have to sign up with RO first and then request a button for your site.

SUBSCRIPTIONS

Subscriptions are a way of making your visitors pay for your content. Generating revenue this way has been a bit hit and miss for the newspaper industry – particularly as most news sites which are now behind paywalls started off by offering all their content for free. So I guess tip number one is to start as you mean to go on. If you are planning to put some of your content behind a paywall, do this from the beginning, because as the past few years have shown, changing the culture from free access to paid-for access has been difficult. You just have to look at a couple of publishers who reversed their decisions to put content behind a paywall because of drastic declines in visitor numbers. The *Sun* (News UK) springs to mind – the paywall was introduced in August 2013, and you couldn't read anything but the headline and the standfirst before being asked for cash. Just two years later, in December 2015, the paper reversed this decision, opening up to free access again, and saw a readership increase of 108% (SimilarWeb figure calculated from June 2015 – paid access – to May 2016 – free access).[10]

This is in contrast to another News UK paper – the *Times* – which has successfully transformed free into paid: the paper went behind a paywall in 2010 and is now reportedly doing very well.

And if you look to the States and the *New York Times*, which in its first-quarter report for 2017[11] showed an enormous spike in subscribers (approximately 2,201,000 at the end of the first quarter of 2017, a net increase of 348,000 subscriptions compared to the end of the fourth quarter of 2016 and a 62.2 percent increase compared to the end of the first quarter of 2016), you would be forgiven for thinking that the subscriber model is the newspaper holy grail.

In a press release to accompany these figures Mark Thompson, president and chief executive officer of the New York Times Company, said:

These results show the current strength and future potential of our digital strategy not just to reach a large audience, but also to deliver substantial revenue. We added an astonishing 308,000 net digital news subscriptions, making Q1 the single best quarter for subscriber growth in our history.

He went on to explain that it was not just the subscribers who had contributed to such a positive report:

Digital advertising revenue grew 19 percent year-over-year, a vindication of our decision to pivot towards mobile, branded content and a broader suite of marketing services, and to focus on innovation. Despite continued pressure on print advertising, we were able to grow overall revenues by 5 percent in the quarter.[12]

The *Guardian* is one of the biggest newspapers resistant to the paywall. The paper's response is its membership scheme, as I have already mentioned, which is based on rewards – giving you extra if you pay to be a member rather than penalising you if you don't pay.

So, a couple of pathways for you to consider: subscriptions and membership. There are a number of plugins that will allow you to generate a revenue stream in this way on WordPress. It's for you to decide which model will work best for you.

Subscriptions & Memberships for PayPal – developer Scott Patterson

This plugin will allow you to sell subscriptions and/or memberships, or it can be set up to sell memberships and limit content on your site. You can sell subscriptions in terms of a set number of days, months or years, and have subscriptions continue forever. You can also offer your customers a trial price.

s2Member Framework (Member Roles, Capabilities, Membership, PayPal Members) – developer s2Member/WebSharks

A complex plugin which allows you to create areas on your site that are open to all and closed to some. Divide your site into membership areas and charge different rates for different levels of access. This could be particularly useful if you are running workshops or classes where you want to allow members to access class notes or instructions, but not the general public. Or you can simply restrict by role, allowing some roles to have more access than others – really you can restrict access to anything you like, charged or not charged.

Don't be alarmed at the set-up stage! It looks complicated but there is lots of help and actually it's quite easy once you get your head round it.

Restrict Content – developer Pippin Williamson

A simple plugin that allows you to easily restrict complete posts/pages to logged-in users only. Levels of restriction may also be set. The Pro version offers payment options.

If you want to make membership the core of your business model you should try to find a commercial theme with this functionality already built in. There are lots to choose from; here are a couple of suggestions:

- **Kickcube** – Membership & User Content **Sharing Theme** – developer An-Themes, and
- **Blogosphere** – developer Userthemes01.

ADVERTISING

There are a number of ways that you can use advertising to generate revenue on your site – none of them particularly lucrative unless of course you have considerable traffic. The traditional forms of advertising – 'banner ads' in your headers and footers, 'skyscrapers' in your sidebars and 'box ads' – are the easiest to configure but the hardest to make cash from, particularly as there are so many ad blocker apps now. This type of advertising is called display advertising and has its roots in print. This is not your only option though: you can also have link adverts in your actual posts/pages, sponsored editorial (branded content) and pre-roll/post-roll/mid-roll ads on your videos (and now audio too).

Here are the various ways you can get advertising on your site.

Classified adverts

If you want to sell advertising space yourself on your site you may want to use a plugin such as **WPAdverts** (developer Greg Winiarski). This plugin will allow you to create adverts yourself and post them anywhere on your site. This is very much a manual tool as opposed to something that is going to pull in an automatic feed of ads from a third party. It is good for individual adverts from your contacts and it allows you to create an ad from a post. It's quite easy to set up and you can connect it directly to your PayPal account. If you wanted to charge your users for creating ads on your site, for example, this is a good plugin (Figure 9.1).

Display advertising

If you want something a bit more automatic you need to tap into one of the ad networks. There are lots of plugins on the market to manage your various accounts with these networks; for example, **Advanced Ads** (developer Thomas Maier).[13] However, this can be confusing when you first start out so my advice is to pick one of the ad networks to concentrate on and install one of the plugins specific to that ad network. Once you get used to using one, you can look to find something that will feed more than one source to your site, such as Advanced Ads.

A note on ad networks: an ad network is essentially a company which acts as an intermediary between you and an advertiser. They are aggregators – they pull in advertising

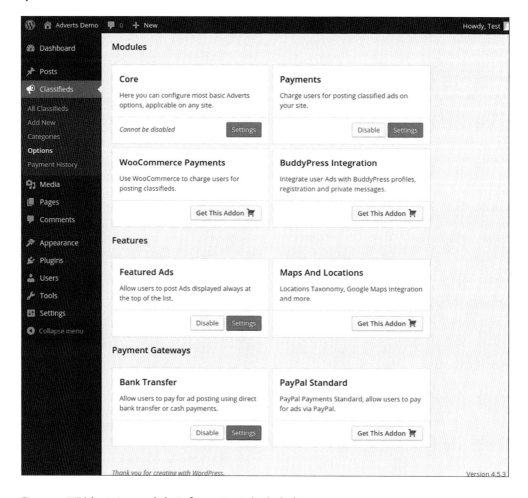

Figure 9.1 WPAdverts is a good plugin for creating individual ads.

for you to place on your site with one feed. The biggest one is **Google AdSense** – this is free and boasts nearly 2 million users.

First, sign up for Google AdSense with your Gmail account (use the one you have created for your website). Add your website, and then you will be asked to add some code to your core WordPress files between the <head> and </head> tags. See page 117 for help with where to find your head tags, or add the plugin **Per Page Add to Head** (developer Erik von Asmuth).

Once you are all connected (this sometimes takes a day or two) select the ad you want on your site, choose where you want it to appear and then just copy and paste the embed code into a post or sidebar. It's that easy.

It is worth noting that Google AdSense also offers you a chance to overlay ads with your video content, and gives you access to a lots of local and global video advertisers.

There are plenty of plugins that you can download to help you with Google AdSense (though I think it is pretty easy to use). If you do want a plugin, a good one for getting AdSense on your site is **WP QUADS** (developer René Hermenau, WP-Staging).

Branded content

Also known as sponsored editorial or native advertising, this can be a bit of a grey area. This is when you write a post or create a piece of content for payment. You can be quite clever about how you do this: often the way the content is approached is a lateral connection to the advertiser rather than a direct link, so instead of writing an article about the release of a new car – let's say a BMW – the sponsored editorial might be a feature about romantic road trips that you can do over a weekend . . . The feature can be a quality feature – with great content – but the money to pay for this content being created is from the advertiser BMW, so the car you use in the feature is the new BMW.

Have a look at the *Guardian* Labs' 'How to solve a murder: a detective's dilemma' – this is a great example of branded content to support Amazon Prime Video's third season of 'Bosch'.[14] It's paid-for content (so essentially advertising) but it is great quality.

AFFILIATE MARKETING

Affiliate marketing is simply when you refer someone from your site to click on a product/service and that person buys from that link. You make your money from commission – you get paid for the introduction. All the WordPress plugins work on pretty much the same basis: create an affiliate account with a company that you think you will be able to send your visitors to, and then download a plugin – either one like Amazon's that is bespoke for it or one such as **ThirstyAffiliates**', which can handle lots of different accounts. Connect your site and your payment information (how you want to be paid). After that you need to decide how, when and where you want the links to appear – this could be in your posts or in your sidebars, or both.

Here are more details:

ThirstyAffiliates – developer ThirstyAffiliates

This is one of the longest-running affiliate marketing plugins and it is very easy to use.

You need to have a list of affiliate links to add first though – so the best thing to do is to research companies that you would like to have an affiliate account with. Ask yourself which companies you think you will be able to send your customers to; for example, you might be recommending a hosting company, so why not become an affiliate of Tsohost via www.tsohost.com/affiliates? When you get an affiliate account you will be given a unique link which you can add to your ThirstyAffiliates plugin.

Then, when you are creating a new post and you are talking about hosting, you can add this link by simply highlighting the text you want to apply the link to (in Edit Post) and then clicking on the ThirstyAffiliates icon in the toolbar. If you have added all your affiliates you will be able to search for the link for Tsohost and it will be applied. Of course, you can do this manually because what we are really talking about is just adding a hyperlink – but if you have a number of affiliates this is the best way to manage them.

Amazon Associates Link Builder – developer Amazon

This is the official plugin from Amazon for embedded links. Before you download and activate this, go and create an account with Amazon Associates via https://affiliate-program.amazon.co.uk. This will give you all the relevant info you are going to need to hook your site up with the plugin. Once you have activated the plugin and it is working with your site, you will see when you create a new post that you have an Amazon link tool in your Edit Post toolbar, so adding links is easy. It works in pretty much the same way as ThirstyAffiliates – but instead of adding lots of links you can search for relevant content on Amazon via the toolbar and then when you find something relevant, you can highlight and link the text.

A good start is looking at homeworkinguk.com/affiliate-programs/for companies which offer affiliate programmes that you can join.

REFERENCES

1   Jackson, J. (2017). *Guardian's* Losses Hit £69m But It Gains More Than 50,000 Paying Members. [online] The *Guardian*. Available at: www.theguardian.com/media/2016/jul/27/guardian-losses-members [Accessed 18 Nov. 2017].

2   Viner, K. (2017). Thank You for Your Support, Which Is More Important Now Than Ever. [online] The *Guardian*. Available at: www.theguardian.com/membership/2017/mar/13/thank-you-for-your-support-which-is-more-important-now-than-ever[Accessed 18 Nov. 2017].

3   Deloitte. (2016). UK News Media: An Engine of Original News Content and Democracy. A Study on the Economic Contribution of the UK News Media Industry December 2016. [online] Newsmediauk.org. Available at: www.newsmediauk.org/write/MediaUploads/Investigation%20Gallery/Final_Report_News_Media_Economic_Impact_Study.pdf [Accessed 18 Nov. 2017].

4   Constine, J. (2017). Facebook Beats in Q1 with $8.03B Revenue, Faster Growth to 1.94B Users. [online] TechCrunch. Available at: https://techcrunch.com/2017/05/03/facebook-q1-2017-earnings/ [Accessed 18 Nov. 2017].

5   YouTube.com. (2017). Press – YouTube. [online] Available at: www.youtube.com/intl/en-GB/yt/about/press [Accessed 18 Nov. 2017].

6   Berg, M. (2016). The Highest-Paid YouTube Stars 2016: PewDiePie Remains No. 1 With $15 Million. [online] Forbes.com. Available at: www.forbes.com/sites/maddieberg/2016/12/05/the-highest-paid-youtube-stars-2016-pewdiepie-remains-no-1-with-15-million/#2ec65f227713 [Accessed 18 Nov. 2017].

7   SocialBlade.com. (2017). Estimated YouTube Money Calculator. [online] Available at: https://socialblade.com/youtube/youtube-money-calculator [Accessed 18 Nov. 2017].

8   BIAKelsey. (2017). Digital Revenues for U.S. Radio Industry Continue to Rise As OTA Numbers Remain Steady at $14.1B in 2016. [online] Available at: www.biakelsey.com/digital-revenues-u-s-radio-industry-continue-rise-ota-numbers-remain-steady-14-1-b-2016-according-new-biakelsey-report [Accessed 18 Nov. 2017].

9   WooCommerce. (2017). WooCommerce Showcase. [online] Available at: https://woocommerce.com/showcase [Accessed 18 Nov. 2017].

10   BI Intelligence. (2016).The *Sun's* Readership More Than Doubles After Removing Paywall. [online] Business Insider. Available at: http://uk.businessinsider.com/the-suns-readership-more-than-doubles-after-removing-paywall-2016-7 [Accessed 18 Nov. 2017].

11   Business Wire. (2017). The New York Times Company Reports 2017 First-Quarter Results. [online] Businesswire.com. Available at: www.businesswire.com/news/home/20170503005744/en/New-York-Times-Company-Reports-2017-First-Quarter [Accessed 18 Nov. 2017].

12   Investors.nytco.com. (2017). The New York Times Company Reports 2017 First-Quarter Results. [online] Available at: http://investors.nytco.com/investors/investor-news/investor-news-details/2017/The-New-York-Times-Company-Reports-2017-First-Quarter-Results/default.aspx [Accessed 18 Nov. 2017].

13   Maier, Thomas (2017). Advanced Ads. [online] WordPress.org. Available at: https://en-gb.wordpress.org/plugins/advanced-ads [Accessed 18 Nov. 2017].

14   *The Guardian*. (2017). How to Solve a Murder: A Detective's Dilemma. [online] Available at: www.theguardian.com/how-to-solve-a-murder-a-detectives-dilemma/all [Accessed 18 Nov. 2017].

Glossary of terms

Aggregation 'Aggregation' in reference to content simply means the collection of information/stories around keywords. This is mostly an automated process set up by entering a number of keywords. A content aggregation tool will then use these words to search the web, pulling in all content that matches them. The simplest example of this process is a search engine results page (SERP).

Algorithm When a user puts in a search term, the search engine will use an algorithm (a computer process) in order to decide which sites best match the search, and will rank them in order, using various determining factors such as trustworthiness, reputation and authority. This is a complex process and not easy to understand. Google, for example, relies on more than 200 unique clues to process a search. These clues could be keywords on your website or they could be the freshness of your content, or they could be based on location. How these algorithms work is continually changing and being updated, so trying to guess what the search engines are looking for is nigh-on impossible.

Alt Tag This is an abbreviation of the term 'alternative attribute' on an image tag and refers to the information you add to describe the image when you upload an image into your media library. Essentially the words you use in the alt tag can help with search engine optimisation so you should always add an alt tag with descriptive keywords. Beware, though, of just adding loads of keywords (Google identifies this as 'keyword stuffing'). The words should describe the image. The information you put in here will also be displayed if for some reason your image doesn't load properly; whatever you put in the alt tag will show as a text box in place of the image. There is a third reason for adding an alt tag to an image: for accessibility. The alt tag is used by screen readers to inform visitors who are visually impaired what's on the screen. This is particularly useful for buttons and commands attached to images. If you have a contact button, for example, the alt tag could say 'Click button to send an email' – the description of what the button does will be read out by a screen reader.

Augmented Reality (AR) This refers to technology that takes an existing environment and overlays information on the top. For example, Google Glasses will show information about whatever you are looking at through the lenses – if you were looking at a building, information about the architects or planning permissions could appear. AR is different to **virtual reality (VR)**, which creates a completely artificial environment. The term 'AR' was coined by Boeing researcher Thomas Caudell in 1990.

Back Link Someone linking to your site from theirs creates a back link. Getting a back link to your site on someone else's pushes up your Google ranking and in essence means your site becomes more visible in searches.

Backdoor   A 'backdoor' refers to a way a hacker can access your site through malware or outdated code. Hackers often hide code in inactive themes, giving them a backdoor straight into your site, so delete any theme or plugin that you are not using.

Bandwidth   Consider how much bandwidth you are allowed – now, trying to work out how much bandwidth you will need is a bit tricky because the calculation is dependent on knowing how big your page size is, and this can vary greatly depending on what content you have on it. So, for example, if you had lots of images on a page, the size of the page is going to be much bigger than if it was just a page of text. Let's say by way of illustration that your average page size is 50kb, and let's say each of your visitors to your site is going to look at 10 pages per month. Your average bandwidth per visitor per month is then 500kb. So, if you have a maximum bandwidth allowance of 5GB then you'd have to have 10,000 visitors each month to hit this limit. This seems an enormous amount of traffic – way beyond what most people enjoy in terms of monthly visits. However, this calculation does not take into account all the other factors that add to the bandwidth usage, namely: larger file sizes; email usage; FTP activity; search-engine crawlers; spam bots … All of these will push your usage up and it is surprising just how quickly the 5GB limit can be reached, even with a relatively basic blog. My advice is to go for 10GB and above. Bandwidth usuage, like most things online, can be scaled up or scaled down according to your use, so there is nothing to stop you starting off with the lowest bandwidth and therefore the cheapest hosting package.

Body text   When you create a post/page the 'body text' refers to the box where you post/type your content. It is the main box underneath the headline.

Bounce Rate   This can refer to both a single page or a whole website and can be tricky to work out – it basically refers to how many pages a visitor is clicking on, compared with how many visitors arrive on your site. So, for example, if 100 visitors arrive on your homepage but only 50 go on to other pages, this gives you a site bounce rate of 50%.

Browser   A browser is an application which allows a visitor to view web content. Examples of browsers are Internet Explorer, Google, Chrome and Safari.

Cache   A 'cache' refers to the information about a website/page that is stored on a computer – usually so that the site can run more efficiently. There are a few common caching terms that you will come across, including 'browser cache', 'memory cache' and 'disk cache'. If you are experiencing problems with changes that you have made not appearing, try clearing your browser cache. One of the quickest ways of increasing the website's speed is by leveraging browser caching. This basically means not loading every single element on your page afresh – for example, a logo is going to be the same each time the site is accessed, so instead of having to download that logo each time a visitor hits one of your pages, a plugin can tell the browser to save the logo and use the saved version instead. This may seem like an insignificant feature but when you consider how many different elements a page consists of, having a plugin that only needs to download fresh content will make a huge difference in how much time a page takes to load.

Cascading Style Sheets (CSS)   The concept of CSS was proposed in 1994 by a member of the World Wide Web Consortium (W3C), Håkon Wium Lie. The proposal was in response to the problems developers and designers were beginning to face due to the phenomenal growth of websites. Essentially, the creation of CSS allowed for site-wide changes to how the content was presented. Colours, font type, font size, styling around images, etc., could be controlled by one page – a .css file.

Categories   Your whole WordPress site is made up of posts and pages. No matter what content you create, you will be required to create a new post or a new page. The way you organise all of that content so that it can be found by visitors is by using categories and tags. Categories are your top-level sections. So, for example, I might want to organise my content into the following categories: News, Reviews, Video, Audio.

Chatbot   A computer application which simulates a human conversation – an online virtual assistant. Siri and Alexa are examples of chatbots.

Child Theme   A child theme inherits the functionality and styling of the parent theme (the original theme). You often have a parent theme which is modified for different uses on a multisite install – so you might have the main site running the parent theme and then the other networked sites running modified versions of this theme (child themes).

Clickbait   This refers to headlines which are created just in order for you to click on them, but when you click through you find that it isn't what you expected or what the headline suggested it is. A technique used to market products.

Content Curation   Running a news and features website is not just about producing original content – it should also be about providing a central point for your audience for all the great content online surrounding your topic area. You as a website owner should be across all trending discussions, all breaking news and every mention of something relevant for your audience. The term to describe this is 'curation'. When it is done effectively it can elevate your website to a position of authority on a topic. To do it successfully needs a certain level of automation as there is far too much content online for you to keep across, but it also requires you to choose the content to

share. (And remember – the more you share the more connected you are.)

Content Management System (CMS)   Essentially a CMS allows someone with little knowledge of websites to create and publish content online – it is the user-friendly dashboard where you can create posts and upload images and the system that will then translate what you have uploaded into code and files stored in a database. It is like a translator for people who do not understand code and do not have the knowledge to build the architecture needed for a website to function properly.

cPanel   A control panel on your website host which allows you to manage your website.

Creative Commons License   A Creative Commons (CC) License enables the free distribution of copyrighted work. If you are looking for images that you want to use on your site, search for images which have signed up for a CC License. Do check exactly what you are allowed to do with that image: there are different grades of permission, from allowing you to use the image freely – including editing and modifying it – to restrictions on the types of website/content it can be used with (generally there is a distinction between commercial and editorial sites).

Demo/Dummy Content   This refers to the content you can download along with the theme you have bought to populate your site. Having dummy content will make your life a whole lot easier as it will mean when you activate your theme you will be given the option to recreate the site so that it looks exactly like the demo version. So, if you are able to upload the dummy content your site will show dummy posts, images, headlines, videos – all of the content on the demo version which you will have seen when you bought the theme. All you have to do then is save your own content of top of the theme creator's. If you buy a theme without dummy content, you will have no structure at all when you activate the theme and you will have to build the whole thing from scratch. You will essentially just have a skeleton site. Much easier to learn how a theme works from a demo than from the instructions. Please note: do not use the images supplied in the demo/dummy content on your own site. You do not have permission for these images – they are purely for demonstration. You must replace any images with your own before going live (that goes for any video and audio content too).

Domain/Domain Name System (DNS)   A domain name (or DNS) refers to the friendly naming convention for web addresses. Websites actually have Internet Protocol (IP) addresses, which are a series of identifying numbers. A domain name simply represents those IP addresses.

Ecommerce   In terms of websites, this simply refers to a website where you can buy/sell something.

Feed   A feed on a website refers to a way of getting content from other sites 'fed' onto your site – usually through headlines and excerpts.

File Transfer Protocol (FTP)   FTP is a way for you to easily transfer files from your local computer to the server where all your WordPress files are stored. In other words, an FTP server links your computer to your host. An example of an FTP application is Filezilla.

Footer   This is a content area at the bottom of a website – it is usually a widget-ready area and quite often has links to the static page content such as the About page, contacts and addresses.

Header   This is a content area at the top of a website – it is usually a widget-ready area and quite often has adverts, menus, logos and news tickers.

Homepage   This is your main/front page – the portal that houses your most recent content and/or your most important links. Think of it like your shopfront.

Host   A website host is a company which provides the services needed to keep a website running successfully. This includes a database and a filing system. Essentially, when you host your site with a company all the files your site needs to work properly are kept by it. It looks after all the technical things such as how your content is found.

House style   Deciding how you want your posts and pages to look is to decide on your house style. You should have a rule for everything – including which fonts to use in which circumstances and how to write the date, for example: are you going to write *27/09/17* or is it going to be *Sep 27, 2017* or is it going to be *27th Sep, 2017*? Once you have decided, you need to stick to it, standardising throughout the site. Will your posts have one image or two? Will you use any landscape images or will you only use portrait? Where is your caption going to go: underneath or on top? Or on the side? Or at the bottom of the post? Keeping everything to a house style will give your website professionalism and, therefore, will help its credibility.

Hyperlink(ing)   A hyperlink is a way of connecting your site to someone else's through linked words or pictures or buttons. The purpose of hyperlinks is twofold – first, to provide extra information, context and validity to a post, and second, to connect your post with other sites on the web, increasing the chance of visibility. Someone linking to your site from theirs creates a back link – all good **SEO**. One of the fundamental jobs for journalists is to provide extra information to a post – good-quality links show research and can afford credibility to the article. Any stat or report mentioned in a post should be hyperlinked back to the original – not another article, if possible, but to the actual source. For anyone who is named, try and find their own website or something they have written which adds further insight to your own post. Any locations, places of interest and events should all be hyperlinked. If you are hyperlinking people/work/events find a contact email and send them the URL of your post. This will encourage the possibility of a back link and increase the likelihood of your content being found and read.

Hypertext Markup Language (HTML) HTML is the language a browser understands. This language allows you to put anything you like on a web page – images, text, videos, etc. – and it also is a way of allowing websites to connect with each other through links (**hyperlinks**). It works by using short codes in a text file. On a page/post in Edit mode, click on the Text tab to see the HTML.

Hypertext Tranfer Protocol (HTTP) HTTP is the way linked content is retrieved from across the web.

Malware This is short for 'malicious software' and refers to anything that can cause harm to your site – viruses, worms and corrupt code.

Menu This is where the navigation for your site is controlled from. Depending on your theme your main menu may run across the top of your site or it could be hidden behind a tab or run down the left side of the screen. The menu allows a visitor to move through your site to find content.

Multisite A multisite is a system of allowing many separate websites to run off one domain with one WordPress installation but with the ability for each site to run mostly independent of one another. So one main website can run a network of other sites, using the same domain as the root with the addition of a site name. For example, http://yourdomain.com/newsite1

Page view A page view is counted when a visitor loads a related page. A visitor is counted when we see a user or browser for the first time in a period (day, week, month).

Parent theme This term refers to the original theme you are using if you have modified versions running – see **child theme**.

Permalink A permalink is simply a URL which is automatically created when you create a new post or a new page. For example, instead of a new post that you have just created being given the URL http://your

site.com/?p=45 – which is the default way WordPress handles content – you will have a link created that uses the title of the post and date, so it would look more like this: http://yoursite.com/2017/07/this-is-my-first-post. This has obvious benefits in terms of searches and archiving – using keywords is much better than random numbers.

Plugin A plugin is a bit of code that can extend the functionality of a standard WordPress install. There are thousands of plugins to explore.

Search Engine Optimisation (SEO) SEO is the way you improve your website so that it shows up in searches and therefore increases your traffic (visitors). An example of a search engine is Google, Bing or Yahoo. How people find your site is dependent on the search engines pulling up your domain when someone puts in a search word (the words people search with), and how these words match your site forms the basis of SEO.

Sidebar This is the area at the side of your post which is normally widget-ready and where you can add extra functionality through plugins. Depending on your theme, the sidebar may be on the right or left side of the post or you may have the option to have both right and left sidebars.

Site Map A site map is essentially a list of all the pages/posts that make up your site, collated into one document which allows search engines to crawl your site more effectively. There are many free plugins that will create your site map for you, and premium versions of plugins too, such as Yoast.

Static Page This simply refers to a page which holds content that is not updated, for example a contact page, an About page or a terms and conditions page.

Tag Categories and tags are the way in which you organise the content of your website and a way for your content to be found through keywords from search engines. Categories are your top-level sections and tags are the keywords attached to an individual post. For example, an article on Brexit and whether it is the best or worst decision for the UK would naturally fit in the top-level category News but would generate tags such as 'UK', 'Cameron', 'Teresa May' and 'EU'. Usually a piece of content will generate around 5–10 tags. These tags can then be used to further organise your content – so you could, if you like, have a section on your website that pulls in all of the articles which mention Cameron or the EU.

Theme   A theme dictates how a site works and how it looks. It is essentially the face of your website – what the public sees and interacts with; the front end as opposed to the back end, which is what you use WordPress to control. A theme is not just about how the theme looks, however: it is responsible for the whole user experience, so it is very important that you pick a theme that is suitable for the content you are going to be producing. Some themes are organised in a way which is more suitable for video content, for example, while others are better for displaying images or data or text. When you begin to look for your theme, this is what

you need to keep in mind – the function. What do you want your site to do? Everything else – the colours, the fonts, the elements – can be changed.

Top-Level Domain (TLD)   This refers to the '.com', '.co', '.uk', etc., at the end of a domain.

Traffic   When you talk about visitors to a site, you talk about how much traffic the site has.

Uniform Resource Locator (URL)   This is the term to describe the full details of a web address, including the **domain name**.

User-Generated Content (UGC)   This refers to any content created by the general public as opposed to a journalist working for a publication. Any video shot by someone at an event, for example, which is uploaded and used by a news site is regarded as UGC.

Virtual Reality (VR)   A computer technology that creates a virtual environment through 3D effects.

Widget   A widget is a piece of code that adds extra functionality to your site. They can be added easily into areas on your website called **sidebars, footers** and **headers**. WordPress by default comes with several widgets, including: Categories, Tag cloud, Calendar, Search and Recent posts.

Useful resources

In this section you will find a list of themes, plugins and websites recommended in the book, for your reference.

COMMERCIAL THEMES

- Beaton – developer wizedesign – good for events
- Benaam – developer scriptsbundle
- BeTheme – developer muffingroup
- Blogosphere – developer userthemes01 – good for subscribers
- Bucket – developer pixelgrade
- Flex Mag – developer MVP Themes
- Gameszone – developer Themefuse
- GrandNews – developer ThemeGoods
- Gridspace – developer Graph Paper Press – photography
- Infographer – developer Qode – good for data
- IronBand – developer IronTemplates – good for events
- Joker – developer Monkeysan – good for photography
- Kickcube – developer An-Themes – good for membership
- Kloe – developer Select-Themes
- MikMag – developer themedutch – good for a community
- Multinews – developer Momizat
- NewsMag – developer tagDiv
- Newspaper – developer tagDiv
- Newstube – developer CactusThemes – good for video
- OneVideo – developer upcode
- Right Now – developer RenkliBeyaz – good for audio
- SimpleMag – developer ThemesIndep
- Snaptube – developer Cohhe – good for video
- Soccer Club – developer PixFill – good for events
- SoundWave – developer wizedesign – good for audio
- Top News – developer MVP Themes
- Ubergrid – developer pukkathemes – grid-based theme
- UnitedCommunity – developer Diabolique – good for a community

- unPress Magazine – developer favethemes – good for ecommerce
- VideoPro – developer CactusThemes
- WPVoyager – developer purethemes – good for maps
- X The Theme – developer Themeco

PLUGINS

- Akismet – developer Akismet – for spam
- AMP for WP – Accelerated Mobile Pages – developer Kaludi, A. and Kaludi, M.
- Avatar Manager – developer Baris
- Black Studio TinyMCE Widget – developer Black Studio
- Bulk Password Reset – developer Woudsma
- Contact Form 7 – developer Takayuki Miyoshi
- Custom Sidebars – developer WPMU DEV – create distinct sidebars for different areas of your site
- Disable Comments – developer Shah
- Facebook Auto Publish – developer xyzscripts.com
- Gravity Forms – developer Gravity Forms
- Hide My WordPress – developer WPPlugins
- Jetpack – developer Automattic
- Limit Login Attempts – developer Eenfeldt
- MailPoet 2 – developer Bonheur – newsletters
- Maintenance – developer Fruitfulcode – take your site down from view while you are making changes
- ManageWP Worker – developer Kemp – manage multiple WordPress sites
- Polldaddy– developer polldaddy.com
- Simple Wp Sitemap – developer Webbjocke
- Smush Image Compression and Optimisation – developer WPMU DEV
- Typeform – developer Typeform
- User Switching – developer Harris
- W3 Total Cache – developer Townes
- Wordfence Security – developer Wordfence
- WordPress 2-step verification – developer as247
- WP Fastest Cache – developer Vona
- WP Full Auto Tags Manager – developer Guillemant David
- WP Mega Menu – developer Mythemeshop
- WP Mobile Menu – developer Takanakui
- WP Super Cache – developer Automattic
- XCloner, Backup and Restore – developer Ovidiu
- Yet Another Related Posts Plugin (YARPP) – developer Adknowledge
- Yoast SEO – developer Yoast

USEFUL WEBSITES

123-reg.co.uk. (2017). Domain name registration and web hosting services. 123 Reg. [online] Available at: http://123-reg.co.uk [Accessed 12 Nov. 2017].

Dynatrace.com. (2017). Digital performance management. [online] Available at: www.dynatrace.com [Accessed 12 Nov. 2017].

Envato. (2017). Digital assets and services. [online] Available at: https://envato.com [Accessed 12 Nov. 2017].

Google Developers. (2017). Page speed tools. [online] Available at: https://developers.google.com/speed/pagespeed [Accessed 12 Nov. 2017].

How To Story. (2017). Must-read for storytellers: Pixar in a box! [online] Available at: http://howtostory.be [Accessed 12 Nov. 2017].

Inc., H. (2017). Hootsuite social media marketing and management dashboard. [online] Available at: https://hootsuite.com [Accessed 13 Nov. 2017].

Internetlivestats.com. (2017). Total number of websites and Internet live stats. [online] Available at: www.internetlivestats.com/total-number-of-websites [Accessed 12 Nov. 2017].

Isithacked.com. (2017). Check if your site has been hacked. [online] Available at: www.isithacked.com [Accessed 12 Nov. 2017].

Knightlab (2017). Soundcite inline audio. [online] Available at: http://soundcite.knightlab.com [Accessed 15 Nov. 2017].

Meenan, P. (2017). WebPagetest – website performance and optimisation test. [online] Available at: www.webpagetest.org [Accessed 12 Nov. 2017].

Nelio Software. (2017). Nelio content for WordPress. [online] Available at: https://neliosoftware.com/content [Accessed 13 Nov. 2017].

Pingdom. (2017). Website and performance monitoring. [online] Available at: www.pingdom.com [Accessed 12 Nov. 2017].

Reynolds, A. (2017). Affiliate programs – Home Working UK. [online] Available at: www.homeworkinguk.com/affiliate-programs [Accessed 18 Nov. 2017].

Search.google.com. (2017). Mobile-friendly test. [online] Available at: https://search.google.com/test/mobile-friendly [Accessed 13 Nov. 2017].

Socialblade.com. (2017). Estimated Youtube Money Calculator. [online] Available at: https://socialblade.com/youtube/youtube-money-calculator [Accessed 18 Nov. 2017].

Storymap.knightlab.com. (2017). StoryMap JS. [online] Available at: https://storymap.knightlab.com/select [Accessed 15 Nov. 2017].

Telling The Story. (2017). Telling The Story: A look at how journalists – and all of us – reach the world. [online] Available at: http://tellingthestoryblog.com [Accessed 12 Nov. 2017].

TSOhost. (2017). TSOhost. [online] Available at: www.tsohost.com [Accessed 12 Nov. 2017].

W3schools.com. (2017). W3Schools Online Web Tutorials. [online] Available at: http://w3schools.com [Accessed 12 Nov. 2017].

Whoishostingthis.com. (2017). Web hosting search tool, reviews and more. [online] Available at: www.whoishostingthis.com [Accessed 12 Nov. 2017].

WPMU DEV. (2017). WordPress toolkit. [online] Available at: https://premium.wpmudev.org/project/issue [Accessed 12 Nov. 2017].

Index

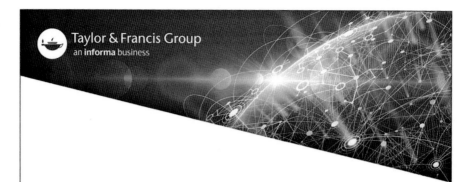